RIGHTLY DIVIDING
THE WORD OF
TRUTH

C. L. Chapman

Rightly Dividing the Word of Truth Book 1: On Defense: Decloaking Cults, Cultists and False Teachings, Book 2: Reaching Forth: Becoming Fruitful and Victorious in Christ

Order this book online at www.trafford.com
or email orders@trafford.com

Most Trafford titles are also available at major online book retailers.

Printed in the United States of America.

ISBN: 978-1-4269-3918-1 (sc)
ISBN: 978-1-4269-3919-8 (hc)
ISBN: 978-1-4269-3920-4 (e)

Library of Congress Control Number: 2010911505

Our mission is to efficiently provide the world's finest, most comprehensive book publishing service, enabling every author to experience success. To find out how to publish your book, your way, and have it available worldwide, visit us online at www.trafford.com

Trafford rev. 10/1/2010

 www.trafford.com

North America & international
toll-free: 1 888 232 4444 (USA & Canada)
phone: 250 383 6864 ◆ fax: 812 355 4082

Table of Contents

Rightly Dividing the Words of Truth
Book 1
On Defense
Decloaking Cults, Cultists and False Teachings

Rightly Dividing the Word of Truth

Book 2

Reaching Forth

Becoming Fruitful and Victorious in Christ

Rightly Dividing the Words of Truth

Book 1

On Defense

Decloaking Cults, Cultists and False Teachings

What is This
Information All About?

The Purpose of *Rightly Dividing the Word of Truth: Book 1—On Defense* and *Book 2—Reaching Forth* is to assist you, the reader, to establish a viable personal relationship between yourself and your Father-God.

There are hundreds of churches, fellowships, other organizations and groups, as well as individuals, who claim to be involved with God and His Word the Bible. Along with these church type fellowships, there are the television and radio ministries, the internet ministries and those of this type that are print based ministries to either embrace or avoid. Most of them teach and/or practice things that separate themselves from other outreaches of the same genre.

Looking at the broad spectrum of teachings promoted by all of these various groups of Christians and folks who call themselves Christians, all of them fall into one of two categories: True and Untrue.

These two categories of teachings are each divided into subcategories:

True teachings are either Relevant or Irrelevant.

The True-Relevant teachings play a vital role in a believer's relationship with his or her salvation and the Redeemer who wrought it.

The True-Irrelevant teachings may be interesting, but they will not be of any value relating to one's salvation, growth or development. Even though the subject matter may be considered educational, if it does not affect the relationship between the believer and the Lord, it is of no real value.

Untrue teachings are either Irrelevant or Harmful.

The Untrue-Irrelevant teachings do nothing beyond pique a person's interest (much like the True-Irrelevant teachings).

The Untrue-Harmful teachings are to be shunned because believing them will

1. Plant seeds of doubt in the Lord,

2. Separate one's confidence from the Lord to something or someone else, or

3. Establish a false premise of works or appeasement of God.

At a glance you can tell that many of the arguments people have over the messages of the Scriptures are of no matter whatsoever! It is sad to see people get all upset over a moot topic! By searching the Scriptures and following some guidelines you will be able to separate or divide teachings and practices so you can either avoid, ignore or embrace them. It could be called "culling teachings and practices," because that is exactly what you will be doing automatically before you know it!

One thing all the Bible teachers have in common: They all claim to believe and practice the Bible. There are so many of these ministries to choose from, and so many of them have little or no scriptural foundations for some of their stands (whatever they use to differentiate between themselves and others), yet so many of them claim to have a single-handed monopoly on the whole of God's Truth.

For people who are particular about the results they want from fellowshipping with someone, selecting a place or type of ministry with which or with whom to fellowship over other like ministries is often mind-boggling. Regrettably, often the choice of a ministry is made based on convenience rather than any actual concern regarding with whom they will fellowship or what is taught in that ministry.

Adding to the conundrum is that in these days when someone is seeking a ministry for fellowship, one may select a ministry of a familiar type of organization or denomination, whose name is recognized, but they often find a whole new and unusual program, agenda, line of doctrines and / or practices than what they expected. Does he or she like the change? Is it a change for better or worse? Which ministry is better? Which one is right? If one ministry is right, which one is it? More importantly, *why* is a ministry right or wrong?

Often the decision of selecting a ministry affects a whole family. That makes the decision infinitely more important. If you expose your children to something radical, how will that affect that person in the long-term? That makes every decision important!

The pitiful part of this whole issue about right vs. wrong, and truth vs. error and the confrontations they are causing as they oppose each other is that almost everyone concerned actually believes themselves to be on the side of right and truth. Yet, looking at the issues objectively, the probability of a single organization to be correct on all aspects of Bible teachings is minuscule. If that were not the case, the majority of the various churches would not be in conflict with one another!

Meanwhile, people tend to follow what they were reared with. What if the position they were brought up on was the wrong side on some vital True-Relevant issues? Or what if they are following some Untrue-Harmful teachings?

Simply put, the questions raised here need to be answered and only you, the advised and informed Bible-student, can answer these questions correctly. You may not necessarily be a Bible student, but you better be one to the extent of defending yourself and your loved ones against the deceitful teachers that abound in this modern and mostly godless society! The answers you form may cause you to make the church-move that you have wanted to avoid, but necessity often demands such a move. You need the correct biblical information! And you will need the will and strength to respond appropriately, as led by the Lord.

You need to know how to avoid biblical errors and deception.

You need to know how to separate Truth from error.

You need to know how to deal with the errors, both those ignorance-based errors and the intentional ones.

You need to know how to deal with those who propagate and promote the errors in Bible teachings, doctrines and practices.

You need to know how to glean the Truths of the Word of God as they relate to you and your family apart from the influence of errors.

You need to know how to grow, mature and become both victorious and fruitful in the Lord.

These are the things that these two books are all about—helping you to know how to determine the Bible's message to you and yours.

This first book, *Book 1: On Defense,* has two main thrusts:

> It is designed to show students of the Word how to discern the difference between good sound biblical information and the bogus and erroneous misinformation that so many are embracing, not knowing that they are embracing error.

> It will illustrate both errors and intended misinformation about the Bible and its contents and it will further show you how to deal with both the misinformation and those who spread it.

The second book, *Book 2—Reaching Forth,* explains how to glean the basic information that you need to grow on, mature in and profit spiritually from the Bible and its message.

Introduction

There is one very important difference between the Scriptures and literature: THE MESSAGE IN THE SCRIPTURES (the Bible) IS A SPIRITUAL MESSAGE. That is, the message is from a spiritual God to His people's spirits with spiritual applications and aimed at spiritual results. Literature is not.

If there is anything you should realize with all clarity, and with absolutely no reservations, it is this: THE BIBLE IS THE WORD OF GOD.

There is no other truth on earth more absolute. God is not a liar, nor is He a man that His Word is without Power, Direction, Omniscience, and Eternity. There is nothing in the universe so important to believers as the Word of God. It is absolute and living Truth and should never be taken as a mere story, fable, lesson, moral, myth, history, secret, mystery, or any of the other things that men often see in connection with the Word of God.

The Bible does not need decoding; it only needs to be understood and its message embraced! This is the concept that we hold to and follow in this composition. It is the Word of God that produces life, health, peace, victory, prosperity, deliverance and abundant blessings for believers even in these tumultuous end-times.

There are eight perspectives addressing the reasons for and advantages in studying the Bible, the Word of God (or, simply, the *Word*). These perspectives are found in Appendix 1. One of these perspectives may make an impression on you, showing you why you are here reading this in the first place. If nothing else, read the introduction to Appendix 1 and see some of the marvelous roles that the Word of God has had on His followers.

7

The Nature of Man

God is a spirit. Man was created in God's image, therefore above anything else, *man has to be a spirit, too.* We, as individuals, think and act independently; therefore we have minds of our own. Of course, we all have our own bodies to house our minds and our spirits. So we are (as Scripture teaches) comprised of spirit, soul (or mind) and body. The relative importance of our components is also in that order: Spirit, soul and body (I Thessalonians 5: 23).

This should open up the realization that there exists another whole universe that consists of spirits of many sorts: God (good); Satan (evil), angels (those from God, as well as those fallen ones that are bound in chains of darkness), various elements of both God's and Satan's kingdoms, (which will include not only demons and their Strongholds, but Principalities, Powers, Spiritual Wickedness in High Places and Rulers of Darkness) as well as human spirits, both the renewed (re-created or regenerated) and the un-renewed (un-recreated). It is the role of redeemed man to reign supreme over all of these spirits except man's Redeemer, God, by the use of the name of Jesus.

Now, repeating, *The Bible— the Word of God— is a spiritual book.* In our educations, we have been taught to read and comprehend with our minds. However, regarding the Word of God, we are supposed to comprehend it with our spirits. This is the reason so many people find the Bible hard to understand and why there are so many churches, ministries and cults teaching so many widely separated views and so many absolutely weird things. This is also why so many have tried to "decode" the Bible and its content, and have failed miserably in so doing!

If we try to understand the Bible using only our intellects, then we will have divisions of thought, various opinions, complicated versions, inadequate paraphrasings, many churches and an even wider selection of individual beliefs, forms, formulas, and practices, and hence, RELIGIONS.

Right here, right now, know this: Christianity is not a religion. Christianity is a living relationship between the Father-God and His Children, established by the shed blood of His Son, Jesus Christ, and maintained by the Holy Spirit through the spirits of God's children.

When people add to that relationship their formulas, practices, rituals, memberships, and all the other things churches, ministries and cults teach and practice, religion results. The point is for you to take advantage of this information by being Christian rather than religious.

> Note: If you are not a Christian, a believer (one who has made a choice to accept Christ as both Savior and Lord according to Romans 10: 9 and 10), follow the instructions found in those verses:

> That if you shall confess with your mouth the Lord Jesus, and shall believe in your heart that God has raised Him from the dead, you shall be saved. For with the heart man believes to righteousness; and with the mouth confession is made to salvation.

> Essential Point: The belief in the heart is absolutely necessary before the confession with the mouth is valid. Anyone may say something to indicate that they have received Christ, but it may not be of the heart. Because, as you will soon see as you read, faith is not an emotion. You can make sure that your confession of Christ with your mouth is valid by making a conscious decision to accept as absolute fact that Christ was crucified in your place for your sins, and that because He did that for you personally, you will live for Him personally. As you will also soon find out, living for Christ is done by allowing Him to live in and through you.

Other things that you may have associated with accepting Christ as Savior will be dealt with later: Baptism, church membership, Communion and other privileges and duties, real or imagined. The main thrust in this note is to ascertain that you are indeed capable of taking full advantage of this introduction to the Scriptures!

> Notice: All Scripture references in this document are modernized King James Translation unless otherwise noted.

<u>Notice</u>: The Scriptures listed for you are usually not the only ones that say the same or similar things. If you desire more than one Scripture to confirm a point that has been made, refer to your concordance and you can probably find other Scriptures.

First Thoughts

What difference does it make if a person knows all there is to know about God and spiritual things or not? Knowing all about God and spiritual things is a mighty big stretch and it may be too much to try to handle. However, not knowing what blessings are available for someone may cause that person to miss out on those blessings. Equally important (and maybe more-so) is the basic relationship between God and a person who may certainly be stressed when that person believes and/or practices error.

> Jesus said, "'You shall love the LORD your God with all your heart, with all your soul, and with all your mind.' This is the first and great commandment. And the second one is like it; 'You shall love your neighbor as yourself.' On these two commandments hang all the Law and the Prophets." (Matthew 22: 37—40)

So this viewpoint expressed by Jesus lays the groundwork for this premise: Any doctrine, practice or concept that assaults the principles of either of these commandments is a false doctrine, illicit practice or destructive concept (an Untrue-Harmful teaching!).

Philosophies, doctrines, concepts or practices that

1. Reduce God to man's level,

2. Elevate man to God's level,

3. Contradict God's role as God, His Word as Truth, or His Redemptive Works as either natural or unessential for salvation,

4. Emphasize someone or something that can be positioned between God and His redeemed ones, or

5. Assault the trust, assurance or love that enlivens the relationship between God and man shall be considered vain philosophies, false doctrines or misguided practices according to what Jesus said about the First Commandment.

By looking at the promise that is connected to the relationship between the Father-God and His redeemed ones, it will be easy to assess the importance of a direct relationship with Him rather than allowing anyone or anything to stand between you and Him. (John 14:11–23)

Jesus spoke to His disciples a few hours before He was crucified. Here are the points that He made:

John 14:11 "Believe Me that I am in the Father and the Father in Me, or else believe Me for the sake of the works themselves."

First, one is to believe Jesus and the Father are united, even if he has to look at the physical evidence rather than take Jesus' words for it.

12. "Most assuredly, I say to you, he who believes in Me, the works that I do he will do also; and greater works than these he will do, because I go to My Father."

Next, you are promised the ability to do as Jesus had done and more-so because He was going to the Father to see to it.

13. "And whatever you ask in My name, that I will do, that the Father may be glorified in the Son."

Directly related to that promise is another: Whatever you would ask of the Father in Jesus' name, the Father would do.

14. "If you ask anything in My name, I will do it."

Added to that promise is yet another: Jesus would himself do whatever you will ask of Him in His name.

15. "If you love Me, keep My commandments.

16. "And I will pray the Father, and He will give you another Helper, that He may abide with you forever, even the Spirit of truth, whom the world cannot receive, because it neither sees Him nor knows Him; but you know Him, for He dwells with you and will be in you. I will not leave you orphans; I will come to you."

Then He gave the simple charge to keep His commandments if you love Him (V. 15). This is followed by yet another promise (Vv. 16–18):

Jesus will pray for you and the Father will send the Holy Spirit to you as a Helper who will live, not only with you, but in you forever. He is the Spirit of Truth who will lead you into all truth. Jesus Himself promised to return to you.

19. "A little while longer and the world will see Me no more, but you will see Me. Because I live, you will live also."

The last promise is a guarantee: Because Jesus lives, you will also live!

20. "At that day you will know that I am in My Father and you in Me, and I in you."

Not only will you be alive because He is alive, but you will understand the unity between yourself, the Father and the Son.

21. "He who has My commandments and keeps them, it is he who loves Me. And he who loves Me will be loved by My Father, and I will love him and manifest Myself to him."

Then Jesus lays down the principle that when you keep His commandments, it is because you love Him, and furthermore, because of your love for Jesus, the Father will love you and Jesus will manifest Himself to you.

22, 23. Judas (not Iscariot) said to Him, "Lord, how is it that You will manifest Yourself to us, and not to the world?" Jesus answered and said to him, "If anyone loves Me, he will keep My word; and My Father will love him, and We will come to him and make Our home with him."

Verse 23 reaffirms the principle and Jesus promises that both Jesus and the Father will come and live with you. In this principle, notice it is Love that produces obedience to His commandments.

Notice: The two commandments in Matthew 22: 37–40 (above) are included along with all of His commandments (or His Words)!

Just be sure to read the content of this passage carefully. No one else is mentioned in these relationships or accompanying promises: No doctrines, churches, saints or anyone or anything else. The promises and the relationships involved here are for only you, from the Father, the Son and the Holy Spirit!

While the First Commandment to which Jesus referred deals with man's relationship with God, the Second Commandment regards man's relationship with other men. When man creates regulations and dogmas that elevate himself or some other person over other people whereby he presents himself or some other person as being superior over them, especially over the Lord's people, whether it be by title (real or imagined role of superiority), knowledge (education, special knowledge—real or imagined), strength, gifts (whether real or imagined), numbers (whereby one group outvotes or otherwise outnumber the other group), or any other means to control, disrespect, dishonor, besmirch, insult, dominate or regulate or any type of slavery or any other subjugation, those regulations and/or dogmas are false doctrines according to this Second Commandment.

The following confrontation between Jesus and Peter serves as an example of the latter case. Peter evidenced a mindset to interfere with the relationship between John and Jesus, but Jesus would not have it. Jesus is the Chief Shepherd and the Father-God is the Head Supreme of everything; anything or anyone who attempts to alter these roles and their relationships is trespassing against them! This incident is recorded in the last chapter of John's Gospel when Jesus gave some last-minute messages to various disciples, including Peter and John. He concluded speaking to Peter by saying, "Follow Me" (John 21: 19).

Then John records this:

Peter, seeing John, asked Jesus, "Lord, what shall this man do?"

Jesus then told Peter, "If I will that he tarry till I come, what is that to you? Follow Me."

Verse 23 records the turn of events this way:

Then went this saying abroad among the brethren, that that disciple [John] should not die. Yet Jesus said not to him, "He shall not die;" but, "If I will that he tarry till I come, what is that to you?"

This is an example of how people—honest, well-intending though they be—twist the facts. The first element of certainty one should recognize in this passage is that a person has his or her own relationship with the Lord and it is not subject to anyone else.

It was none of Peter's business what the Lord was about with John. This may upset some church elders or ministers who try to control their parishioners, but what the Lord does with one person is not another person's affair!

In the same vein, the Lord does not deal with groups. He deals with individuals only, and when people think that they receive blessings from God because they belong to a particular group, even though that group may be a church, they are sadly mistaken.

The second truth illustrates the tendency for people to repeat what Jesus says. It is only natural to cling to every syllable that comes from the lips of the Master. However, it is desirable that every clung-to syllable should be a correct syllable, too! That is why the Word emphasizes exactly what the Lord said rather than allowing a misrepresentation or an assumption to usurp the intended meaning.

In this case the whole message got twisted. This is not unusual. This is one of the main problems regarding biblical understanding: Misquoting or misapplying the Word. Misquoting Scripture is one of the main fountains that produce a stream of biblical error, whether the simple misquotation or designed perversion of the Word. Misapplying the words is also a major problem. People do not seek out to whom the words were addressed; they only assume they were addressed to the reader.

Finally, the lesson in this passage establishes the necessity for the absolute best translations of the Scriptures. You should use a Bible that is as close to a literal translation as you can find. (For study purposes, avoid the paraphrased editions; they are only man's opinions of what the Word is saying. Some opinions may be good, but the vast majority of them are bad. By using paraphrased editions, a person can make the Bible say anything they may want it to say. Many paraphrasing editors are on an agenda and may not even know the Lord.) Be sure to get a reliable translation of the Bible and use other translations and dictionaries (preferably Greek and Hebrew dictionaries) to establish the validity of every relevant passage! Many Bibles have notes and references in them that indicate the meanings of key words, sometimes using literal translations or words from other translations in them.

The goal is to really know and understand what the Lord is saying to and about you as best you can. Paraphrasing and generalizations will not cut it!

Rightly Dividing the Word of Truth

BOOK 1

On Defense

1

THE GUIDEPOSTS OF BIBLE-STUDY

Many people have some unhealthy attitudes and practices regarding their habits of reading and studying the Bible. Because they know the Bible is God's Word, they think there is something mystical or magic about it. They think they are reading something with magic powers and the words there are somehow able to know who is reading them and therefore these words reach out and grab the reader giving him or her something special, unique or overpowering.

There have been times when these special, unique or overpowering revelations have come to the Bible-reader, and these events have come unexpectedly and without premonition by the Holy Spirit. But to plan on such revelations or to depend on them is not wise and will most likely eventually lead the reader who does this into error. Going willy-nilly on a shot-in-the-dark search for wonderful truths is foolish.

The thing to do is to actively seek the Holy Spirit's guidance and blessing on your study of the Word and have a plan. The best way to read or study the Bible is to follow a plan of study, whether a topic by topic study, a chronological study, a book-by-book study, a Read-the-Bible-in-a-Year study or another type of plan.

Whichever method you select, you need to abide by some guidelines as you proceed with your plan of study. After you find out what the Word is all about, then you will have the above mentioned adventures of revelations, truths and thrills that the Heavenly Father and His Word have for you.

So let's look at those guidelines. The guidelines consist of seven guideposts, besides the one previously mentioned (getting the words in the right order to begin with). These guidelines could have been called rules, regulations or standards, but these terms all sound so dogmatic that they were rejected. Guidelines sounds more friendly, yet firm enough to let you know they are there for a sound reason.

The Guideposts are few (seven) and simple, based on common sense. These are things that you are to consciously avoid as you delve into the Word of God.

Guideline 1. Do not take a portion of Scripture out of its context.

Guideline 2. Do not appropriate Scriptures that do not regard you by address, topic or proper analogy. Misappropriation is not a good thing to do in any case.

Guideline 3. Do not redefine the words of the Scriptures. Because of how much languages have evolved and the words have changed their meaning over the years, go back to the original meaning of those words as best you can, discern their original meaning and embrace those definitions.

Guideline 4. Do not add to the Scriptures. Assuming something is meant when it is not stated leads to error. This is a mistake made by most paraphrasers of Scripture.

Guideline 5. Do not take from or delete the Scriptures or portions of them. Disregarding the portions of Scripture that you may need for your edification or deliverance also leads to error, as well as incapacitation in the Word.

Guideline 6. Do not embrace doctrines, teachings or messages about God or His ways or activities that are contrary to the Scriptures. Remember, there is nothing new under the sun—not even when a friend tells you so!

Guideline 7. Do not assume the Word is saying or meaning something that is not obvious in the message. Be careful to make sure that any teaching or message you embrace is based on the Word of God. Do not trust your experience(s), emotions or human reason to believe anything that the Word of God does not specifically re-affirm.

There, that wasn't hard was it? Seven guideposts, although they overlap somewhat, all are simple; all are logical. If you will follow these guidelines and make sure that those who would teach you also follow them, you will be safe from false doctrines and teachings that would lead you into some sort of foul bondage of the enemy (Satan).

> <u>Notice</u>: If you find that you are already involved with a group that has made their way by not following these guidelines and you are already following a religious sect, fellowshipping with the people or in captivity by them, you should go directly to Appendix 2 where these matters are discussed. Even if you suspect that you have been engulfed or someone you know has been swept up into one of these groups, whether cult or cult-like church, look at Appendix 2 on the topic of Cocooning and see what the problem may be and how to deal with it.

The Guideposts Expounded

To amplify the guideposts, let's look at some lessons and examples of how some Bible-teachers have been broken them. Going outside the guidelines leads to errors, one error leading to another. The first missed guidepost is the removal of Scripture verses from their context. Most everyone has been guilty of this at one time or another.

Guidepost 1:
Do not remove a Scripture from its Context.

Removing a Scripture from its context probably accounts for more biblical misinformation than any other single cause. It accounts for many of those biblical disagreements that people argue over. It accounts for the vast majority of the alleged contradictions in Scripture. It accounts for those confusing positions distinguishing right from wrong. It accounts for those rambling and inconclusive answers generated by misinformed folks about the Bible and its doctrines. As you will see, there are several ways to move a portion of a message to a place where it doesn't belong!

The first and most basic thing everyone needs to know is this: Not every word of God's Word is for every reader's benefit. When people do not realize this, they are destined to miss several Bible study guideposts.

Look at II Timothy 2:15:

Study to show yourself approved to God, a workman who needs not to be ashamed, rightly dividing the word of truth.

Take notice of the words *rightly dividing*. These words are taken from a Greek word that means *cut straight*. Although the Word of God is a unit, inseparable, there are several groups of people addressed in God's Word. One person or group should not attempt to appropriate the part of the message addressed to someone else. That is where you should make your cut—cutting straight to separate what concerns you from what does not.

Many modern wills (testaments) have several audiences or addressees in them. The will is a unit, with only one intention, but several people may be addressed within the passages of that will. Messages and gifts are distributed according to the will and desires of the deceased.

Those in attendance of the reading of such wills know enough to not claim a gift or message left to someone else. Joe can't claim Jane's gift or message and she can't claim his. Although it is only one will, the several messages and gifts may not be the same for any two people.

So it is with God's Will. A saint of the New Testament shouldn't attempt to obtain something that belongs to an Old Testament saint (although many do make such erroneous claims). And certainly an Old Testament saint could never claim a New Testament believer's blessings. (But some of those of the Old Testament who had a glimpse of salvation would have loved to appropriate for themselves the New Testament blessings!)

Some of the audiences in the Scriptures are the following:

The saints (servants) who were never born-again (Old Testament),

The saints (sons) who were born-again (New Testament),

Those who were under the Law (Jews),

Those who were never under the Law (Gentiles), although some do not know it,

The ones to whom Jesus spoke who were not saints at all, and never would be,

The followers of Jesus who later became saints,

Those who were born-again after the Church-age opened (us),

And many individuals in various circumstances.

Some of these groups were spoken about in messages addressed to someone else—such as the prophecies or historical discussions. We are to *cut straight* and embrace the portions of Scripture that apply to us, are addressed to us, or directly affect us and set other portions aside, knowing they refer to or are addressed to someone else. What portion is ours—meaning "for our use"—serves for our edification and what portion addressed to others serves other purposes, possibly only our learning.

As a matter of fact, it is common knowledge that each of the four Gospels was written for the special benefit of a certain group of people:

> *Matthew* was written for and to the Jews who were under the Law, emphasizing Christ as their Messiah;

> *Mark* was written to the Romans, emphasizing Christ as authoritative and powerful;

> *Luke* was written to the Greeks, emphasizing Christ as intelligent, educated and cultured; and

> *John* was written to all mankind, emphasizing Christ as the Eternal Redeemer and Lover of the soul.

It is foolish for someone who is born again to attempt to appropriate a message addressed to a non-believer. Yet that is exactly what many believers, as well as unbelievers who only profess to be believers, do on a regular basis. Many people simply do not know that a topic discussed in the Bible may have a different perspective from each potential reader of that text, depending on who that reader may be.

If you are a believer—one who has accepted Jesus Christ as Savior and Lord (Romans 10: 9, 10)—would you read the Book of Exodus and start making the Old Testament Tabernacle all over again and start making animal sacrifices? Of course not! No one is so out of touch! Yet some people will cling to some Old Testament principle, ritual or custom because the Law has told the Old Testament Saints to do that ritual or custom, allegedly establishing a principle for New Covenant folks to follow.

We believers often eat pork or catfish, and generally do our church services on the first day of the week. Most of us know that the laws governing food and days were strictly for the Children of Israel.

So were all the Old Testament Laws. No positive reference is made anywhere in the New Testament about the believers keeping or living under the Law! On the contrary, Paul called the Old Testament Law "the Law of Sin and Death" (Romans 8: 2) and he wrote in his epistles directing believers away from the necessity of observing the O. T. Law.

Many believers regard laws of conduct as indicators of the condition of their relationship with God. The relationship between the Father and His children is purely spiritual and no outward manifestation, especially a drummed up one, will have any bearing on that relationship. What someone *compels* himself to do—regardless of which Testament he may use to justify his actions—is a Law.

We believers live by *faith*, and the conduct that we demonstrate should never be worked up or consciously developed as a ritual or act of appeasement of God. Our conduct is based on New Testament guidelines—*Love*—(John 14:15) and that conduct whether good or bad is the fruit of *Faith* (John 14:12), whether that conduct proceeds from an un-renewed and fleshly mind or one that is fully viable and pliable in the Holy Spirit.

When you read a message from someone, anyone, whether God or mortal, identify the addressee or intended recipient of that message, and if you do not fit the identity of the addressee or intended recipient of that message, do not receive that message as your own. If the message is about someone else, let the topic remain someone else's information!

Audience Analysis

On the other end of the spectrum of addressees in the Word is the concept of "Audience Analysis." Audience analysis is important to the speaker or writer because of the message. If the message is not received, or not received well, the message is not effective. Paul specifically mentioned his analysis of the addressees when he wrote to the Corinthians and Galatians. In I Corinthians 3: 1–3 Paul evaluates his readers and their ability to receive his words.

Again in Galatians 4: 9–11 he mentions the readers' attitudes and conduct that reflect their need of the message to them. It is important then to see, not only the needs of the addressees, but their ability to accept the message and its results in their lives—or lack thereof if the audience is not correctly evaluated.

Why did not the Father address the Children of Israel in the same way Jesus spoke to the masses or like Paul addressed these New Testament people? The Children of Israel would find flying much easier than understanding anything of the new birth if regeneration messages had been given to them. Likewise, Paul's epistles to believers would have snowed under the typical Jew that Jesus ministered to, and even Jesus' messages were hard for their un-renewed minds.

The message must apply to the hearer or the hearers effectively have no ears! New Testament believers should be concentrating their reading-studying endeavors in the New Testament (especially the epistles) to find out who and what they are rather than attempting to identify with Old Testament characters and Old Testament circumstances.

Many New Testament, born-again believers see themselves as Old Testament believers, not realizing that Old Testament saints did not believe! Indeed, they could not believe because they were never born-again! Jehovah's responses to Old Testament saints were based on elements that were from outside the person—a God-Servant relationship rather than a New Testament Father-Son relationship. The resultant miracles of the Old Testament were God revealing Himself to them. Indeed, He had to show Himself to them because of their unbelief! In contrast, New Testament miracles were and are the Father being a father to His children.

Some biblical messages may be personal. For instance, the story of Elisha and Naaman tells of a healing of leprosy by washing in the Jordan River seven times (II Kings 5). We know that it worked for Naaman after his struggle with disobedience. It would not work for anyone else, nor will it work today—or there would not be any leprosy left in the world. There would have been a parade of lepers to the Jordan River that would have caused leprosy to disappear from the planet! However, the lesson was for Naaman to be obedient to the Word of the Lord—which we are also to do today *if* that message is clearly addressed to us.

If the message is to unbelievers, we, as believers, should not receive that Word. When we believers attempt to obey God's Word that He has given to unbelievers, we are subtly calling ourselves unbelievers and insulting the Lord and His work in our behalf.

Example One:

> The Lesson: *Suicide is good, all of us should do it, and we should all do it right away.*

The Foundation of Error:

> The Bible says in Matthew 27: 5 that a man (Judas) hanged himself.

And he [Judas] cast down the pieces of silver into the sanctuary, and departed; and he went away and hanged himself.

> The Bible says in Luke 10: 37 that we also are supposed to hang ourselves.

And Jesus said to him, "Go, and you do likewise."

> The Bible says in John 13: 27 that we are do be timely about hanging ourselves.

Jesus therefore said to him, "What you do, do quickly"

Now look at what you have been taught: Judas hanged himself; you should hang yourself, and you should do it immediately! Of course this teaching is ridiculous, but it is exactly what many people do with their Bible-study and Bible-teaching methods. Three verses of Scripture were taken out of their context, then joined into an unholy relationship that culminated with a diabolical message.

Sometimes this maneuver is not intentional, but often it is. The cults use this tactic continually. As a matter of fact, they thrive on this sort of nonsense. Many honest Bible-believing Christians do the same thing because they do not know better.

> An Aside: A symptom of being a cult is that the cultists' attitude asserts that they are the only ones to have the truth (or a truth). They have the attitude that everyone else is wrong! *We are the only ones with the truth and if you are not one of us, you are in deep trouble*!

> When someone reflects this attitude, it is certain that they are at least leaning toward being a cult. Many mainstream churches fall into this category. If you know of someone involved with a group that is like this, go to Appendix 2, "Cocooning."

> Another Aside Regarding Cults: There is a tendency in cults and private dissenters against the Gospel that they must add something to the way God deals with man. They often look at the Old Testament and label it "Plan A," and label the New Testament as "Plan B." They teach that Plan A did not work, so God went to Plan B. Then they invent another plan in the name of God (Plan C, whether it comes by dream, vision, hallucination or science of mind) and call it something that will allow the participants to approach God on some level that neither Plan A nor Plan B would do, since both plans failed so miserably!

> These folks do not realize that the Old Testament has so many illustrations, pictures and other types in it referring to the New Testament that it is obvious that there is only one plan—man's redemption and re-creation. They also do not realize that the teachings in the New Testament refer back at the Old Testament as a precursor to the New—making the two Testaments a united composite of the Word of God.

> While both Testaments refer to each other, neither Testament refers to or acknowledges a Third Testament. (One cult claims that the "other sheep" mentioned in John 10:16 refers to another generation of

followers who come to Jesus by following their book. However, Jesus was speaking to Jews who were hearing the Word for the first time and He was speaking in prophecy of us—His Gentile converts.

Other cults have imagined revelations of a third or fourth or umpteenth Plan and have so preached it to the lost, thus deceiving many.)

So when you hear people claiming the Old Testament did not work (Plan A), so God went to the New Testament (Plan B) and because it failed, too, they have to come up with yet another plan (Plan C), discount them as cultists! The Old Testament bore witness to the New Testament and the New Testament finished the plan for man's redemption as hinted at in the Old Testament. There is no need for further plans, C, D or any other!

Many cultists have claimed revelation knowledge of additional means whereby man can elevate himself to God whether written books or verbal messages. Such additions to God's Word are false and bogus and need to be ignored.

Back to Guidepost 1, if you will notice, some words in these isolated verses are often omitted. In the last two verses, *"to him"* was key. People who deliberately mislead others in their teachings, as well as those who are ignorant of the rules, will leave out or overlook key words of Scripture in order to make their points. There are many valid points that one can make using only portions of verses, but to remove the verse from its context to make that point is deception—often diabolical. (See Antecedents, Chapter 3, *Book 1.*)

You can prevent this error by reading the context and ask yourself some questions about the words being emphasized. Just because something is Scripture, it does not have to be a spiritual truth, not to you or to anyone else. It depends on who said it, to whom it was said, and under what circumstances it was said. The first three questions to ask then are these:

> *Who said it?*
>
> *To whom was it said?*
>
> *What were the circumstances?*

Who Said It?

In the above passages, twice the messenger was identified as Jesus. Did Jesus say those things? Yes.

To Whom Was It Said?

The first question leads to the second question: To whom was He speaking? He was speaking "to him." Because both verses were taken out of context, each *"to him"* means different people. In the account in Luke, Jesus was speaking to an inquisitive lawyer. In the account in John, Jesus was indeed speaking to Judas instructing him to proceed with the betrayal. Jesus knew that the enemy was tempting Judas to betray Him and Jesus allowed him to proceed to that end.

But Jesus did not tell Judas to hang himself. Matthew was recording the events in Jesus' life and recounted that Judas had hanged himself over his remorse for his betrayal of Jesus, thus partly fulfilling prophecy (Jeremiah 18: 1–4; 19: 1–4; Zechariah 11: 12 and 13).

In any event Jesus was not directing the words to the reader! You can readily see the dangers of removing the words from their contexts and even more dangerous to scramble the message like in this example. But some people, even Bible-teachers, do it on a regular basis.

If you are a Christian, and the message is not to Christians, do not receive the message as relevant to you. If you are lost, do not attempt to claim the promises of Christians until you become one.

This demarcation of identities between being a Christian and not being a Christian is very important. That is why believers need to know who they are in Christ and what they are in Christ as well as the other benefits of being a believer. After you know that you have eternal life and the nature of that life (besides being eternal) you will realize that the commands issued by Jehovah through Moses and others of the Old Testament as they spoke to the Israelites exclude you because you are not an Israelite. More on this later.

What were the circumstances?

Example Two: Job 25: 6 says that men are worms. Read it.

How much less is man, who is a worm; or the son of man, who is a worm?

This passage borders on blasphemy because Jesus referred to Himself as *Son of Man* (Matthew 8: 20; Luke 9: 58). Yet here in Job, someone called Jesus a worm! Who said it? Bildad, the Shuhite—a pagan, who had little, if any, knowledge of God at all!

Was Bildad actually referring to Jesus when he said the son of man is a worm? No, absolutely not! He was speaking of man in general as being a low form of life compared to God.

To whom was Bildad speaking? Bildad was replying to Job, who had complained about the violence on earth.

Continuing the same illustration, what were the circumstances under which Bildad made his remark? Why did he say it? Bildad was one of Job's "miserable comforters" (Job 16: 2). He was letting Job know that Job should be more humble because, as Bildad saw it, in spite of Job's charges against life's problem-makers, Job was too proud. Was the pot not calling the kettle black?

You have now seen an illustration of Scriptures out of context, separated by textual isolation. This mistake is so very common that attempting to list more of them would be futile. This mistake is easy to avoid and every person reading or studying the Bible should learn to avoid this type of error on virtually everything they read, especially the Scriptures.

Refer again to the questions:

Who said it?

To whom was it said?

Under what circumstances was it said?

And now, more specifically, add another question: *Is the message to or about me?*

Is the message to or about me?

If someone reads or quotes verses to you, always make sure that you make them read or quote several verses before and several verses after the emphasized verse in order to check the context. Then, if you do not fit the description of the addressee in the Scripture, do not accept the message of that passage as your own.

The easiest way to avoid removing Scripture from its context is to always read the surrounding verses along with the referred one(s). Read the whole chapter (or book!) if need be, but find out who said it, to whom was he (all the writers of Scripture were males) speaking, and what were the circumstances. If you do not find yourself in that message, do not identify with that message. Leave it for the ones to whom God is speaking.

Breaking Lists:

Another Way to Take Scriptures from Their Context

We are still on the topic of isolation Scriptures from their context. Everyone, individual and group alike, wants to consider himself, herself or themselves as having the best there is to have. We want the best home, the best car, the best clothes, and so on.

This seems to be especially applicable to people regarding their relationship with their politics and their God, their religion, their church and their understanding and operation in these relationships.

When someone applies for a job or position that they really want but are not sure they are qualified to do, they often stretch their qualifications by omitting any possibly negative information about themselves or by embellishing their qualities. If the list of qualifications has a dozen points to it, they may highlight only ten of their better qualifications and omit the other two that they may not have or are weak on.

Like a job-seeker or a braggart, it is pitiful to what level some political minded people will stoop to in order to make a political statement or to get elected. In such cases lying is not excluded! Even more pitiful are those religious people (even Christians) who stoop to unknown levels to make themselves appear different from what they really are.

These religious people may not be seeking a public office, but their goal for gaining influence is just as loathsome. Some of the tactics they use include attempting to change the qualifications for their position as believers. They will highlight their achievements in the Lord and disregard the Scriptures that point to some lack on their part. It defies logic, but one of the tactics used to do this is simply omitting or explaining away the things in Scripture that they do not manifest or do not practice as believers. Often they start out by breaking the Bible-study principles.

In order to make themselves look better, they will break up a list, claiming that some of the things on a list are either done away with at the end of the New Testament (or the death of John) and are not needed today, or that the things mentioned have been excluded by the Lord.

Specifically look at the lists in Mark 16, Romans 12, I Corinthians Chapters 12 and 14, and Ephesians 4. The Mark 16 list (Vv. 17 and 18) comprises of these five elements, the signs that should accompany believers:

They shall cast out demons;

They will speak in new tongues;

They shall take up serpents;

If they shall drink a deadly thing, it shall not hurt them; and

They shall lay hands on the sick and they shall recover.

The Romans 12 list (Vv. 6-8) has on it these items, the gifts according grace:

Prophecy,	Ministry,	Teaching,
Exhortation,	Giving,	Leading, and
Showing Mercy.		

The list in I Corinthians 12: 7-11 consists of nine of the gifts of the Holy Spirit:

Word of Wisdom,	Word of Knowledge,
Faith,	Gifts of Healing,
Working of Miracles,	Prophecy,
Discerning of Spirits,	Unknown Tongues, and
Interpretation of Tongues.	

The list of the offices of the church in Ephesians 4: 11 include these:

Apostles,	Prophets,
Evangelists,	Pastors and Teachers.

Many ministries and church denominations teach their followers to embrace some items and to disregard other items on these lists. Those items most often omitted are these:

All items on the Mark 16 list.

Only one item is challenged or avoided on the list in Romans:

Prophecy.

Often shunned items on the I Corinthians list are these (8 of 9):

Prophecy,	Word of Wisdom,
Word of Knowledge,	Gifts of Healing,
Working of Miracles,	Discerning of Spirits,
Unknown Tongues,	Interpretation of Tongues.

Often avoided items from the list in Ephesians are these:

Apostles, and   Prophets.

Intermingled on these lists, except the one in Mark, are items that nearly all churches approve of and claim to have:

Ministry,	Teaching,	Exhortation,
Giving,	Leading,	Showing Mercy,
Faith,	Evangelists,	Pastors and
Teachers.		

By the way some ministries and church denominations have divided these gifts, operations and offices up to suit themselves you would think that there are two sets of lists!

Regarding the items on these lists more specifically, the functions on the list found in Mark 16 are all signs that are supposed to accompany believers. According to this passage, if someone claims to be a believer, these signs should accompany him or her as needed.

A few churches and ministries use and practice the signs on this list, while some groups abuse these signs and make a show of them, making a spectacle of themselves while they do it. In spite of the open and obvious manifestation of these gifts in question by many people, there are many other churches, ministries and individual believers who deny the operation, existence, presence or blessings of these signs in any and all forms. They act as if because these particular people do not manifest these signs, these signs should simply go away so that these people do not appear as if they have any lack in their spiritual lives.

Looking at the context in Mark, it is obvious that the Lord intended that all believers manifest these signs as needed in their lives. After the Lord's resurrection, Jesus met with His disciples: Mark 16: 15–18:

And He [Jesus] said to them [His disciples], "Go into all the world, and preach the gospel to the whole creation. He who believes and is baptized shall be saved; but he who disbelieves shall be condemned. And these signs shall accompany those who believe: In My name they shall cast out demons; they shall speak with new tongues; they shall take up serpents, and if they drink any deadly thing, it shall in no wise hurt them; they shall lay hands on the sick, and they shall recover."

There were no exclusions mentioned, nor was there a time element present to make these signs appear to be a temporary or limited promise. Jesus plainly said these signs would accompany believers. If these signs do not accompany a believer as needed, something is wrong somewhere. The problem will not be with the message or with Jesus. That means whoever the person is who claims to be a believer yet does not have these signs follow him or her is suspect.

This suspicion is what these list-breakers want to avoid. They want to look good to their neighbors and especially to prospective converts, regardless. The avoided items are averted in any way they can be averted. Some have said the items simply ended; other said they are no longer needed; and some have tried to see to the removal of these verses from the text of the Bible. (See Appendix 3 where the last objection is discussed in detail.)

Referring to the list in Romans 12, (Prophesy, Ministry, Teaching, Exhortation, Giving, Leading, Showing Mercy) Paul is writing of the body of believers being one Body in Christ. This, too, has no reference to time or other limitations. In the preceding verses (3–5), Paul writes of this unity of the Body, and then he presents the list of gifts that are obviously for the whole Body of Christ.

Following the list in Romans 12: 6–8 is another list (Vv. 10–21) that is seldom, if ever, broken into pieces. On that list are items of Christian character, all of which appear to be above reproach because all are so logical, even if every individual may not manifest all of them.

It may be obvious to some of us that the items on the list of gifts are needed in order to produce or perform the items on the other list! In other words, the things on first list empower the believer to produce the items on the second list!

The problem arises and becomes obvious when people expect the items on the second list to develop but they do not. The reason they do not develop is because the items on the first list are not being practiced or otherwise manifested! You cannot have the items on the last list without the abilities on the first list—the one that has so often been ignored or mutilated!

The list in I Corinthians has been mutilated by some people because they accuse the Corinthian Church of having so many problems within its membership and was thus not only a "primitive" church, but a fleshly one, too. The problem with an argument that uses these excuses is so illogical that it is difficult to comment on in brevity.

> <u>One</u>: If the Corinthian Church was so primitive, why has not the denomination or ministry that condemns or omits the Gifts of the Holy Spirit ever manifested the items on the list even briefly as they develop past the primitive stage? In the same vein, why have

not those who hold their superiority over the primitive Corinthian Church ever surpassed these Gifts with bigger and better gifts?

<u>Two</u>: Paul enumerated problems with individuals in the Corinthian congregation and made solid recommendations to fix the problems. What ministry or denomination that mutilates this list of gifts of the Holy Spirit does not have equal or worse problems within its membership? Then, when these modern problems surface, how does that church leadership deal with them? Excommunication? Fines? Dismissal? Censuring? Shunning the offender(s)? Penances? Condemning the offender(s)? Cover-ups? Musical assignments (Move the offender to another church)? What? How? Or maybe they merely ignore the problem(s)!

The churches and ministries that so readily point to the fleshliness and primitiveness of the Corinthian Church and its membership respond to their own fleshliness and primitiveness in an absurdly immature and childish manner! Titles, degrees, culture, pluralities and splendor in materialism do not amount to spiritual advancement. If one is not gifted by the Holy Spirit, be honest enough to admit it and seek the Father-God's remedy.

Some churches and ministries have taught that tongues and prophecies have discontinued by using Paul's comments in I Corinthians 13: 8, a verse found in the middle of the Love Chapter. This verse also has a list that these folks who teach this doctrine are breaking up:

I Corinthians 13: 8 Love never fails: but whether *there be* prophecies, they shall be done away; whether *there be* tongues, they shall cease; whether *there be* knowledge, it shall be done away.

There is the list: Prophecies, Tongues and Knowledge. Those who do not believe in practicing the gifts of the Holy Spirit teach that prophecies and tongues have been done away with in the modern church. They overlook the fact that if prophecies and tongues have been done away with, so has knowledge!

They also usually fail to see the next verses where Paul tells when these things will be removed.

I Corinthians 13: 9–11 For we know in part, and we prophesy in part; but when what is perfect has come, what is in part shall be done away.

11 When I was a child, I spoke as a child, I felt as a child, I thought as a child: now that I am become a man, I have put away childish things.

Some folks have asserted that the "perfect one that is to come" is man's complete understanding of the Bible. Therefore we are able to reason as mature men and women. So we do not need these two gifts—the tongues and prophecy. (But there are three gifts on that list.)

Furthermore, if Paul meant that this perfect one that is coming is man's revelation of the Bible's full meaning, why are there so many denominations? If our understanding of the Word is already perfect all the churches would be one! Why do we have so many translations of the Word if our understanding of it is already perfect? Why are there so many Bible commentaries if our understanding is already perfect? Why did I write this document and why are you reading it?

Here is something that cannot be passed off as lightly as simply making a statement, regardless of how simple or complex the rationale behind that statement may seem. In our daily convoluted personal situations, we often need to know the direction we are to take in our family lives, in our businesses or in our academic, professional and social lives. Where are our specific instructions in the Bible? Where are the really tough questions about personal decisions answered in the Bible, the Word of God?

These questions are not answered in the Bible. Such leading has to come from the Lord and Him alone. It is the Holy Spirit who answers those life-leading, life-changing questions. The only recourse believers have often comes by divine leading through the gifts in operation, prophecy, tongues and their interpretation, Word of Wisdom or Word of Knowledge.

As further proof of the identity of Perfection that Paul referred to in Verse 9, read Verse 12 of the same passage:

I Corinthians 13: 12 and 13 For now we see in a mirror, darkly; but then face to face: now I know in part; but then shall I know fully even as also I was fully known.

13 But now abides faith, hope, love, these three; and the greatest of these is love.

Where is the face of the Bible? It has no face! Looking at all of the characteristics alluded to in this passage, only the Lord Jesus can meet all of these criteria when He returns as Redeemer to reign as King of Kings and Lord of Lords!

You see, there is a lot of information available if the Scriptures are simply left in context when you read and study them. The list in question in Ephesians is another example of items needed to produce items on yet another list. The first list consists of items that are intended for the whole Church-Body as it matures in Him. This list of church offices and their functions are designed to produce or make manifest the items on the next list, one that is seldom, if ever, mutilated, the equipping and edifying of the Body of Christ. As long as there is a Body of Christ on Earth, these offices and their functions will be needed. The offices are these:

Apostles,   Prophets,   Evangelists,

Pastors and Teachers.

The beneficiaries of these offices are members of the Body of Christ so that the membership would manifest these things:

Our unity in the Faith;

Our knowledge of the Son of God;

Our becoming mature men and women;

Our manifestation of the measure of the stature of the fullness of Christ;

Our being no longer children tossed about and carried away with every sort of doctrine;

Our speaking the truth in love;

Our growing in Him, who is the Head—Christ.

The bottom line is that lists have been broken at the convenience of those who feel the need to avoid their responsibility before the Lord. In spite of what the Scriptures may include on this list or elsewhere, these folks have abused breaking lists in order to make themselves appear to be more than they are or appear to be different than they are.

It follows then that many of these people who eliminate items on these various lists would be the very same ones who establish their own human-inspired programs and human facilitated programs to replace those gifts, operations, administrations and offices that the Father has established. In other words, they would rather do things led by the human flesh than do those things according to the leading of the Father and His Word. In yet other words, Christianity would be replaced with *religion*!

Guidepost 2:
Do not misappropriate the message of the Word.

Removal of the verses from their context leads right to the next logical guidepost: Do not misappropriate the Word.

Example One: *Wisdom*

One of the many cults that claim to be the only true followers of God holds the following teaching: Man is an ageless being, moving from one evolutionary existence to another and to another and finally as they get closer to being godlike, they manage to go be with God. One word defines their stance: *Reincarnation.* Here is one of the distortions of the Word they use to prove their teaching. They point out these verses in Proverbs 8, starting with Verse 22:

22 Jehovah possessed me in the beginning of His way, before His works of old.

23 I was set up from everlasting, from the beginning, before the earth was.

24 When there were no depths, I was brought forth, when there were no fountains abounding with water.

25 Before the mountains were settled, before the hills was I brought forth;

These verses that supposedly prove pre-existence continue for several more verses. The proponents of reincarnation make their argument sound almost appealing and reasonable. *Someone was with God before creation came about. Why not everyone?*

This sounds great—until the verses are put back into their context. To put the verses into their context, you need to go all the way back to the first verse of the chapter. There the context identifies to whom *"I"* and *"Me"* refer. *I* and *Me* refer, not to the reader, nor to an individual, nor to people as a whole; it refers to *Wisdom*—a personification of one of the attributes of Jehovah.

Not only have these misguided folks run over the first guidepost by removing the Scripture from its context, but they smashed into the second one: Do not embrace Scriptures that do not regard you by address, topic or subject. They appropriated the verses that refer to someone or something else for themselves.

In the above example, had they not taken the verses from their context, they would never have embraced the message and believed that the one who was mentioned as being pre-existent was themselves. Any reader of any message should not assume that a pronoun refers to the reader unless that pronoun is "*you*." Even then the context may indicate that the reader is still not the "*you*" who the writer addressed. (See <u>Antecedent</u>, Chapter 3, *Book 1*.)

Another case of misappropriation of Scripture has misled many believers. They read Luke 21: 12 and believe that Christians will go through the great tribulation predicted by Christ.

> **But before all these things, they shall lay their hands on you, and shall persecute you, delivering you up to the synagogues and prisons, bringing you before kings and governors for My name's sake.**

Yes, the word *you* is found there, but does it mean you, the reader? Look at the context. First the topic is the Great Tribulation of "Last Days" and "Prophecy" fame. Second, look at the addressee. Jesus was speaking to Jews, the un-regenerated, lost sheep of the House of Israel—not to believers! Simply put, you (the reader of this document) will never be taken to a synagogue for judgment.

You will never be brought before a king for any reason. You may in these last days be brought before an American council or other (maybe even a vile governor) and accused of something, and may even go to prison, but being brought before the synagogue or king, never!

Jews were Jesus' addressees. Jesus never in His earthly walk spoke to a believer—not one! He spoke of believers often, but not to believers. No one became a believer until after the resurrection of the Lord Jesus, not even His disciples. So He could not have communicated with any believers before He became Redeemer to all who have accepted Him as such. Therefore, if someone believes that we believers are going through the Great Tribulation, they better find other Scripture sources for reinforcement. These verses in Luke will not confirm their fears.

Example Two: *Fall Away*

Yet another instance of misappropriation caused by isolation of verses from their context is found in Hebrews. First of all, the Book of Hebrews is addressed to those who were not only Jews by birth, but the Jews of that day who had actually been under the Old Law. The topic deals much with the Law, the prophecies, and Christ who fulfilled both and how He did it.

It is imperative that readers see to whom the message was intended. The addressee of the message will be found in the context and is often in the verses cited if the reader reads carefully. Repeating, there are many addressees in the Word of God: The Hebrews of the Old Testament, as well as the New, pagans, believers, disciples and many individuals.

Many believers overlook the addressee and the topic and see Chapter 6, Vv. 4–6.

> 4 For as touching those who were once enlightened and tasted of the heavenly gift, and were made partakers of the Holy Spirit, and tasted the good Word of God, and the powers of the age to come, and *then* fell away, it is impossible to renew them again to repentance; seeing they crucify to themselves the Son of God afresh, and put Him to an open shame.

The errant believers know that they themselves had been enlightened, and that they themselves had tasted the heavenly Gift and had partaken of the Holy Spirit. They assume that these verses apply to them based on their own experience in the Lord, which may have been real and genuine. They came to the conclusion that they were the topic of the discourse. However, if you will read carefully the message, you will see that believers are not the addressee here, nor are they the topic!

First, read Hebrews 3: 1 where the addressee is identified as "*Hebrews*"— Holy Brethren, partakers of the heavenly calling. That addressee does not change in the whole Book of *Hebrews*.

If that isn't enough to convince you that these verses are not to be used to warn believers of their falling away, read the passage carefully. Look at the pronouns in the text quoted:

Those—who were once enlightened

They—if they shall fall away

Them—renewed again to repentance

They—crucify to themselves

Themselves—who crucify the Son of Man afresh.

These are all third person pronouns. First person pronouns are *I, me, my, mine* and *we, us, our, ours*, pronouns that refer to one's self, whether singular or plural.

Second person pronouns are *you, your, yours,* pronouns that refer to "you." The second person pronouns for you are always plural in usage but can be either singular or plural in meaning. (The verb attending *you* even when *you* is singular in meaning is always plural, such as "You are" or "You have" in contrast to the improper singular usage of "You is" or "You has.").

Third person pronouns are *she, he, him, her, it, they, those, them, themselves,* and any other pronoun pertaining to anyone or anything not of "*me*" or "*you.*"

The writer of Hebrews is not writing of himself—not first person. In the cited passage he is not writing to you as a New Testament believer. He is writing about *those, they, them, they* and *themselves* (the previous list), Jews who were considering Jesus as Messiah, either having already committed themselves or are considering so doing. His topic or subject is those Jews who are considering Christ, their Messiah, third person.

Further proof is in verse 9:

> But, beloved, we [first person] are persuaded better things of you [second person], and things that accompany salvation, though we thus speak:

The message here in Hebrews before verse nine is not concerning believers because the subjects "*they*" and "*them*" did not have salvation and they did not relate to things of salvation. In verse nine the addressee changes to "you who have salvation and relate to the things of salvation." Only believers have salvation and only believers relate to the things that pertain to salvation! This address to *you as having salvation* appears in contrast to *they, them,* and *those* and *their unbelief* and *their falling away* of the previous verses.

Many people believe that a believer can become lost again. If that is true, other verses than these must be used to teach that message.

There are many other things we can learn and questions that can be answered by keeping the Word in its context. The context can not only reveal who said it and to whom, but also the circumstances that inspired or provoked the message. The context can show where the address was presented, when it was presented and why it was presented. All of these factors should be considered when planning to incorporate the lessons of the Bible into your life.

If the passage was Old Testament, unless it was prophetic, it is unlikely that believers can identify with the message except through type and foreshadow (which are forms of prophecy). Of course we can see in the Old Testament what conduct may please or displease the Lord by understanding what He determines to be good and decent conduct and we can respond appropriately. However, to respond with a legalistic idea of earning the Father's endorsement is not correct.

Most of what we New Testament believers should identify with are the letters or epistles in the New Testament. Many of the things Jesus said apply to us and we can embrace, but many things He said He spoke to the Jews who were there in front of Him when He said it. We cannot take of these things without carefully weighing the message to see if it is relating to us as believers. The epistles are all addressed to believers and it is upon them that we can most readily rely.

It is essential that believers realize that the Old Testament Laws were addressed solely to the Jews of that day. Christ fulfilled all of those Laws and in so doing gave those who know Him as Savior the ability and power to say "No" to all the temptations that sin may have on their lives. (There is more on this topic. [See <u>Shifting from Old to New</u>, Chapter 2, *Book 2*.])

Guidepost 3:
Do not redefine the words of the Scriptures.

The vocabulary and the meanings of the words of Scripture are very important. When there is no clarity of those definitions, confusion follows. Confusion leads to error and error leads to loss of blessings, including never having eternal life if the error is that far removed from its truth.

Some erroneous doctrines come from the practice of re-defining terms to suit the needs or desires of the teacher and his point of view. Many people do it; some out of ignorance, but some for the same reason that people break lists—to make themselves look good!

If changing the meaning of words were to become legitimate and acceptable, there are no bounds on what people could logically teach regarding the Word of God. So let's pick on a word that many denominations and ministries have allowed to change meaning.

Prophecy—Prophesy

The word we select is *prophecy,* (the noun) or *prophesy,* (the verb). According to dictionaries, *Strong's Exhaustive Concordance of the Bible* (Strong's), and Scripture references, the noun *prophecy* means *"a forecast"* or *"a prediction"* and the verb *prophesy* means *"to foretell"* or *"to predict."*

In spite of the real definition, some groups define the verb as *"forth-tell."* (The noun could possibly be called *bull*.) The definition *"forth tell"* for *prophecy* fulfills their desires in having prophecy in their churches according to I Corinthians 14: 39, "Covet to prophesy . . . ."

A true *prophecy* as meant as a gift of the Holy Spirit is a message anointed by the Holy Spirit that makes a prediction, while *forth telling* is any utterance, intelligent or not, anointed or not.

Of course the *redefined prophecy* means that they can assess themselves to believe in all of the Scriptures, yet without operating in the true gift of prophecy—or usually any of the other gifts of the Holy Spirit.

All of the prophetic books of the Bible were written by or about the prophets of God, and these people did prophesy (foretell the future or some aspect of it). None of the false (pagan) prophets really prophesied because they could not. Only one of God's prophets in the Scriptures did not predict the future to some extent and that one prophet was not assigned as a prophet of God, but was assigned as a prophet of Moses—a man. In the conflict with Pharaoh, God gave Aaron the position of Moses' prophet because of Moses' slowness of speech. All Aaron ever did was exactly what Moses told him, but he did not function long. By the time the plague of flies came on Egypt, Moses was speaking by himself at God's instruction. Aaron was only a bystander for the rest of the confrontation with Pharaoh (Exodus 7: 1–10: 29).

The word *prophecy* is linked many times to words previously spoken about later events—predictions. Some people contend that the *Word of Wisdom*, the *Word of Knowledge, Messages in Unknown Tongues* along with the *Interpretation of Tongues* (all four being gifts of the Holy Spirit) are forms of prophecy. They could be right because these utterances are inspired directly from the Holy Spirit just like prophecy is. These gifts did not appear in the Old Testament on a regular basis because they are specifically for use in the church age. However, these gifts are not merely "forth-telling!"

Those churches, ministries and teachers who define *prophecy* as *forth-telling* seldom, if ever, experience any of the gifts of the Holy Spirit as portrayed in the Scriptures. If they have to re-define the words in order to qualify as being an example of the scriptural church, they have abandoned the real gifts of the Holy Spirit—thus also abandoning the Word of God. Ego causes their loss of objectivity, not only leading them to defend their church-doctrine so unwisely, but even in their downright self-promotion and bias.

Some churches have it doubly difficult. Having two shoes on the topic of the gifts of the Holy Spirit really makes them look foolish—both shoes being on the wrong feet! If prophecy were to be done away with as some allege in the breaking the list in I Corinthians 13: 8, how in the world would they prophesy in any case in their services thus fulfilling I Corinthians 14: 1?

Those who use the new definitions of *prophesy* and *prophecy* do not realize what any of the gifts of the Holy Spirit really are and how they come to be performed. The only thing they know about the Holy Spirit is what they read in the Scriptures (which they obviously do not really understand) or are taught by their fellows in their ignorance. (The blind do indeed lead the blind at times!)

Reading about swimming does not automatically teach someone how to swim. They have not been filled with the Holy Spirit and when they try to emulate His operations, they miss the mark. The gifts of the Holy Spirit are not show-off manifestations.

Some people on the other side of the issue (those who condone and promote the gifts of the Holy Spirit) are liable to counterfeit the gifts to show themselves to be more than they really are.

The gifts are for ministering purposes only. When a need is present or about to manifest itself, one of the gifts can be used to remedy the situation—whether by healing, deliverance, instruction or teaching through prophecy—even when the person(s) do not know what is hampering them or what is about to hamper them. The Holy Spirit knows about the enemy and his activities and He heads him off with the use of these gifts. It is indeed a shame when people make His gifts a sham, a mere point of doctrine to be disputed!

Simply Re-defining or out-and-out Lying? - Tithing

This example of redefinition of words is really bewildering. It is so widely accepted as fact, so often preached and taught, and presented as so reasonable and logical that virtually no one challenges the definition or the concept.

Almost every church and ministry, regardless of their stance on the Old Testament Law, embraces this concept of re-definitions. The topic is *tithing.* Even churches that teach that the New Testament is the only way to go for believers will forget all about the obsolescence of the Old Testament Law and teach the necessity of tithing.

> Malachi 3: 10 "Bring you the whole tithe into the storehouse, that there may be food in My house, and prove Me now herewith," says Jehovah of Hosts, "if I will not open you the windows of heaven, and pour you out a blessing, that there shall not be room enough *to receive it.*"

There is the promise, loud and clear. But the subtle thing is the context, the addressees and the definitions—all three guideposts smashed here in a single swoop!

Who was speaking (or writing)? Malachi was writing in the Name of Jehovah.

To whom was Jehovah addressing His message? He was addressing the Israelites.

What were the circumstances under which Jehovah was addressing these Israelites? Jehovah was speaking to those Jews who were instructed to rebuild Jerusalem (particularly the walls and the temple there) after their return from Babylon.

Exactly what was the message? Breaking the message down one point at a time, the first part of the message was instructing these Israelites to bring their tithes to the storehouse. The storehouse was where the people brought the wherewithal for the workers who were to continue to rebuild the city's walls and the temple and sustain themselves.

Where do New Testament people have a storehouse? The church is not a storehouse. The church's bank account is not a storehouse. The parsonage is not a storehouse. What is the New Testament storehouse? The only storehouse we New Testament believers have is the LORD—the Father-God Himself!

Are we supposed to give of our substance to the Lord? Yes, repeatedly we New Testament believers are taught to give. But how much are we supposed to give? The Word does not mention anywhere the tithe as a duty of the New Testament believer. "Let him give as he purposes in his heart" (II Corinthians 9: 7) is a decision left between the believer and the Holy Spirit. We should give according to what blessing we receive of Him and how we are led by the Holy Spirit. The whole matter is discussed in the 9th Chapter of II Corinthians.

The main principle on giving in the New Testament is according to a passage in Luke:

> Luke 6: 38 Give, and it shall be given to you; good measure, pressed down, shaken together, running over, shall they give into your bosom. For with what measure you mete it shall be measured to you again.

So our giving is determined somewhat by how we are blessed and somewhat by the way we want to share. There is a saying that is not

Scripture but is still very believable: "You cannot out-give God." As far as is known, it has never been done. Some folks have set up to attempt it on a trial basis and have failed. The Father always rewards the giver with more than he or she gives. This is confirmed in II Corinthians 9: 6-11:

6 But this *I say*, He who sows sparingly shall reap also sparingly; and he who sows bountifully shall reap also bountifully. *Let* each man *do* according as he has purposes in his heart: not grudgingly, or of necessity: for God loves a cheerful giver. And God is able to make all grace abound to you; that you, having always all sufficiency in everything, may abound to every good work: As it is written, "He has scattered abroad; he has given to the poor; his righteousness abides forever."

10 And He who supplies seed to the sower and bread for food, shall supply and multiply your seed for sowing, and increase the fruits of your righteousness: you being enriched in everything to all liberality, which works through us thanksgiving to God.

So the message of giving is valid, and so is the subsequent. promise of blessing. The means and methods used to urge people to give using Malachi's message is NOT valid. It is deception and laying an unnecessary guilt trip on the believers. Look at the verses just before the tenth verse.

Malachi 3: 8 Will a man rob God? Yet you rob Me. But you say, "Wherein have we robbed You?" In tithes and offerings. You are cursed with the curse; for you rob Me, even this whole nation.

The assumption is that we believers are recipients of this message—our robbery of God, our becoming thieves and robbers, our missing of the blessings of the open window and the flood of goodness from it—and we have thus developed into some sort of a nation by robbing God if we do not establish a method of tithing!

The real addressees of the message in Malachi were the Jews in the reconstruction days. The storehouse is not the church, nor vice-versa. There is no food in the church that is brought in by the parishioners. That food was to sustain the workers building the city walls and the temple. This wholesale re-defining of terms and functions on such a near universal scale proves that the modern churches are often more big business than a ministry of God! The Father doesn't need to brow-beat believers to have them give to support Him and His work. Only men in their carnality do such low business!

However, there is a viable counter-response to the charge that the giving of the tithe is under the Law. It was not factually under the Law.

Abraham (Abram) established the principle of giving a tithe long before the Law came by Moses (Genesis 14: 20). Moses was given the Law from the LORD later, as recorded in Exodus 20. So, strictly speaking, the tithe is not a part of the Law; tithing pre-dated the Law.

Therefore, if you want to give ten percent of your income to the Father, He will accept it and bless you for it. He will do likewise with 12%, 20% or 5%. He is your Father and He has blessings in store for you that you cannot count! He appreciates your faithfulness and consideration, but you are not to be bound to a church, ministry or other party to accept your tithes, offerings or anything else you may be urged or coerced to give.

You are to give to Him according to the way He leads and to whom He may instruct. He may lead you to give some amount to a church or ministry, but He may also lead you to give to an orphan, to a widow, to someone who is ill, to a missionary, or maybe to someone who is simply in need or out of work for a time!

If you give all your offerings (tithes) to a church or ministry, how can you give to the other parties in their need? The Lord will instruct you to whom to give. After all, He, not the organized church, is the owner of the tithe, if that is still your position (Leviticus 27: 30).

So far we have looked at the guideposts that deal with isolation of the Scriptures from their context, misappropriation of these Scriptures and redefining the words of Scripture. The examples given are by no means the only instances when these rules have been broken, but you now should know what these rules are and what they mean. And you should begin to see how to examine the various teachings of people and compare them to Scripture.

Guidepost Four:
Do not add to the Scriptures.
and
Guidepost Five:
Do not take from or delete the Scriptures.

We will now look at the other guideposts. The events that lead to the fall of man are based on avoiding the next two guideposts. The first one is the addition to the message of the Word of God and the second one is the counterpart, the deletion from the message of God's Word.

In the Garden

After the creation of Adam and Eve, before they were expelled from the Garden of Eden, the enemy, Satan, lured Eve and she then lured Adam into their decision to disobey Jehovah and partake of the forbidden fruit of the tree of the knowledge of good and evil.

Before Eve was created, Jehovah had instructed Adam to not eat of the tree of the knowledge of good and evil.

Genesis 2: 16 And Jehovah God commanded the man, saying, "Of every tree of the garden you may freely eat: but of the tree of the knowledge of good and evil, you shall not eat of it: for in the day that you eat thereof you shall surely die."

After Eve came on the scene, Satan, disguised as a serpent, came to her and seduced her to eat of the forbidden tree.

Genesis 3: 1 Now the serpent was more subtle than any beast of the field that Jehovah God had made. And he said to the woman, "Yea, has God said, 'You shall not eat of any tree of the garden?'"

2 And the woman said to the serpent, "Of the fruit of the trees of the garden we may eat: but of the fruit of the tree that is in the midst of the garden, God has said, 'You shall not eat of it, neither shall you touch it, lest you die.'"

Notice what Jehovah had said: "You shall not eat of the tree." (Genesis 2: 16) Then compare that with what Eve said He said: "You shall not eat of it or even touch it." (Genesis 3: 2) The fact is this: Adam and Eve were to be keepers of the garden. They had to have been allowed to touch the tree or they would be guilty of neglecting the tree. But Eve said that God had forbidden not only the eating of the fruit of the tree, but the touching of it as well. She added to God's command.

Then the serpent (Satan's instrument of deception) contradicted Jehovah by calling Jehovah a liar and countermanded His ordinance.

Genesis 3: 4 And the serpent said to the woman, "You shall not surely die: for God knows that in the day you eat thereof, then your eyes shall be opened, and you shall be as God, knowing good and evil."

Satan blasphemed and said Jehovah-God had lied to them because they would not really die. Satan made his contradiction sound reasonable because of Jehovah's alleged ulterior motive—not to allow Adam and Eve to become like Him, knowing good and evil.

The contradiction is not really all that reasonable to begin with. Jehovah created them and that creation was intended to create someone with whom

He could fellowship. Why would He create someone or something that He would be averse to or that would conceivably develop into something to which He would become averse? He knew what was going to happen before it happened and to think He was concerned about the works of His own designs is absolutely ridiculous!

Satan reinforced his deception with a "revelation:" Eve saw that what the serpent said was true. So, not every revelation is from the LORD. Satan has his revelations, too! She ate and shared with Adam.

> 6 And when the woman saw that the tree was good for food, and that it was a delight to the eyes, and that the tree was to be desired to make one wise, she took of the fruit thereof, and ate; and she gave also to her husband with her, and he ate.

At this point it was too late. They found out that Jehovah had not lied and they found out that only part of what the Tempter had said was true: They did indeed know something more than they did before!

What they learned was not good: They saw their own inadequacies. Furthermore, they enacted a plan to remedy their inadequacies with works of their own hands. Their "revelation" led them to see two things:

They saw themselves as lacking, and

They saw Jehovah as limited.

Both of these "revelations" fell into the category of Untrue—Harmful Teachings. Then they compounded the problem. They tried to hide what they had done. They assumed God was not as He is and they tried to fool Him! They couldn't hide what they had done any more than they could fly. What they had done caused them to become something other than what Jehovah had created. They gave up their immortality and became mortal! All of this robbery by Satan happened because they had failed to follow God's Word.

When they tried to hide what they had done, they established a trend that has lasted ever since: Natural un-regenerated man has tried to make a means to reach God on man's own terms.

Like Adam and Eve, and this episode in the Garden, masses of egocentric men, too, have failed. But they had to try it. And many are still trying it!

> 7 And the eyes of them both were opened, and they knew that they were naked; and they sewed fig-leaves together, and made themselves aprons.

8 And they heard the voice of Jehovah God walking in the garden in the cool of the day: and the man and his wife hid themselves from the presence of Jehovah God amongst the trees of the garden.

The rest of the event you know. If you do not know, you should be careful to take the time to read it. The LORD put His eternal plan into motion. He did four things:

He came to them and expelled them from the Garden,

He limited their time of existence on earth,

He laid the blame on Satan, as it should have been, and

He made the very first promise of redemption through Christ. He predicted Satan's doom by the Seed (Christ).

Eve added words to the LORD's command to not eat of the tree. Where did they miss the other guidepost? No one mentioned the result of the breaking of the command—the immediate death of Adam. Adam died the day he ate of the forbidden tree.

That death was not obvious on one hand. He remained vertical, looked at the grass from the green side, talked, functioned, reasoned, fathered children, responded and carried on as if normal (except he was outside the Garden!), but he was actually dead as a sun-dried carp! He had died spiritually.

Not only did Adam die, but Eve died, too. That is why they realized they were naked. The presence of the LORD on their lives and their relationship with Him had protected them from the realization of their nudity. Indeed, Jehovah and His glory on them must have hidden their nakedness.

Some people emphatically teach that there was an aura that covered Adam and Eve during this time—an aura from the relationship with Jehovah. There is no known scriptural reason for this doctrine (outside the one we are discussing), but there was something that kept them decent that was missing after they disobeyed the LORD. They had died. Their spirits were no longer connected to or related to the Divine and they were spiritually dead.

Adam and Eve's alteration of that portion of God's Word was not mentioned verbally, but it was certainly obvious to everyone that the LORD's Word was dominant in these events: They died!

Death dominated all of man until the New Testament age when new life was given to believers through Jesus Christ. Spiritual death's condition was manifested so thoroughly in the Old Testament people that the spirit of man was never mentioned until Christ brought it to the attention of His followers. The Sadducees of Jesus' day did not believe in any form of spiritual life. The Pharisees believed only in an after-life that was spiritual. The Old Testament writers did not understand spiritual life much, if at all, so any mention of it was only a hint.

Someone may have added to God's word; someone may have deleted or ignored another portion of His Word; but no one has ever invalidated any portion of it!

There are other instances of addition, deletion or otherwise altering the Word—too many to mention because almost everyone does it—either knowingly or unknowingly. It is hard to know all there is to know about a biblical topic; therefore, it is not hard to be misinformed regarding that topic. The remedy is to be as well informed as you can on relevant topics of the Bible.

You may want to look at Appendix 3 to see other problem areas that are due to changes in the Bible's text. There is also more information coming up in Chapter 2 under "Mistranslations."

Editorial or Translational Additions to the Text of the Word

The translators and/or editors have taken on the responsibility to make Hebrew, Greek and Aramaic into logical and correct English. Both of the principle languages of the Bible, Hebrew and Greek, as well as some more modern languages, have a limited use of the *Be* verb. They do not use a *Be* verb except to emphasize the meaning of it, such as the tense of the verb.

The *Be* verbs, in case you have forgotten, are these*: Is, am, are, was* and *were*, along with the future indicators used with the word be (*will be, shall be)* and the infinitive, *to be.*

Thus, a sentence in one of these languages would mean "The boy is tall," but would be said in their language simply, "The boy tall." In that language, the *Be* verb will simply be omitted.

Bible translators or editors have inserted the verb form that they believed to be correct to make the sentence good to English readers. Usually they were correct in so doing, but in some places, they changed the basic meaning of the sentence when they added the *Be* word (or other verbs).

<u>Italics</u>
Many Editorial Additions
Are Noted by Printing Them in Italics.

Examples: Romans 5: 15 and 16:

15 But not as the trespass, so also *is* the free gift. For if by the trespass of the one the many died, much more did the grace of God, and the gift by the grace *which is* by one man, Jesus Christ, abound to the many.

16 And not as *it was* by one that sinned, *so is* the gift: for the judgment *was* by one to condemnation, but the free gift *is by* many trespasses to justification.

You can see that these additions need to be there in order to make the English sentences complete. Reading the verses without the added *be* verbs make the sentence structures a little odd!

15 But not as the trespass, so also the free gift. For if by the trespass of the one the many died, much more did the grace of God, and the gift by the grace by one man, Jesus Christ, abound to the many.

16 And not as by one that sinned, the gift: for the judgment by one to condemnation, but the free gift many trespasses to justification.

Besides shortening the passage, the passage becomes a mystery for rapid and complete understanding without the added verbs. Some editors have replaced the *Be verbs* with other verbs, but the additions need to be placed there for propriety's sake in English. There are countless additions like these that are ethical and aboveboard.

On the other hand, there are those editorial additions that taint the message. Either a word is added when it should not be or an incorrect word is added.

Romans 1: 1, 4 and 7:

1 Paul, a servant of Jesus Christ, called *to be* an apostle, separated to the gospel of God,

4 who was declared *to be* the Son of God with power, according to the spirit of holiness, by the resurrection from the dead; *even* Jesus Christ our Lord,

7 To all who are in Rome, beloved of God, called *to be* saints: Grace to you and peace from God our Father and the Lord Jesus Christ.

Note that each verse has the italicized words *to be* in them. The editors have added these infinitive forms of verbs intending to make the sentences better. However, in adding these verbs, they weaken the effect of the other verb already present. Read each verse without the added *to be*, and see the change in meaning.

1 Paul, a servant of Jesus Christ, called an apostle, separated to the gospel of God,

4 who was declared the Son of God with power, according to the spirit of holiness, by the resurrection from the dead; *even* Jesus Christ our Lord,

7 To all who are in Rome, beloved of God, called saints: Grace to you and peace from God our Father and the Lord Jesus Christ.

They have potentially tampered with the identity of those people in those verses. Paul was definitely an apostle; Jesus was definitely the Son of God with power, and the addressees of the Book of Romans were definitely saints! You may believe this to be nit-picking, but as you develop the knowledge of the Word of God and know the authority of God's Word, you will see the potential importance of these little changes. The *to be*s would express some doubt regarding the completion of the calling of the Father-God on the subject except for one factor. That factor relates to the immutability of God and His Word. It is moot whether the *to be*s are present in these particular sentences or not because if the Father-God said something about someone, that matter is a fact, regardless of how much doubt editors or translators may subtly insert into the message.

The only difference is the wording of the message itself. Without the *to be*s, there is little doubt regarding the identity of the subjects in the eyes of the Father-God. The only difference is in the mind of unwitting readers where there could be an element of doubt about the accuracy of these identifications.

Again, there are other examples of these additions to the text of the Bible. It isn't hard to read the text both ways, both with and without the italicized words, and see what change in meaning the added words may make. That is why they call it studying!

However, it is hard to know how far the italics have become important to the texts of Scripture. There is at least one place where italics were used a few years ago that italics are not usually used now. (Many of the most recently published Bibles omit the phrase altogether.) They are the last ten words in Romans 8: 1 in the King James Version:

There is therefore now no condemnation to those who are in Christ Jesus, *who walk not after the flesh, but after the Spirit.*

Notice the implication that if one does not walk after the Spirit, condemnation will come on that person. But if those words were not there, the meaning would be changed to "There is therefore now no condemnation to those in Christ Jesus." Which then is more important, the walking after the Spirit, or being in Christ Jesus? Does not the presence of those italicized words in the first verse nullify the meaning of the second and third verses?

> For the Law of the Spirit of life in Christ has made me free from the Law of Sin and Death. For what the Law could not do, in that it was weak through the flesh, God sending His Own Son in the likeness of sinful flesh, and for sin, condemned sin in the flesh.

In these verses, what we are (in Christ Jesus) overshadows what we do (walking after the Spirit). In the fourth verse the concept of the righteousness being fulfilled in us brings the stipulation of "not walking after the flesh." So the ten word phrase in question belongs very logically in the fourth verse, but does not in the first.

If we were saved by works, it could belong in the first verse, but we are not. We are saved by grace or we are not saved at all! How long have those words been like that? Was it that way from the original King James translators or was it more recent Bible publishers who made the changes? Who knows? Who really cares? The goal is simply to find out what the Word is saying to us now and go on. Many newer translations omit the ten words altogether, which is better than even having them in italics.

No one has the right to add to, to subtract from, or to alter in any way the meanings or the messages in the Scriptures. When you read Romans 8: 1, and those ten words are in the text, it is better to omit them in your mind because these words were not present in the original text.

There is another example in I John 2: 23 where nine words are italicized in many Bibles and not in others. The verse reads

Whosoever denies the Son, the same has not the Father; *he who acknowledges the Son has the Father also.*

It should not be a given that a statement that is 180 degrees out of phase with a truth is automatically another truth. The mental-assent person (one who mouths a confession of salvation without the involvement of the faith in the heart) would not necessarily have the Father.

Adding words is not the only changes people make. Some folks change the order of the words. Most English declarative sentences arrange the components of a sentence starting with the subject, followed by the predicate, which is then followed by the rest of the thought. In an interrogative sentence, the order is usually reversed; the predicate coming first. These arrangements are not so in other languages. Re-arranging these sentence components from one language to another to make the sentence easier to read in English is reasonable. However, when someone re-arranges the order of sentence components that causes a change in the meaning of the sentence, an error is nearly always created!

One dear lady said the "Holy Spirit of promise" (Ephesians 1: 13) was the same as "the promise of the Holy Spirit." How can one even hope to explain the difference? The difference is too obvious to comment on intelligently.

Guidepost Six:
Do not embrace doctrines, practices, teachings, customs or messages
that are contrary to the Scriptures.

There are many churches, ministries, teachers and ministers who preach and teach things that are contrary to God's Word. Some of these contradictions are due to ignorance; some are blatant, yet the church or ministry often maintains their course of error, some even after others have warned them of their error. Sadly, many people follow these errant churches.

Religious Titles

One of the most often abused offenses is the assumption that the ministers have a divine title. In Psalm 111: 9 the Bible says: "Holy and Reverend is His name," referring to Jehovah. Why then do mere men refer to themselves and each other as Reverend? Why do some mere men address themselves and other mere men as "Holy someone," such as *"Holy Father"*?

If the Bible says that "Holy" and "Reverend" are names of Jehovah, is it not presumptuous for mere men and women to claim these titles? Because it is done habitually and almost universally does not make it an acceptable thing to do in the eyes of the Heavenly Father.

That isn't the only case like this. There are those churches that promote the title of "Father" be given to their pastors or priests. Jesus gave the scribes and Pharisees a bad time more than once. On one occasion, He gave them a scathing rebuke for the titles they gave each other. Matthew 23: 1–3 and 6–12:

1 Then spoke Jesus to the multitudes and to His disciples, saying, "The scribes and the Pharisees sit on Moses seat. All things therefore whatever they bid you, *these* do and observe: but do not do after their works; for they say, and do not. . . .

6 They love the chief place at feasts, and the chief seats in the synagogues, and the salutations in the marketplaces, and to be called of men, Rabbi. But be not called 'Rabbi:' for one is your teacher, and all you are brethren. And call no man your 'father' on the earth, for one is your Father, *even* He who is in heaven. Neither be you called 'masters,' for one is your master, *even* the Christ. But he who is greatest among you shall be your servant. And whoever shall exalt himself shall be humbled; and whoever shall humble himself shall be exalted."

This passage is repeated in other books: Mark 12: 38–40 and Luke 20: 45–47. The above passage was edited for brevity's sake, so you may read this and the other passages to see if you still think some man or woman should address another mortal as Reverend, Holy, Rabbi, Master or Father or Mother.

> An Aside: In Verse 8, Jesus used the words "all of you are brethren."
> He was speaking, as emphasized, to the Jews in front of Him. He
> was not laying the foundation for universal brotherhood of man.

If this lesson were placed on the front pages of newspapers and broadcast so that everyone would recognize these facts, do you really think this will change people's minds about how they address their church dignitaries? Probably not, because men love the high offices and the high official names, just as Jesus said of the scribes and Pharisees! You, dear reader, are the only one who will be expected to have a change in attitude.

This is only the tip of the proverbial iceberg. Some churches teach so many things that contradict the Scriptures that it is embarrassing to point them out because you will think we are church-bashing!

So, let's mention only one typical example at this point and other examples will be highlighted later.

It is widely taught that Peter was the first Pope. First of all, *"Pope"* means *"Father."* The above passage should shoot the very concept of a Pope in the head. If we are not to call any other person on earth *Father*, *Papa* or *Pope*, why is there someone who calls himself *Pope*? And why does the alleged "father" turn around and have a covey of men to perpetuate the ill-advised tradition? If this doesn't open your eyes, look at other sound reasons why Peter is not who or what many people think he is as taught by millions of these "fathers."

The basis upon which these teachings exists in Matthew 16: 18:

"And I [Jesus] also say to you, that you are Peter, and upon this Rock I will build My church; and the gates of Hades shall not prevail against it."

Jesus was speaking to Peter. He was telling Peter that he (Peter) was a rock, but it was upon "this Rock," referring to Himself, that He would build His church. There are differences in the two words found in this passage that mean "rock." Peter is derived from *petros*, which means *stone*. The Greek word Jesus used for "this rock" was *petra*, which means *a huge rock*. The difference is obvious in Greek, but to English speakers it is subtle.

In further explanation, the key word is "*this*." Jesus did not say, "Upon *you* I will build My church." He was indicating Himself as the One upon whom He would build His church. If this antecedent confusion is not clear to you in this passage, let's look elsewhere for clarification.

The first passage is found in I Corinthians. There you will see that it was Christ Jesus who was the Spiritual Rock from whom the Israelites drank while they were in the wilderness.

I Corinthians 10: 1–4 For I would not, brethren, have you ignorant, that our forefathers [the Israelites] were all under the cloud, and all passed through the sea; and were all baptized to Moses in the cloud and in the sea; and all ate the same spiritual food; and all drank of the same spiritual drink: for they drank of a Spiritual Rock that followed them: and the Rock was Christ.

So that was Old Testament; what about the New One? Look at Ephesians 2: 19–22:

So then you are no more strangers and sojourners, but you are fellow-citizens with the saints, and of the household of God, being built upon the foundation of the apostles and prophets, Christ Jesus Himself being the Chief Corner Stone; in whom each several building, fitly framed together, grows into a holy temple in the Lord; in whom you also are built together for a habitation of God in the Spirit.

Nowhere in either passage is Peter mentioned. It was Jesus as the Rock of the Old Testament, and it is Jesus as the Rock—the Chief Cornerstone—of the New Testament.

What did Peter himself say of the matter? I Peter 2: 1–8:

1 Putting away therefore all wickedness, and all guile, and hypocrisies, and envies, and all evil speeches, as newborn babes, long for the spiritual milk that is without guile, that you may grow thereby to

salvation; if you have tasted that the Lord is gracious: to whom coming, a Living Stone, rejected indeed of men, but with God elect, precious, you also, as living stones, are built up a spiritual house, to be a holy priesthood, to offer up spiritual sacrifices, acceptable to God through Jesus Christ.

6 Because it is contained in Scripture, "Behold, I lay in Zion a Chief Corner Stone, elect, precious: And he who believes on Him shall not be put to shame."

7 For you therefore who believe is the preciousness: but for such as disbelieve, "The stone that the builders rejected, the same was made the head of the corner; and, a stone of stumbling, and a rock of offence; for they stumble at the Word, being disobedient: whereunto also they were appointed.

In this passage Peter is not speaking of himself, but of Christ. It is Christ who fulfills all of these points:

> You have tasted that the Lord is precious; coming to Him as a Living Stone; rejected by men, but chosen by God;

> God laid in Zion a Chief Corner Stone, elect, precious and upon whom believers have no shame and are not confounded.

Peter himself pointed to Jesus as the Rock of Salvation. So where does that fact put the teaching that it was upon Peter that Jesus would build His Church? OUT! Where does that put the teaching that the Pope is a legitimate office of the Body of Christ? OUT!

There is still one more point to make on this topic. If there were a position on earth as a Pope, why was Peter selected as the first one? The people who promote the concept that Peter was the first Pope selected Peter simply because he was convenient.

It was not well thought out to choose Peter as the first Pope because Peter was an apostle called to the Jews (Galatians2: 7, 8). Are most of those who hold that Peter was the first Pope Jews? No. They are mostly descendants of people from the Roman Empire and the people from the lands conquered by those descendants of the Roman Empire. There are not many Jews or former Jews among those who look at Peter as the first Pope.

As a matter of fact, some of the Popes and other Catholic dignitaries have been noticeably anti-Semitic through the ages! Only recently have the Popes attempted to put up an image of openness to the Jews and peoples of other religions. They have made like gestures to the Muslims.

Tradition teaches that Peter was crucified upside down, not feeling fit to end his life as Jesus had ended His earthly life. How true this is or how false is not important. Scriptures are silent about these things.

What the Scriptures do teach is that Jesus defeated death, sin and the grave. Peter never rose from the dead! Peter never was a propitiation for our sins. Peter was never seated at the Father-God's right hand where he makes intercession for us. As we believers sit in the heavenlies, it is not beside Peter! It is beside Jesus, the King of Glory!

There are many other teachings that contradict and countermand the Word, but let us move on to more about the guideposts. The other teachings that disregard the messages of Scripture will be dealt with later.

Guidepost Seven:
Do not assume the Word is saying or meaning something that is
not obvious in its message.

Just as surely as you cannot assume that the Scriptures teach the same things as your church teaches, you cannot assume that the Scriptures use all terms consistently from one context to another context. It may be true in many cases, but there are some words that have several connotations.

Example: *Baptism*

The word *Baptism* or *Baptize* is a word with many applications. Many people hear or see the word *baptism* or *baptize* and they immediately think of water. However, the words *baptize* and *baptism* relate to media other than water more often than they relate to water.

One of the most controversial doctrines in the Bible is the one on baptism. Every Christian should be baptized—the Scriptures plainly teach that. The question is IN WHAT?

Strong's refers to 101 uses of *baptism* and related words in the two Testaments. The use of the term in connection with the *baptism of John the Baptist in the Jordan River* and *repentance* combine for some 42 of those references. But, the Lord did not tell us to either baptize or to be baptized in either John's baptism or in the Jordan River.

The other references to baptism are usually assumed to be in water, but water is not mentioned except in connection with John, the Jordan River and the eunuch whom Philip baptized (Acts 8: 36–40). These are some of the other references to baptisms but omitting the term *water*:

Buried with Him in baptism (Romans 6: 4; Colossians 2: 12)

Baptized into *One Lord* (Ephesians 4: 5);

Baptized in the *Name* of the *Lord Jesus* (Acts 8: 16);

Baptized in the *Name* of *Jesus* (Acts 2: 38);

Baptized into *Christ* (Romans 6: 3; Galatians 3: 27);

He will baptize you with the *Holy Spirit* or *Spirit* (Matthew 3: 11; Mark 1: 8; and Luke 3:16), and

An assortment of other uses in which there are no associating nouns.

When Jesus commanded that converts be baptized in the Name of the Father and of the Son and of the Holy Spirit, where does He mention water (Matthew 28: 19)? We often assume He means water, but does He? He didn't say so.

When believers were baptized in the Name of Jesus Christ (Acts 2: 38); in the Name of the Lord Jesus (Acts 8: 16; 19: 5); and the Name of the Lord (Acts 10: 48) was it also in water? If Jesus did mean for baptism to be in water, using the formula (Matthew 28) "in the name of the Father, and of the Son, and of the Holy Spirit," why did He not say water? And why did the Apostles NOT follow His formula when they baptized believers (Acts 2: 38; 8: 16; 10: 48; 19: 5)? Not once does the formula of the names of the Father, the Son and the Holy Spirit appear in the New Testament Church history of baptism outside of Jesus' instructions.

Because baptism means *immersion* or *dip into*, several other questions arise. Did the converts' homes have baptisteries in them for converts who were baptized in the middle of the night (Acts 16: 33)? It is doubtful. Or did the group go at odd hours to the local creek or beach to get baptized? That is possible, but . . . .

Or were the converts sprinkled? Sprinkling is not *immersion* or *dipping into*. Does the tradition of sprinkling equate with baptism? If *baptism* does mean *dipping into*, by what or whose authority does sprinkling become effective? Assumptions do not answer these questions adequately.

In Strong's there is one reference to Moses' baptism "in the cloud and in the sea" (I Corinthians 10: 2), which we can accept as being types (illustrative foreshadows) of New Testament baptisms. Moses' baptism was two episodes of one baptism; one referred to the cloud that followed the Israelites by day and led them by night (Exodus 13: 21, 22), and the other referred to the Israelites' crossing of the Red Sea (Exodus 14: 19–22).

Was water involved with either of them? Yes, of course, the Red Sea is water. How wet did any of the Israelites get in either of the episodes of Moses' baptism? According to Scripture, the Israelites followed Moses across the Red Sea's bed on dry ground.

No, they did not get wet (Exodus 14: 22). When Jesus commands to baptize and be baptized, can we still assume that He means it to be in water?

In I Corinthians 10: 1–12 Paul declares that God was not pleased with those who partook of Moses' baptism. God's displeasure was not caused by the presence or absence of water, but because of the people's unbelief. So, do baptisms mean anything if there is no real belief in the heart? Is baptism valid in God's eyes only in cases involving belief (faith)?

Infant baptism is then a vain and empty ceremony because an infant cannot have his or her own faith! Active personal faith is then a requirement. Philip certainly insisted that the eunuch whom he baptized believe (Acts 8: 37).

I Corinthians 12: 13 asserts that the Holy Spirit baptized us all [Jews and Gentiles] into One Body—the Body of Christ. John the Baptist prophesied that Christ would baptize in the Holy Spirit (John 1: 33). We then have two divine members of the Godhead cross-baptizing believers into each other—the Holy Spirit immersing converts into Jesus (for salvation) and Jesus immersing believers into the Holy Spirit (for anointing power).

When Jesus said to baptize in the Name of the Father, the Son, and the Holy Spirit, was He speaking of one of the two divine baptisms?

Or did He refer to both of them? Or did He mean baptism in water as is usually assumed? Or did He mean all three baptisms as one complete baptism for the whole spirit, soul, and body of the believer? Can we still assume anything without thoroughly studying the question?

So every time baptism is mentioned, question how it is meant.

Assuming it means in water every time is absurd. A large segment of Christianity knows nothing about any baptism except the one in water, yet God has promised great benefits for those who experience the other baptisms (the context in I Corinthians 12).

Now do not misunderstand the purpose here. Baptism in water is a sound doctrine and practice—doing it in the name of the Father and of the Son and of the Holy Spirit, and in the name of the Lord Jesus Christ, as the Apostles baptized as recorded in Acts. Baptism in water has a purpose beyond merely obeying Jesus' command. But the other baptisms in the

New Testament are important, too—yet without water. So if you have made much of baptism, do not think that it is being made insignificant.

The purpose is to make you think and then for you to find out what the Scripture is saying rather than assume it is saying something it may or may not be saying.

Communion

While mentioning one ordinance of the church, let's mention the other legitimate one: Communion. There is confusion regarding the nature of Communion, the Lord's Supper. While the Lord did say that the bread was His Body and the fruit of the vine (wine or grape juice) was His Blood, some people believe that these earthly things consumed by believers mystically become the literal Body of Christ and His Blood (Matthew 26: 26–28; Mark 1: 22–25; Luke 22: 19–20). Others say these earthly commodities are mere symbolism with little (if any) valid meaning.

It is highly impractical to try to defend the concept of such a conversion of these elements—the bread literally becoming His Flesh and the fruit of the vine literally becoming His Blood as the literalists view things. Jesus is alive and well as He sits beside His Father on His throne in Heaven. He would not continue to flake off His Flesh or transfuse His Blood for such an ordinance. That would serve no good purpose. The act of redemption is complete and done.

On the other hand, those who hold the view of mere symbolism have also missed the mark. Some have missed it so far as to have leavened bread in their ceremony and others have inserted other drinks besides the fruit of the vine. To say the ceremony is purely symbolic is to regard the Lord's words as a meaningless exaggeration!

Paul wrote some warnings about the misuse of the Lord's Supper. The celebration should be taken seriously and with respect to what the Lord did at Calvary (I Corinthians 11: 23—34).

The Simple Truth of Baptism and Communion

The truth of baptism lies in the spirituality of baptism. Baptism, like communion and like re-birth, is a spiritual event in one's spiritual life. That is why there are no specific instructions on how to do them. Baptism is a picture of the death, burial and resurrection of the Lord. When we re-enact those events in our baptism, we are not only celebrating the things Jesus did on our behalf but we are uniting with Him in it—becoming one with Him. That is why water is so seldom mentioned.

We were baptized into His death—uniting with Him in it; we were baptized into His burial; and we were joined with Him in His resurrection to newness of life! We are then identified with Him in His victory over sickness (Matthew 8: 17), sin (Acts 2: 38) and death (I Corinthians 15: 55, 56). We should also be baptized in the Holy Spirit as He baptized in the Book of Acts (Acts 1: 5).

The correct way to do any of these things is to seek the Lord and follow His Word as best you can. He will honor your efforts by His Grace. The important thing is to realize that baptism relates to media other than water and you should embrace these baptisms as well as the one in water.

The secret to Communion is the spirituality of the Lord's Supper. The Lord's Supper is spiritual—not physical and not symbolic. Jesus as Bread of Life sheds His Life qualities into the believer as the believer consumes the bread and the Lord shares the qualities of His Redemption with the believer upon the drinking of the fruit of the vine. These operations are done in the spirit realm and are as valid and real as the world around us. The Lord's Supper is a spiritual aspect of celebrating the Lord's substitutionary work in redeeming His own.

The reason there are no specific instructions written relating to baptism or communion is because they are spiritual. If there were instructions, these ordinances would very quickly become mere religious affairs. They would never please the Lord!

Another Example of Assumption
Two Natures

Another assumption of facts that the Scriptures do not support is the doctrine that many ministries teach regarding the "Dual-nature" of believers. Of all the erroneous messages and teachings that are almost universally accepted as truth in the New Testament Church, this is one that is the most devastating to the individual believer. Believers who accept this point of doctrine as true become limited in their relationship with the Lord and their identities in the Lord. They are taught to accept defeat, sickness and poverty as a way of life because they still have their old man and his fallen nature within them.

The error begins when they assume that the warfare Paul mentioned in Romans Chapters 7 and 8 concludes that believers have both the nature of God and the old sinful nature at the same time. Careful study of these chapters will show you two things: One is that the old nature that wars against the spirit is in the "*members*" (Romans 7: 23). These members are NOT the members of the physical body.

The second thing is that Paul was writing of his own biographical experience. In Chapter 7 of Romans, Paul expressed his warfare with his un-regenerated self as he tried to live according to the Law and please God by his own efforts.

Paul explained his plight. Between Verse 11 and Verse 12 he changed tenses from past to present, thus making his plight more dramatic and more real to the reader. But notice the subtle change of tenses again as he closes his narration in Chapter 7. This time, from his frustrated present tense, he pleads for a future—one that has a deliverer for him: "Who shall deliver me?" Thus he came to a conclusion and resolution to his plight as found in the last verses of Chapter 7 and first verses of Chapter 8!

> Romans 7: 9–Romans 8: 4: [Past tense] And I was alive apart from the Law once: but when the Commandment came, sin revived, and I died; and the Commandment that was to life, this I found *to be* to death: for sin, finding occasion, through the Commandment beguiled me, and through it slew me.
>
> 12 So that the Law is holy, and the Commandment holy, and righteous, and good. Did then what is good become death to me? God forbid. But sin, that it might be shown to be sin, by working death to me through what is good;—that through the Commandment sin might become exceeding sinful. [Shift of tenses from past to present]
>
> 14 For we know that the Law is spiritual: but I am carnal, sold under sin.
>
> 15 For what I do I know not: for not what I would, that do I practice; but what I hate, that I do.
>
> 16 But if what I would not, that I do, I consent to the Law that it is good.
>
> 17 So now it is no more I that do it, but sin that dwells in me.
>
> 18 For I know that in me, that is, in my flesh, dwells no good thing: for to will is present with me, but to do what is good *is* not.
>
> 19 For the good that I would I do not: but the evil that I would not, that I practice.

20 But if what I would not, that I do, it is no more I that do it, but sin that dwells in me.

21 I find then the Law, that, to me who would do good, evil is present.

22 For I delight in the Law of God after the inward man:

23 but I see a different law in my members, warring against the law of my mind, and bringing me into captivity under the Law of sin that is in my members.

24 Wretched man that I am! <u>Who shall deliver me out of the body of this death?</u>

25 <u>I thank God through Jesus Christ our Lord</u>. So then I of myself with the mind, indeed, serve the Law of God; but with the flesh the law of sin. [Subtle change to a conclusion and resolution of the conflict]

8: 1 <u>There is therefore now no condemnation to those who are in Christ Jesus</u>.

2 For the Law of the Spirit of life in Christ Jesus made me free from the Law of sin and of death.

3 For what the Law could not do, in that it was weak through the flesh, God, sending His own Son in the likeness of sinful flesh and for sin, condemned sin in the flesh: that the ordinance of the Law might be fulfilled in us, who walk not after the flesh, but after the Spirit.

Paul was absolutely delivered of his plight by the Lord Jesus Christ and the issue of the struggle within him was settled. The Lord Jesus Christ is our deliverer, too—our only deliverer. The deliverance is complete: There is no condemnation to those who are in Christ Jesus.

Some Bible translators and commentators assume that the term *members* (V. 23) refers to body members and some have even inserted the term *body* to go along with *members* in their Bibles' texts. But careful study shows that the term *body* is not in the passage. The Word says that the old nature that wars against our spirits is *in our members*.

If the reference to *members* mentioned in Romans 7: 23 is not our *body members*, what members does Paul refer to? Read in Paul's letter to the Colossians (3: 5–9) and you will find a few of them listed:

Fornication,   Uncleanness,

Inordinate Affection,   Evil Desire,

Covetousness,	Anger,
Wrath,	Malice,
Blasphemy,	Filthy Communication, and
Lying	

These are not *body members* but actions, deeds, activities, habits and lifestyles—things that the lost do and practice as they walk through life.

Furthermore, II Corinthians 5: 17 tells us that old things have passed away and all things have been made new. If this verse is true, (and it is), how can a believer have two natures?

Nothing in the whole wide world has two natures at the same time. A tadpole changes into a toad or frog, and larvae turn into insects.

People have an even more drastic change when they change from a hopelessly lost sinner to a born-again son or daughter of the Living, Loving Father-God by the work of His grace! We drop off one nature and take on another. Then we learn how to get along in our new nature. Just like the metamorphosis from fuzzy-worm to butterfly transpires, we believers may tend to walk at first. But the aim of the Father-God for us as believers is to fly!

If someone accepts the notion of believers having both the old and the new natures at the same time, he or she will accept the role of a fumbling, stumbling, weak-kneed child of God, unable to live a life pleasing to the Father, and thus unable to develop into the victorious, consistent and all-conquering, fruit bearing son or daughter of the Living and Loving Father-God!

> Do not assume the Scriptures refer to something simply because of one or two words when there are other important possibilities.

2

Other Bible-Study
Dos and Don'ts

There are other things involved with the comprehension of Scripture besides the guideposts that we have mentioned. These are topics of using common sense on what is often common knowledge. Some of these things are not always common knowledge, but they should be. So let's look at some of them.

The Meanings of the Words

Let's consider the meanings of the words that we see in type on the Bible's pages. Words change their meanings over time. As one minister noted in the 1950's, "Fifty years ago *jam* was made of peaches and put in jars. Now *jam* is made of traffic and it is in the streets." Moving into the 21st Century, *jam* is something kids do or, pluralized, they could be something kids wear!

As we see, time causes words to change their meanings within a language, but those changes are nothing compared to the changes in meanings between languages. Any translation has some changes of word-meanings from one language to the other language whether spoken or written.

The Bible, being a translation, is no exception. Look, for instance, at the simple word *believe*. According to most of us, when we hear the word *believe*, we think of "assuming something to be true" and so we mark it down in our minds as fact and go about our business. According to the Amplified Bible, as well as the scriptural applications regarding the word, *believe* is "*believe*" plus "*trusts in, adheres to, relies on.*"

Thus, *belief,* as it is used in the New Testament, is more than mere mental assent to a fact, but it means *a commitment to that fact as a truth and a necessity in life.* Commitment leads to a course of action, which is what James meant when he said, "Faith without works is dead." (James 2: 20) In that same passage James used *Faith* and *Belief* interchangeably because both English words come from the same Greek word.

James explained that *faith* (or *belief*) produces *works*—or a better expression—produces *action.* Thus, when you believe scripturally, you act on what that belief dictates. You believe in Christ scripturally and you dedicate or commit your life to Him. It is more than merely acknowledging that He died for you on the cross.

Realize that words, their usage and meanings change from year to year, from age to age, from culture to culture, and certainly from language to language. Be sure to do your best to realize what intent the Father had in mind when He inspired the Word in the beginning. His message is the one that we should believe—thus act on!

The Definitions of the Words

There was a young man who, a year or so before he graduated from high school, started a school Bible club. Upon graduation, he chose a girl to continue the work he had initiated; and this she was doing. Another young man objected to a girl being the club's president. He cited the Scripture that a woman is not to usurp authority over a man. (1 Timothy 2:12: "But allow not a woman to teach, nor to usurp authority over the man, but to be in silence.")

The young man was told to go look up the word *usurp*; which he did. He found that the girl had not usurped her position, but had been duly appointed—a legitimate option of the student who was graduating. The troubled young man had not known that *usurp*, since it looked and sounded so much like *use*, does not mean *use* but it means *steal* or *misappropriate.*

Words may look much alike or sound much alike, but sometimes they aren't even closely related. Make sure you know the meanings of words in Scripture, especially controversial words.

The Mistranslations in the Word

Not to criticize the translators because their task is a very difficult one, but there are dozens of terms in the Bible, especially the King James Version

(KJV), that were either mistranslated or have changed meaning since they were translated. The King James Translation is four centuries old and many terms have changed meaning since their translation.

The biggest single problem with the KJV is that the translators, while trying to make the translation a work of beautiful literature, added style that made it hard to understand when they could have made the text somewhat easier to read. The *"thees"* and *"thous"* pronouns, and the *"est"* suffixes on the verbs sound nice, but they often confuse the modern reader. Recently educated readers are not the best qualified readers in the world and working on a piece of art for the Father-God's Truth can turn into a real struggle.

The King James translators who had in mind to make the Word of God a work of art stretched to use as many words as synonyms as they could! Be careful not to take literally every tidbit of difference between the words they used then and what we would use today.

For instance, in Mark the Lord told a parable of the sower and the seeds of the Word being planted. The translators used *"birds of the air"* or *"fowls of the air"* (typifying demons) as villains to eat the first seeds planted. When seeking the difference between birds and fowls, it was found that both terms in the Greek were identical and simply meant *"birds."* The additions of *"of the air"* were not in the original message and were inserted to make the Bible flowery and really great poetry! The translators abandoned the KISS principle (Keep It Simple, Stupid)!

There are topics already mentioned under Guidepost Five in reference to Editorial and Translational Changes regarding definitions of words and there are several more instances of obvious mistranslations pointed out in Appendix 3.

Connotative Meanings

Our minds often assume a meaning by a word's use (or misuse) and a mental picture develops. When people hear the word *"car,"* everyone gets a mental picture of a car. However, no two cars in these mental pictures are alike in the various minds of the hearers. Thus, when we hear a term used, often we connect it mentally with an image that sets out a mental process apart from what the messenger intended. Sometimes this even puts words in the mind that one may think are synonyms, but aren't in that particular usage. Be aware that virtually everyone does this and differences do occur. These differences will not necessarily make someone correct and someone else incorrect in their imagery. They will simply be different.

Some points of differences are of absolutely no importance and should be treated as such rather than differing parties getting their noses all out of joint. Sometimes a consensus is not necessary because the differences are insignificant. If a point is important in the here and now relationship with the Father-God, then a consensus should be reached, but sometimes even then a consensus may not be reached.

Example: *Millennialism—Pre-, Post-, A- or None!*

One argument exists among four groups of theologians. Some believe the Rapture (the catching away of the Church in the end time) will occur before the Millennium (the thousand years of peace); these are the Pre-millennialists. Some believe that the Rapture will occur after the Millennium; these are the Post-millennialists.

Another group believes that there will be no Millennium at all; these are the Amillennialists. Yet another group does not use the term *millennium* at all because the Scriptures do not use the term *millennium*, but uses the expression "a thousand years."

The last group is simply outflanking good reason. This is a case of semantics and the meaning is the same regardless of a particular word and its definition. So this group doesn't really count in our equation. Thus, only one of the other three positions can possibly be right on this point of doctrine.

Pick a position. If that position happens to be right, what does it matter? How does it change anything? Pick another position. If the second position is right, how does that matter? How does that position change anything? That leaves only one more opinion. How does that position matter and how does it change anything?

This whole debate is a useless waste of time because what will happen will happen and anyone's knowledge of the sequence of events will not affect the sequence of the events one way or another! The topic is moot! Why argue about it? Getting all torqued out of shape about it is ridiculous! Yet some have obviously done it anyway!

Another Example (one that does matter):

Covenant

A term that many people misunderstand due to its similarity to *oath, contract, promise, agreement* or other term generally used in business and legal relations, is *covenant.* The usual usage indicates that *covenant* means *contract, oath,* or *agreement,* and the dictionary agrees (Webster).

However, if you will study the *covenants* in Scripture, you will find that the covenant's terms were established by only one party. There was no sit-down to discuss the terms, not even to agree or disagree. One party set all the terms and the other party was silent. (Of course it was Jehovah who established most of these covenants and who wants to discuss terms, especially to argue, with the Omnipotent!)

Thus, the second of Webster's definitions (*oath*) is more closely correct. The LORD typically would establish the covenants' terms and the Israelites would merely accept them. However, the Israelites never lived up to the terms of any of the covenants.

The Israelites did make one covenant to the LORD. But Israel never lived up to the terms that covenant, either. It appears that even Josiah, the king who had initiated the covenant, died in defiance of God's will (II Kings 23).

There are eight primary covenants mentioned in Scripture, but only one of them relates to the believers—the New Testament (or New Covenant, which are the same in Greek). Chapters 8–10 of Hebrews teach some very important things about the New Covenant:

1. The New Covenant was established between the Father and the Son. We believers are not mentioned in the Covenant. We come on the scene later as benefactors by grace.

2. The Covenant is sealed by the Blood of Jesus, (all covenants were sealed with blood, the Old Testament blood offerings typified the Blood of Jesus). Thus, they were binding even to the point of death for either party in the covenant.

If you will study it, you will find that the New Covenant was issued on the basis of God saying "I WILL" rather than on His saying "*IF* you will," (as He spoke in other covenants). Then the Covenant was sealed with Christ's Blood (Hebrews 9: 19—10: 18). *Covenant* is only one word, and there are many terms that every Bible student needs to be familiar with. There is no need to panic over the vocabulary, but be diligent to learn them as you can.

There are volumes written by competent authors about the Blood Covenant. You may want to read more about the topic.

The Synonyms of Scripture—or Lack Thereof

In English there are substitute words for many of our words. Most communicators use synonyms often to keep the audience from becoming bored. Look at our English dictionaries—especially the unabridged ones! They have hundreds of thousands of terms in them. Compare the English vocabulary with the vocabularies of either Old Testament Hebrew with its 8700 words or New Testament Greek with its 6000 words. English may have a bountiful supply of synonyms, but neither biblical Greek nor Hebrew does.

In spite of this simple fact, some Bible scholars and teachers treat Greek and Hebrew words that may be similar or related as if they are interchangeable.

The translators have messed up one topic with its set of teachings so badly that many people are confused about what to believe. The topic I speak of here is the *"spirit, soul, mind, heart, life"* controversy. I am not about to get into the debate here, but the translators have often interchanged these terms with each other. If you will look up *spirit* in Strong's, you will find several Hebrew or Greek words from which the translators translated *spirit,* and these terms were used elsewhere for *soul, mind, life,* or *heart.* It follows that all five of these terms have been cross-substituted for each other throughout both Testaments.

Now the argument rages if man is a bipartite or tripartite being, not to mention the rest of the questions people have about the differences in and purposes of the heart, mind, soul, life and spirit. The translators have treated all five terms in the same haphazard way. It will take too much time to prove it to you here, but there are major differences between the meanings of these terms—thus differences how we relate to these terms and how they relate to us.

Ask yourself some relevant questions about what you see on the Bible's pages. Are the ideas presented general or are they specific? Is it your soul that was re-born, or your spirit? Was it your heart that was renewed or your soul—or even your mind—or maybe it was your spirit? When you want to get into God's Word, do you want to put it in your heart, mind, soul or spirit? Who are you, spirit, soul, or mere body?

To some, it will make no difference, but when the enemy comes at you with his lies, seductions, accusations and other attacks you should know exactly who and what you are so you can deal with him more successfully. Because of the way the translators dealt with these terms in a relevant passage, you must research the term to find out for sure which word it really was in the original tongue. (See <u>Single Words for Several</u>, Chapter 2, *Book 1*.)

The problem that translations cause by the loss of the meanings of terms from one language to the next is staggering. If translations did not lose so much in original meaning, there would not be so many different translations of the Bible. It seems that everyone (including me) is attempting to clarify what the Word of God is saying, many of which renderings are prejudiced by ignorance, education, assumption, bias and denominationalism. You have to do some investigation to find which translations of the Bible are best for you.

Using several translations is usually better than using just one, regardless of which one. One should have several translations of Scripture, good dictionaries, or other references on the Greek and Hebrew words themselves. Having a good exhaustive concordance is also important.

Looking up words and references to those words can often clarify a term's meaning in Scripture better than dictionary definitions can. Get some study aids to help you with the meanings of the words in Scripture. Some computer programs have made such studies much easier than the old turn-the-page-in-a-book-and-find-another-book-and-look-at-another-page type of study.

When words' definitions do not conform to what references say or to what you believe, do a research in the Scriptures' uses of the words. Be cautious, but also be honest with yourself in how you deal with your conclusion. Accept the real definition and be prepared to respond appropriately to any conclusion you may honestly come to.

Single Words for Several

Another problem that human-implemented translations from one language to another concerns the abstract expressions in one culture that are not equal in the other. A couple of examples are the terms for *life* and *love* as found in Greek. *Life* comes from one of three Greek words—*bios, zoe, or psyche.* One means a *natural biological life* (*bios*—as in biology); another means *the God type of (spiritual) life* or *universal life* (*zoe*, from which we get zoo or zoology); and the other means *soul* or *mind* (*psyche*, from which we get *psychology* and other *psycho*-terms).

Many of the translators have treated these terms alike. Often the translators placed an "*eternal*" or an "*everlasting*" in front of *zoe* "life" to make a distinction that it was not *bios* or *psyche*.

However, sometimes they did not make that accommodation. Another set of terms are somewhat confusing to the typical English Bible-student: Love (*agape*) and Love (*phileo*). While agape (ah-gah'-pay) means the God-type of Love—His very nature—eternal, unconditional, unchangeable and un-measurable, dispensed by grace love; *phileo* (fee-lay'-o) means the human love, limited, conditional, and temporal love. Both *agape* and *phileo* are translated *love* with no help discerning which is which, except in I Corinthians 13 where *agape* is called *charity*.

This subtle difference is important when you consider the "brotherly love" of *Philadelphia* being only human love in contrast to an idealized non-existent city of *Agapedelphia*. The human love is the limitation put on the Philadelphian Church of Revelation, Chapter 3.

Bible teachers and scholars must then be cautious how they study these terms. The student must look up the word in every passage to see if it is *bios, zoe,* or *psyche* if the term becomes important.

And certainly *agape* should never be treated like any sort of human love. A good exhaustive concordance (either Robert Young's (LL.D.) Analytical Concordance to the Bible, or Strong's, or some other good study aids) and some research of your own will help you get through these words.

Be active in researching the subtle differences in meanings.

Capitals

Another area in which most people assume erroneously deals with capitalization of the term *spirit* (pneuma). What is spirit? *Spirit* (pneuma) basically means *breath* or *wind*. But we are not often talking here of mere *breath* or *wind* when we see the term in the Scriptures. We are usually talking of the term *spirit* as it applies to *the part of man that is eternal*—the *part that is born again,* or *the part that needs to be born again,* the part of man that *is God conscious.*

There are many *spirits* mentioned in Scripture. Is the passage in which you find the word *spirit* referring to the *Holy Spirit*? If the Scripture did not say *Holy Spirit*, do not assume it meant the *Holy Spirit*. Often *spirit* is referring to the Holy Spirit, but even more often it is referring to the re-created human spirit.

A couple of places where the Scriptures refer to the recreated human spirit *as spirit* is in Galatians 5 and Ephesians 6. Sometimes the editors or translators have capitalized the word *spirit*, and it should not be. Make sure that the context affirms the necessity of the capital before you assume the term *spirit* refers to the Holy Spirit.

As you read under Guideposts 4 and 5, God placed Adam and Eve in the Garden of Eden, and gave them dominion over every living thing (Genesis 1:28). He also instructed them to eat anything they desired except the fruit of the tree of knowledge of good and evil: "for in the day that you eat thereof, you shall surely die" (Genesis 2:15-18).

As you know, they ate of the forbidden fruit. Now, either God lied, or they died that day. Yet, it was over 900 years later that they went to their graves. Did they die the very day they ate of the fruit as God said they would, or not? They did; they died spiritually. They could still function physically and mentally, but their spirits were dead—separated from the LORD. That is why Hebrews 6: 1 and 9: 14 refer to "dead works"—activities, even though dedicated to God, that proceed from dead spirits.

That is also why there is no mention of eternal life in the Old Testament, nor even any real indication that the Old Testament people believed in a human spirit. That's why the Sadducees (who did not believe in the human spirit) and the Pharisees (who did believe in the human spirit, at least to a point that there was life after death) were so embroiled in controversy when Jesus made His entry on earth.

Again, that is why Jesus said John 3: 3 and 7, "Except a man be born again, he cannot see the Kingdom of God" and "Marvel not that I say to you, 'You must be born again.'"

Once one is saved, look what the recreated human spirit (born-again) is capable of producing (Galatians 5: 22, 23)!

> But the fruit of the [recreated] spirit, against which there is no law, includes love (agape), joy, peace, patience, gentleness, goodness, faith, meekness, and temperance.

> Notice: The word *Spirit* in this passage does not start with a capital because the context does not mention the Holy Spirit, and the message is not referring to the Holy Spirit. The context refers to the contrast between the recreated human spirit and the flesh. If the *spirit* here referred to the Holy Spirit, the comparison would be unequal—comparing divinity with carnality. So the verse is telling us that the great virtues that we as Christians are to manifest proceed from our recreated spirits. Of course we cannot experience

re-creation without the Holy Spirit in our lives, but it is our spirits that produce the fruit by the works of the Holy Spirit in us.

Do not assume that capital letters belong where there is an element of doubt about it.

Another important example is in Ephesians 6, where we see the phrase *the Sword of the Spirit*. The only reason the *S* in *Spirit* is capitalized is because it is part of a title. It is not referring to the Holy Spirit because the Holy Spirit does not need a sword. Neither is the Holy Spirit putting on the armor of God. The Word of God is the sword that believers use with their re-created spirits to engage the enemy and his forces.

The Scriptures' Figures of Speech: Similes, Metaphors and Allegories

Like normal literature and like much of our ordinary speech, the Bible incorporates literary devices called "Figures of Speech." These are tools used to teach a lesson by revealing examples and illustrations of principles. The first one is the simile.

A simile is a comparison of two unlike items, concepts or ideas while using the terms *like* or *as* to connect the terms. Isaiah 53: 2 contains an example:

For He shall grow up before Him *as* a tender plant, and *as* a root out of a dry ground; He has no form nor comeliness, and when we shall see Him, there is no beauty that we should desire Him.

These comparisons are straightforward—making the qualities of one subject obvious in the other subject. A tender root out of dry ground is solitary, (being the only living thing nearby) visual, (any observant person would recognize the stark contrast of the green among the brown) and mysterious (receiving its nourishment from an unseen source). These notes are the obvious ones—typical of any simile.

A metaphor does the same thing as the simile, but is little more subtle. It does not use *like* or *as* while making the comparison. One such common metaphor is in Proverbs 30: 5:

He [the Lord] is a shield to those who put their trust in Him.

Anyone who can think can readily see that there is a definite difference between the inanimate (dead) shield and the Living Lord! But the resultant function of the Lord is like a shield to those who trust in Him. The metaphor asserts that the Lord and the shield are the same—the Lord is a shield, without the *like* or *as*.

An allegory is also often called a parable—a story whose characters and/or key elements represent something in life. The characters and/or key elements are therefore used allegorically. The events in the Old Testament are often involved in allegories representing qualities, people or things in the New Testament; so do Jesus' parables. The terms for the characters and/or elements in an allegory are called *types* and the living qualities, people or things in the New Testament are called the *antitypes*. The *type* is the foreshadowing character or element in the story, while the *antitype* is the real thing that the type-character or element reflects or foreshadows.

One of the many examples is the story of Abraham and the offering of Isaac (Genesis 22). Abraham, representing in type the Father-God, offered Isaac, who represented in type the only begotten Son (Jesus); and the altar was a type for Calvary.

Yet the final actual offering was made by God Himself, supplying a lamb as Abraham said He would—Jehovah Jireh. This whole event was later carried out by Jesus as He became the Lamb of God, our Sin-offering. So the types and antitypes are these:

Types	Antitypes
Abraham,	God the Father
Isaac,	God the Son—the Lamb of God
The wood Isaac carried,	The Cross
The altar,	Calvary
The ram (offering)	Jesus, the Lamb of God

The analogy of Abraham, Isaac and Calvary is very basic here. There is enough information in the Scriptures to write many pages about the significance of this allegory.

Another example is the parable of the sower (Mark 4: 3-20). It is an allegory in which the sower sows his seed and four different results occur. One immediately thinks of wheat (or some other crop), but Jesus explained that the product sown was "the Word" (v.14). After verse 14, He explains what each of the four results meant.

Incorrect Analogies

There are many parables and there are many types in the Old Testament. The problem comes from the analogies that men and women put on these allegories! For instance: In a publication that mentions the term *backsliding* as a doctrine of the New Testament, the editors use a metaphor in the Similitudes: Matthew 5: 13:

> You are the salt of the earth, but if the salt has lost its savor, with what shall it be salted? It is therefore good for nothing, but to be cast out, and to be trodden under the foot of men.

It must be noted that the term *backslide* is not a New Testament word, nor is there a concept of it in the New Testament. However, the editors of that particular book did not know this and they tried to present the teaching of New Testament backsliding of believers as valid.

In this passage in Matthew, to whom was Jesus speaking? Un-regenerated Jews. He said you [un-regenerated Jews] are the salt of the earth. If the salt [you—un-regenerated Jews] has lost its saltiness, with what shall it be salted? What does *it* refer to? Does *it* refer to salt or earth? Further in the statement, Jesus said, "It is therefore good for nothing." Again, to what does *it* refer?

Those whom Jesus addressed were not yet saved and were part of the unsavory world system. And the world system, because of the unsavory people in charge of it, has been trodden under the foot of men starting long before that original message. Does the savor that was lost refer to salvation? How can it refer to salvation when these people were not saved? Does it not refer to integrity? Or knowledge? Or care? Or any one of a hundred other attributes that cause men and women to conduct themselves civilly? What analogy really fits this allegory?

When one makes an analogy of a scriptural allegory, make certain that the facts are there in the Scripture to corroborate or reinforce whatever point one is trying to make. If the Scriptures (in context) do not back-up that analogy, regard the whole lesson as only someone's opinion. It may be a good opinion or a bad one, but it will be only an opinion as long as Scripture does not directly support the whole concept of what is being taught. *Accepting someone's opinions as truth could lead you to follow error.* Even if the error is in published print, make sure the Word agrees with the conclusion!

The Symbols of Scripture

Types, antitypes, allegories, metaphors, and similes are important in Scripture, but they should not be overdone. Many of the creatures John saw as recorded in Revelation went unexplained. Why?

Though it is possible that these envisioned creatures resemble in type the elements in the world-system as we know it, it is also possible that these creatures with several heads or horns were not as symbolic as many people believe. They could be the actual spirit-creatures of the heavens that empowered the things or events on earth that John recorded seeing. In other words, the creatures John saw could have caused the manifestation of human organizations and governments and their activities on earth and they could have appeared in spirit form exactly as John described them. Because of the nature of the spirit world, there may not be as much symbolism in Revelation as many people think.

For instance, look at Nazism. Nazism, as founded by Adolph Hitler, was a composite of occult beliefs that originated in Old Testament days. (They were not founded on the Old Testament, but originated while the Old Testament was being lived out in time.) The devastation that Nazism perpetrated on mankind was almost beyond belief. In spite of history's accounting of the horrors, the spirit that raised up Hitler and Nazism is now being reared again to attempt a re-emergence. Several men (Idi Amin Dada and Saddam Hussein, for two of many examples) admired Hitler and his philosophy, and again preached the same diabolical message and practiced his cruelty. Some of Hitler's political tactics are being played out in the United States even as this document is being written.

It's because the spirit that led Hitler in his politics and the spirits that spawned the occult activities that Hitler engaged in are not dead or non-existent. Those spirits are trying to revive National Socialism (Nazism) right here in the United States, and Satan is helping. So there may be more reality in what is described than mere symbolism.

There is one cult in particular that has taken an extreme view of symbols. Their view is so extreme that any subject in the Scriptures that they do not understand clearly (and there are many of them), they merely say "It's symbolic." If you ask them what being born-again means, they may tell you, "It's symbolic." If you then ask what it symbolizes, they will change the subject. Anything they do not have a ready answer for, they assert to be symbolic, but they seldom have a rational answer for what that something symbolizes.

This same cult has taken many people and confused them to the point that, in spite of offering only a gospel based on works with no potential for eternal life, many fall in with them. They lean heavily on the 144,000 found in Revelation, citing that these are the only ones who will have life in heaven. They ignore the vast crowd of thousands of thousands that the Scripture mentions just a few verses away.

If you will ask one of these folk if he or she has any hope of being in the 144,000, he or she often says that there is a little hope for him or her to be one of the 144,000. The Scripture plainly identifies these 144,000 people as Jews and lists the tribes of Israel that they came from. But if you ask one of these cultists of which tribe he or she is, the answer will be, "It's symbolic. These twelve tribes are symbolic of Spiritual Israel." If you ask them *how* they are symbolic or of *what* are they symbolic, they become evasive and will want to leave. Their whole religion exists only because they base their teaching on Scriptures out of context, misappropriated verses, or re-defined words. Without these three erroneous treatments of Scripture, this cult (as most of them) could not continue to exist.

Make certain that any similes, metaphors or symbols you find in Scripture are appropriately explained and then use them properly. The guidelines for the meaning of words would be summed up:

Do not assume a meaning.

Do not assume a capital.

Use study aids as needed to make meanings clear.

When in doubt, look up a term's usage in Scripture.

Do not get caught up in the allegories.

Scriptural Preferences and Over-emphases

Because sometimes a Scripture seems to jump out at a reader, the reader seems to get a revelation (real or imagined) of what God means in that passage. Often one over reacts to such "revelation" and other Scriptures seem to become secondary—or even completely irrelevant!

The reader simply gets too excited about that new idea, or understanding of the Word, and loses his or her perspective or spiritual balance.

For instance, one group of churches has new knowledge (to them) of the Scriptures in Mark 11: 22–24.

> And Jesus answered and said to them [His disciples], Have faith in God. For truly I say to you, "That whoever shall say to this mountain, 'Be you removed and be you cast into the sea;' and shall not doubt in his heart, but shall believe that those things that he says shall come to pass; he shall have whatever he says. Therefore I say to you, 'Whatever things you desire, when you pray, believe that you receive them and you shall have them.'"

The truths are there: When you have the God-type of faith and you say to that particular mountain to be cast into the sea, it will happen. If you believe in a heart free from doubt, then you will have whatever you said. And those truths are wonderful! They are precious, no doubt about it. But this group has so emphasized this one Scripture and several others on the same subject that their whole concept of Christianity is wrapped up in "What I say is what I get!"

Their "confession" (that is how they refer to what they are claiming in prayer and in their conversations/confessions according to that passage) seems to have become more important to them than their relationship with their Savior. Their testimonies consist more of what they "confess in" than what the Lord has done for them or who they are in Christ. Because of their zealousness for one doctrine, many other truths are seldom, if ever, mentioned.

This is not unlike many churches that are on a fringe of fundamentalism. One group of churches teaches almost exclusively on the topic relating to being born-again. Another one teaches about the fullness of the Holy Spirit. Another one will emphasize missionary operations. Another one will teach strong lessons on baptism or communion. So on and on churches and their ministries go, specializing it seems in one thing or another.

Keep your awareness open to all aspects of the Word and your relationship with it.

Summing Up

One can prevent over-emphasis or over-zealousness by incorporating an even, consistent attitude toward the Scriptures.

Do not give one relevant Scripture more emphasis than another.

One can regard some Scriptures as more relevant to a believer than others by asking the questions mentioned earlier. This is a good place to review them. These are the questions:

Who said it?

> *To whom was it said?*
>
> *What were the circumstances? and*
>
> *Was the message to or for me?*

If you will continue to ask these questions, you will be able to find out the importance of a particular passage as it relates to you.

Scriptural Blanks (Silences)

Scriptural misunderstanding also goes into the areas of scriptural silence. Some fundamental churches teach rather weak doctrines that they really have no foundation for because the doctrines are based on what the Scriptures do NOT say.

One can neither scripturally condemn nor condone things that the Scriptures are silent about. One can only point out that Scriptures do not mention certain facts or topics, but to teach that the Bible condemns such-and-such because it is not mentioned in Scripture is ludicrous. On the other side of the same sheet of paper, one cannot automatically embrace something that the Scriptures do not mention one way or another. (These are reasons we need the Holy Spirit to guide us!)

Some people hold the teaching that they should not use anything in church not mentioned in the New Testament. Perhaps they should be consistent and walk to church, worship in uninsured churches, disconnect the phone and utilities, build outhouses, and a long list of other daily conveniences found in their churches that the New Testament has no comment about. As a matter of fact, the Word never commissioned the erection of church buildings, not even the outbuildings!

Another topic long abused is the topic of interracial marriage. Some people use the verse of Scripture where it says, "Be not unequally yoked together" as meaning to not marry someone of another race.

This is an example of taking Scripture from its context. Look at the rest of the verse:

> Be not unequally yoked together with unbelievers. For what fellowship does righteousness have with unrighteousness? And what communion does light have with darkness?

The topic that restricts marriage is not relating to race but to <u>faith</u>! A believer is not supposed to marry an unbeliever. There is no mention of either marrying someone of another race or not marrying someone of another race. The topic of inter-racial marriage is not mentioned in the Bible.

There were restrictions in the Old Testament regarding the Children of Israel marrying members of certain pagan nations. It was not based on race but on the religions of the pagan nation that the LORD restricted them from marrying.

> Objective: *Do not condemn or condone something about which the Bible is silent.*

Questioning the Father-God Regarding "Why?"

When something bad happens to people, often people will ask God why. Usually the person(s) with the questions are upset and not in a receptive mood and would not recognize the Lord's voice if He answered.

There are several problems with these types of questions. One is the obvious challenge in the tone of the question. There is often a subtle hint that God has no right to do what has just happened to so-n-so.

The next problem lies in the self-pitying attitude reflected in such questions. This attitude has a firm base on self-righteousness, something the Father-God has no use for.

The biggest single problem about these types of questions is the false premise(s) upon which the questions are based. Look back at Genesis when Adam and Eve were scuttled by the Serpent to establish Satan as the god of this world. Satan, as confirmed in Job, is the perpetrator of the evil things that happen to people. He is the one who kills, robs and destroys—not God! He is the one who blinds men to the Truth of Life! He is the one who causes people to die prematurely—not the Father-God! (John 10; II Corinthians 4: 4).

In conclusion, it isn't God who takes life (or even property leaving people without) from people! God receives His people, but He doesn't take them. It is Satan, the god of this world, who does these bad things for which God too often gets the blame.

To compound the problem, most people do not know the Lord well enough to ask Him why. If they do know Him well enough, they will frame the question properly and He will answer and explain—if they are calm enough to listen. But when He is asked a question based on a false premise, He will not answer. To answer a question based on a false premise gives credence to the false premise and the Father will not do that.

3

Positive Study Tips

Sometimes the Word as presented is confusing, to say the least. Much confusion comes from the way the Word is laid out for you.

Chapter/Verse Breaks

Did you ever wonder what the man who broke the Bible into chapters and verses was drinking when he did it? It was a fine idea, but it was not done responsibly. The chapter/verse breaks in Scripture are terrible in many places. Paragraphs are broken, sentences are broken, and of course the reader must take special care to look for the periods that end the sentence, as well as topic changes for the paragraph changes. This makes it very easy to take a Scripture from its context!

These breaks necessitate care in keeping the thoughts together. Then, too, there is the "follow the antecedent" game, which has some issues of its own (it will be mentioned later).

These breaks in turn have caused editing problems for Bible publishers because they often try to clear things up for the reader. Sometimes they help; sometimes they muddle things worse than they ever were before.

Example: Look at Ephesians, Chapters 1 and 2.

Ephesians 1: 1 and 1: 2 (the greeting) comprise one sentence. The next sentence starts at Verse 3 and ends at Verse 14. The third sentence starts at Chapter 1, Verse 15 and ends at Chapter 2, Verse 3.

The editors or translators tried to shorten the translation of this Greek sentence, which isn't such a bad idea, but the way they did it was disastrous to the message. Some of them have simply placed a period at the end of Chapter 1 and added words (verbs) to Chapter 2 to make the text there grammatically correct. However, in doing that, they reduced the power and impact of the message.

Other translators or editors also added periods in Chapter 1 with other changes, thus ruining the content even more!

In the text, notice that there are many dependent clauses in that passage, each one dependent on the preceding clause. There are more than 265 English words in the translation of this sentence that runs from Ephesians 1: 15 to 2: 3 (at least it was originally one sentence).

The average comprehended sentence in English should be between 15 and 30 words long, depending on the ability of the writer to understand his audience and to write clearly on that level. Each sentence should have only one thought. Compound subjects, predicates, and objects are common and complex sentences are common, but still each correctly structured sentence has only one thought.

Look at the italicized words in Verse 1 of Chapter 2: *Has quickened* (or made alive). Without those words, the passage between 2: 1 and 2: 3 becomes a sentence fragment—an incomplete sentence. This fact proves that the whole passage from 1: 15 to 2: 3 is only one sentence. It is, however, much too long for the average English reader to appreciably comprehend. It may not have been confusing to a Greek reader, but in English, that is much too long.

English readers simply do not usually put that many dependant clauses together on a single topic with a single thought. The manner in which the translators or editors have broken this long sentence into more than one sentence has caused the loss of good and vital information.

Might

There are two *mights* often used in Scripture. One definition relates to *might* meaning *power, strength* or *ability*. The other *might* (as used in John 3: 17, and II Corinthians 5: 21 for examples) relates to the other meaning—the past tense for *may*.

The latter *might*, in today's usage, means that there is an element of doubt in whatever follows. I *might* do this or that or I *might* not. However, in older times *might* was used simply as the past tense form of *may*. It has changed meaning, adding that element of doubt.

There was no such implication in the King James usage. This text uses *might*, it is in the subjunctive mood, which we do not use much any more. The subjunctive mood is used when there is an element of doubt or condition in the sentence. In modern usage, the subjunctive mood is most often used in conjunction with *if.* "If I were going, I would wear a blue suit." You can readily see the doubt caused by *if,* and the subject being *I* (singular), and the verb *were* being both plural and past tense. The subject-predicate rules twist when the subjunctive mood is used.

Example:

John 3:16, 17 For God so loved the world that He gave His only begotten Son, that whoever believes in Him should not perish, but have everlasting life, for God sent not His Son into the world to condemn the world, but that the world, through Him *might* be saved.

This is a subjunctive use of *might* because the condition of being saved was contingent on the first part of the sentence, God sending His Son. When the first condition is met, the second part of the sentence becomes an established fact. The *might* becomes a positive and conclusive verb— *would, could, will* or *shall.*

Thus, when the skeptics see the term *might,* there is no real room for doubt, no matter how much they want doubt to be there. John 3:16 and 17 leaves little doubt in the work of the Father and His plans, nor is there any doubt anywhere else in the Word, even though the word *might* may have been used. Remember the Bible is a translation, thus human efforts are involved. That, in and of itself, lends to some shortcomings.

Antecedents

An antecedent is a word (a noun or pronoun) to which another word (a noun or pronoun) refers, either in the same sentence or a following sentence.

Antecedents may precede their pronoun as much as a sentence or two. Any further separation than that constitutes poor writing (or poor translating). As an example, "The car was red and it was traveling fast!" In this sentence, *it* refers to *the car.*

Ultimately, every pronoun has an antecedent, even though whatever it refers to may be only understood within the context. The first person pronouns (*I* and *we*) are self explanatory. Likewise the second person pronoun (*you*) is self explanatory within the context of the message.

The most confusing are the third person pronouns *they*, and *them*, but especially *it*. The context becomes very important in determining what a pronoun's antecedent is.

If the antecedent is not known, confusion follows. Look at this example: "Mary hit Jane. She was very angry!" Was Mary angry and therefore she struck Jane? Or was Jane very angry because Mary hit her? In our example, we have two possibilities. If the antecedent is not made clear, we simply do not know what is being said in the sentence. Both of them could not have been very angry or the second sentence would have said, "They were very angry."

So it is in Scriptures. Confusion results when the text does not make a pronoun's antecedent clear. To make matters worse, the reader often identifies with some of the people in the account and then the reader often gets the wrong message doctrinally.

As an example, read the 4th Chapter of Romans. If we were to go through this chapter and clarify every pronoun, it would be confusing and laborious reading. But in our minds that is what we are expected to do to really understand the message of God's Word.

1. What then shall we [us, the reader and Paul] say that Abraham our father [again, us, the owner of father] has found according to the flesh?

2. For if Abraham was justified by works, he [Abraham] has something of which to boast, but not before God.

3. For what does the Scripture say? "Abraham believed God, and it [Abraham's belief of God's message] was accounted to him [Abraham] for righteousness."

4. Now to him who works [a worker], the wages are not counted as grace but as debt.

5. But to him who does not work [a non-worker] but believes on Him who [God] justifies the ungodly, his [the non-worker's] faith is accounted for righteousness, 6. just as David also describes the blessedness of the man to whom [receiver of God's righteousness] God imputes righteousness apart from works:

7. "Blessed are those whose [lawless doers] lawless deeds are forgiven, and whose [lawless doers'] sins are covered;

8. Blessed is the man to whom [the man] the Lord shall not impute sin."

9. Does this blessedness then come upon the circumcised only, or upon the uncircumcised also? For we [the readers and Paul] say that faith was accounted to Abraham for righteousness.

10. How then was it [the righteousness] accounted? While he [Abraham] was circumcised, or uncircumcised? Not while circumcised, but while uncircumcised.

By the time you read through Verse 25 of this portion of Scripture, analyzing the pronouns and their antecedents properly as you read, there is a realization that attempting to combine grace with the Law is futile.

There are lines all over some chapters in one of my study Bibles, criss-crossing the columns as I trace the pronouns and their antecedents through the Word. This criss-crossing can establish, re-establish, confirm, reconfirm, affirm and reaffirm the foundation of your salvation and your relationship with your Heavenly Father and His benefits to and for you.

This is only one small passage and there are many more passages just as important and relevant as this one.

4

Extra-Scriptural Topics

Jesus said, "I am the Way, the Truth and the Life. No one comes to the Father except through Me" (John 14: 6). This would indicate that Jesus is the hub upon which the whole wheel of faith rotates. If the wheel of faith is not balanced on the hub, the wheel wobbles and shakes its load. That is why there are so many churches, some of which do not show any indication of knowing one end of the Lord or His Word from the other.

When people do not follow the Bible-study guidelines, the wheel becomes off balance and things get "all shook up!" There is no doubt that the shaking of things is what some folks evidently want. (It is sure the enemy wants things well stirred and shaken!) Hence, there are some parties who want to throw off the balance of the Word and any relationship with the Lord that may result from it. They are being led by Satan, who is using his devices to lure people away from the center of the truth. He may lead them by offering them wealth, power, attention, relevance, false assurances, false promises, false peace and any number of other fallacies that he may scheme up.

> An Aside: Two of the main lures that the enemy uses to derail people are Relevance and Validation. Everyone wants to be needed—to someone or for something. Everyone wants to be acknowledged—by someone or for some accomplishment(s). Because so many people fall into the traps of Relevance or Validation, you may see why so many people come up with their weird concepts of the Bible and its contents. It is for sure that Satan is leading the parade of biblical error and ignorance, and many are following—for these reasons or for whatever other reason!

There are many teachings in churches and various individual ministries that come from missing or avoiding the guidelines for Bible-study; others come from using experience and religious sayings or clichés as foundations for their teachings; still other come from . . . well, who knows!

Some doctrines, teachings and practices are relevant to one's relationship with the Lord and others have no relevance whatever. Therefore, you need to think through very carefully the things you accept as fact!

Traditions

Several religious activities fall into the category of traditions: The non-scriptural chronology of the events surrounding the crucifixion, burial and resurrection of Jesus; the traditions about Christmas; and several other things.

The topics in this chapter will be some of the most obvious of the multitude of deceptions, including some Scripture passages that Satan uses to deceive the people and the other Scriptures that correct the misinformation.

One way of discerning the Lord's preference of how we choose to live is by reading and examining what the Bible says about the topic in question. Look up the word in a concordance and review all of the Scriptures that relate to that topic. To really satisfy your study, also look up the opposite topics in your concordance and study them.

For instance, you may want to find out what you need to do to get saved. Looking in you concordance, you will find many references to the term *"save"* or *salvation*. You may notice a reference to the Philippian jailer who asked that same question of Paul and Silas (Acts 16: 30). They answered him in the next verse. The jailer and his family acted on the opportunity and were later baptized. The whole chapter should be considered when you read this passage because of the subsequent action of being baptized. (See also <u>Baptism</u>, "Guidepost 7," Chapter 1, *Book 1*.)

There will be many other references to *save* in your concordance. There are several connections of *saved* with the term *faith*. There are many references to what Jesus said about *save*. The connection with *save* and *circumcision* in Acts 15 leads to the argument whether a person can be saved or not by fulfilling the terms of the Law.

So, by reading all these references, you may find out how to be saved and that nothing you can do can save you. You will be saved by the grace of the Father through the shed blood of Christ. Nothing else can save you.

You will also find out there are other terms that the translators have rendered "saved" that were used elsewhere as "delivered." In order to really get to the nitty-gritty bottom of the situation, in a concordance, look up the term "*lost*," the opposite of saved. *Lost* is combined with *lose* in one concordance that I have, and there are not nearly as many references to *lose* or *lost* as there are to *save, saved, salvation* or *delivered*.

References to *lose* or *lost* are connected to *sheep, piece of silver*, and the condition of man in contrast to *life*. From there, you may want to see *grace, life, redemption* or any one of several other words that you may want to research in regards to *saved, lost* and their references. After you finish researching, apply the guidelines for study to the information that you have gleaned.

Do these Scriptures apply to me?

Who said them?

To whom were they said?

What were any extenuating circumstances?

Because everyone needs salvation, this topic could be of interest to anyone. Although there are many topics that may pique someone's interest in the Bible, there are many topics not discussed or mentioned in the Bible. Any discussion of a topic will be easier to research if the topic is in Scriptures to begin with.

Some of the things we will be referring to in the next few pages are not in the Scriptures at all. You will see them as we come to them.

Joining the Church—Church Membership

The vast majority of churches encourage church membership, often without knowing anything about whom they are inviting to join them. The only thing the Scriptures say about joining the church is where the Lord added daily to the church those who were saved (Acts 2: 47).

Obviously, the Lord adding someone to the Body of Believers or the Body of Christ (the Church) is one thing, but a man or woman signing a pledge sheet and a membership roll in the local church means nothing outside the political or social power and money the local church gains from the new member. While what the Lord does is spiritual, the actions of signing and pledging only restrict the new member financially and emotionally.

Enrollment of members in a church is an addition that has come into being in the modern church. Its basis probably has more to do with finances and political or social power than any other purpose, real or imagined.

Another logical reason for church membership is for selfish purposes: *"We, the local church, want to brand everyone we can as ours so no on else can claim them!"* This notion is purely selfish and has no virtue in it. Certainly if church membership or joining a church were important, the Bible would have said something about it.

This is the one device that is more indicative than any other that many modern churches are not outreaches of God as much as they are big businesses.

The Vanity of Church Membership

Church leaders often boast of the growth of their denomination or local church as if it a great accomplishment or in competition with other churches. Some acknowledge that God has blessed them, but most of the time even that concession is with some pride as if they deserved God's benevolence.

The same is true on the other side of the coin. Many people join a church simply because they benefit from the image of being good upstanding church members! Many stories are spread through the communities where local members of society are caught between their misconduct and their reputations as moral citizens.

The misconduct of one who claims the name of Christ is where the problems arise. Simply put, some of these people are an embarrassment to the ministry of Christ and those who love Him (II Corinthians 6: 3). Although it is up to the Lord to judge His people, it is up to believing members to see to it that any misconduct is not rewarded, neither with apathy nor license. This is a touchy issue. While misconduct should not be rewarded, the Body of Christ should maintain an even attitude toward the offender(s) and love them beyond these errors and minister to them accordingly—the goal being to deliver the offenders from their offensive conduct.

Although excommunication is an option available to every congregation, it is almost never an acceptable idea to actually use it. Sometimes the membership and their affairs are embarrassing, but that is why the Holy Spirit is needed in the ministry!

One church had an abortionist physician in their congregation who served in the church as an usher and greeter. It was well known who he was and what he did for a living, yet much of the membership accepted him without hesitation or reservation. However, his means of livelihood was definitely offensive to someone. He was murdered.

Other churches have had openly gay activists in their congregation, sometimes as pastors! These things should never happen! Paul wrote to not fellowship with these sorts (I Corinthians 5: 8–13; II Timothy 3: 1–7). The existence of gay ministers has split more than one church!

There is a mystery in the way some people claim to be believers, join a church and call themselves members of that church, after which it becomes known that there are problems in their identities and in their lifestyles in relation to the Lord. Millions of these people, many of them thinking themselves to be believers, do not know the difference between the church they see in front of them and the God these churches claim to represent.

These problem people and their phony IDs is one area that the world sees as the problem it is. As is usually the case, the worldly who see these problem people promptly blame God for them and their problems.

Dealing with people—not just the "problem people," but all people—must come directly from and through the ministry of the gifts of the Holy Spirit. Only He can discern, heal and save individuals and deliver them from their problems!

Being Brutally Frank

Many people watch other people. It is probably a majority of the people watch other people. With some folks, watching other people is a hobby! Often these people-watchers watch others to see personal weaknesses for the purpose of judging them.

That gives rise to gossip and condemnation of nearly everyone by someone. In all probability you are being scrutinized by people at any given point in time.

The principle is this: When one condemns his fellows, he or she is psychologically standing over that fellow in superiority, thus becoming better than that condemned fellow. However, the principle is only psychological and therefore imaginary, having no validation whatsoever. The whole premise is based on diabolical rationale.

Paul writing to the Corinthians mentioned that they (himself and the Corinthians) gave no offense in anything so that the ministry would not be blamed. The term *ministry* was obviously referring to their association with the Lord. Following this statement there is a long list of words relating to their relationship with their ministry of God (II Corinthians 6: 3–10).

Again Paul admonished the Thessalonians to avoid the very appearance of evil (II Thessalonians 6: 3). Having put up these two verses as a basis for the following practical lessons in life, let's sum up the situation:

> We should live our lives as consistently before the Lord as we can because a life lived for the Lord is far more honorable in His eyes than any eyes on earth. His eyes are the only ones that count!

> Although we will be judged (condemned) by our fellow beings, the Lord's judgment is the only one that has any authority! The Lord Jesus already saved us from eternal judgment, becoming our sin-bearer, so the Father-God will not judge believers!

> Those earthlings who judge us see us through eyes with all sorts of influences: Jealousy, strife, contention, lust, hate . . . and no telling what other influences. In conclusion, you and I will never please the vast majority of these earthly judges. We can only please the Lord, and that by His grace.

So brace yourself for criticism from all quarters because the enemy will see to it that you are criticized! The best you can do will dedicate all you do to the Lord and allow Him to bless you as a Father blesses His child. He will lead you regarding conduct before men.

Meanwhile, in order to silence a few critical voices, here are some adjustments that may be warranted.

Aligning Your Christianity with Your Political Voice

Something everyone needs to know: The church is not God and God in not the church. If people do not clearly understand this basic fact, they will soon leave off any acknowledgment of God at all because of people and their observed failures in the church! Therefore every believer should be aware of this and avoid being an embarrassment to the ministry of Christ as much as possible.

In the first place, a church may support political people, policies or programs that do not please the Lord, to say the least. Some large American denominational churches have been involved with aiding foreign governments or rebels against foreign governments with not only food and medicine, but with arms, ammunition and personnel to use them. Some of the factions supported by these large American denominational churches are from the far Left—Communism. Of these, most are (or were) not allies of the US, some even resisting American forces.

Some large American denominational churches support some anti-constitutional positions, such as open borders that allow people to enter the US without authorization. This is illegal and support of the notion is not only against our laws, but places our people in danger of another 9/11 type of attack. Many terrorists have entered the US by this means since 2000, and some churches support their entry, with or without proper authorization.

Of course those involved with these lax measures are aware of the danger to the US and our citizens, but for some reason, they do not care or are willing to take the risk of another 9/11 type of attack.

In the second place, these church-joiners support a church that in turn supports legislation directly, or support people who support legislation that is not moral, ethical or decent. Many allegedly devout Roman Catholic politicians support abortion rights contrary to what the Roman Catholic Church embraces. So do many Baptists, Methodists, Episcopalians and others (although some independent churches may accept the premise of choice).

It is not unusual for politicians of the same church membership to be on opposite sides in moral debates, each voting either for or against moral or immoral legislation on the docket. It is especially bewildering to see and hear these church-affiliated politicians fabricate stories (lie) to make a point, or to make false accusations (lie) against honorable people to gain some political advantage. Then if the church leadership raises an issue regarding the political stand of one of their politicians, there comes forth the cry for separation of church and state!

Not long ago the Speaker of the House made statements about the teachings of the Roman Catholic Church regarding abortion that turned out badly for her. She either did not know what she believed as a Catholic, or she lied about what the RCC's position was on abortion.

In today's convoluted political scene, believers need to look at the issues and the candidates closely to see who meets with the standards of the Christian believers who know the will of the Lord by His Word.

Because the Constitution of the United States of America is not a topic under discussion, the constitutionality of the actions of politicians will not come into play in this document. The propriety of Christendom according to the Word of God does come within the limits of this document and it will be pointed out that there needs to be an awakening of some segments of Christianity that have serious political problems.

There are several issues currently and constantly debated that are hot topics constitutionally speaking: Those open borders and the lax resistance to illegal entry into the US; the support these illegals have after they get here, (illegal employment, public benefits, etc.); and the massive social problems they have caused by being here without paying their fair share. Of course, there is also the problem of not only the illegal personnel, but the drug traffic, weapons traffic, and terrorist traffic that accompany some of them.

This is not the place to say all that could and should be said regarding the invasion from the south. Just realize this: The US is a nation of laws. As long as people react to their emotions, whether that of pity for the invaders or that of greed for their cheap labor, the end will only be confusion, chaos and disorder. Enforcing the laws that we have with level-headed responses is the only thing that will bring these crises to a peacefully and orderly end.

Aligning your Christianity with Your Social Voice

Another set of hot topics relate to our peaceful and un-terrorized existence. Some people would rather spend money on social programs and entitlements than on our national defense.

Although this is a constitutional issue, it also touches on civility of proper Christian conduct, or lack thereof. The Constitution does not mention that the government owes anyone a living or a minimum living standard. The only thing the Constitution guarantees is the people's protection from foreign harm.

Some people who claim to be believers seem to think that a life of freeloading at the expense of the taxpayers is an honorable way to make a living. They seem to think it is okay to embezzle a living from someone who has deep pockets, whether the victim is the government or some private rich organization. The problem of public (government) assistance from state or local sources does not relate to people who cannot make their own living, but to people who will not make their own living.

Not many people have a problem with welfare where it is needed, but most people object to welfare payments to people who simply do not want to work for their sustenance. There is growing resentment regarding the "Less fortunate" people who are in their position because of poor life management skills. Most of the ne'er-do-wells never do well because of an assortment of life choices that laid the foundation for their poverty:

Dropping out of school,

Vagrancy,

Getting / making someone pregnant,

Traffic crimes—DUI, DWI,

Getting married too young (or at all),

Living together w/o marriage,

Crime, theft, larceny

Getting involved with narcotics, alcohol

Abandonment of responsibilities,

And many more.

Many people do not think those people who have made such choices should be bailed out of their messes, thus enabling them in their messes is even worse. Unfortunately, the latter is usually what happens. Only one Word should close the matter: II Thessalonians 3: 10:

If anyone will not work, neither shall he eat.

The Debris of Racism

Some people who claim to be believers cannot allow the past to be the past. Their race has been mistreated in the past and they won't let anyone forget it, especially not themselves. While the Black race was definitely mistreated, so have other races, not only in the US but around the world: Whites, Chinese, Mexican, Native Americans, Europeans, Asians and others. Other abuses have occurred, such as prejudice and name-calling: Po' White Trash, Wetbacks, Spicks, Wops, Limeys, Niggers, Honkies, Jesus-Haters and others who have been looked down on for one excuse or another. It is the way people are—not just some people, but the lost in any society are liable to abuse others. Believers should not do so under any circumstances, not initially nor in retaliation!

Get over it; nothing will right the wrongs of a century past. Those actually guilty of the abuses are long since gone to their judgment before God and resurrecting the same old hate patterns except in reverse accomplishes nothing but negativity! Let the dead bury their dead!

Aligning your Christianity against America's Abominations

There are some 50 abominations mentioned in the Bible. There are two issues that top the list on political debate in America. These two constantly relevant issues are on the talking points in nearly every community in America, and have been for years. Both of them relate to American believers—all American believers: Abortion Rights (Choice) and Gay Rights. If a believer is on the wrong side of either of these issues, that believer needs to repent of these attitudes and actions and get involved with his or her new creation in Jesus Christ!

Without going into a lengthy debate here regarding the evils of the abominations of abortion and homosexuality, and how the Father-God looks at these abominations and those who practice them, just take a look at how the nations of the Old Testament were judged by Jehovah for doing the same things that the abortionists or homosexuals do today. The inhabitants of Sodom and Gomorrah were wiped out for their homosexuality and anti-God stands, and the inhabitants of Canaan were wiped out for child sacrifices. (The only difference between *abortion* and *child-sacrifice* is semantics and timing.)

Later, both of the nations that came from the Children of Israel (Israel and Judah) suffered the LORD's wrath for child sacrifice. Israel ceased to exist and Judah spent 70 years in Babylonian captivity for it. One American political party habitually supports both Choice (for abortion rights) and Gay Rights. Many so-called believers support that same party but are privately against either Abortion Rights or Gay Rights (Gay Rights meaning same-sex marriage and other special benefits giving homosexuals privileges more than other people have.)

Believers, as all people, need to forget political party associations and pretentious obligations and look at the issues and those who support these evils in our society. Churches that are politically active should take account to the Word of God regarding the people they support and the issues they support.

Some politically active church-members must make some tough choices. Often there are three issues facing the political active church-member: Alleged racism, abortion rights and gay rights. The charges have been made that one political party is racist. That party denies it is racist.

Meanwhile the other principle party pushes the two abominations as part of their platform! So we know one party is completely wrong because of its support for the abominations, while some folks believe the other party may be wrong for its alleged racism.

These issues make decisions of support tough. Many people believe both principle political parties in the US are failures that need replacing!

It is certain that supporting a racist (if that party is truly racist) party is obviously not acceptable, it is also certain that a person or organization that endorses a pro-choice candidate or a pro-gay-rights candidate is certainly going against the Lord and His Word in so doing!

Nothing matters to the electorate except the representation he or she receives when that delegate votes one way or another. The representative you elected to represent you, whether local, state or federal, whether Representative, Senator, Governor or President supports issues in your place. If that person practices or preaches racism; or if that person votes to support the murder of an innocent who is being created in God's image, or if that person votes to grant special rights to gays simply because they are gay, you need to make sure you get that person out of public office as soon as possible! Make sure your personal vote does not get this nation any further cross-threaded with the Father-God than it already is!

> <u>An Aside</u>: Not to defend racism (it is absolutely vile), racism is not listed as one of the abominations of the Bible. You should not base your vote on political party, skin-color, gender, previous occupation, physical abilities (or lack thereof), sexual orientation, popularity, personality or any other traits that make a person unique. You need to elect representation who is moral, upstanding and honorable, and who will vote in accordance with the Word of God on any and all issues.

> You may be putting your party affiliation on the line here, but changing party affiliation will not hurt you if you are doing it as to the Lord! You may not have to change parties, but you may need to change your voting habits if you have in the past voted for people who promote the practices of these abominations! One current debate concerns the possibility (maybe even probability) that all political parties are corrupt and not worth anyone's support!

Holidays

Look briefly at the traditions that Christians often hold about Christmas and Easter. Like most of the so-called holidays of America, the holiday (from holy-day) is usually only an excuse for a fancy feed—and a big one, at that! Christmas is popular for secular and selfish reasons, and both Christmas and Thanksgiving are the days that gluttony is permitted regardless of any tendencies away from such conduct!

Easter is less popular because it has not yet been as related specifically to the food aspect as much as Christmas and Thanksgiving, but it has been connected with style and clothing. Only in the last few years have commercialism of food (especially chocolate) addressed Easter. Be sure to realize that many of the teachings about these "Holy Day" events are false and meaningless.

Christmas

Christmas is a treasure trove of things that are scripturally groundless. Starting at the first of the story, there is no scriptural reference at all for the number of wise men who came to Jesus' birth, nor of His age when they got there. Herod figured every male child two years old and under a likely candidate for being the Christ child. The idea that the wise men ever came to the stable where Jesus was born is highly suspect, to say the least.

> <u>An Aside</u>: The Star of Bethlehem has been discussed for years. Some scientists claim that some of the planets lined up in such a fashion that they appeared to be one star.

> Others dispute this notion. Still others deny the star ever really existed. The notion that the Star of Bethlehem was a manifestation of several planets aligned to appear as one is of no earthly value. Even if the planets did align themselves to appear as one body in the sky, how would those following that "star" ever find a single geographical location on earth? They could not do it any more than finding a certain locale on earth underneath the moon!

> The moon is only a quarter of a million miles above the earth. The coalition of planets would be many millions of miles above the earth. If someone could not find a specific location by being underneath the moon, finding the location of the Christ-child by a bunch of aligned planets would be even more farfetched.

That narrows the answer down to being something very special. When science is unable to explain an event, why can't we just go ahead and acknowledge a miracle has happened?

The idea of shepherds being in the field in the middle of winter is outrageous. The birth of Jesus had to be in the spring, summer or, most probably, the fall.

The reasons some people have preferred to believe the birth of Christ was in the fall is two-fold: The number of people traveling made accommodations hard to find as it would have been in the celebration of the harvest. It is also likely that the Romans demanded the census be taken when travel was relatively easy—at least regarding weather. Regardless of logical rationale or not, the rationale for the birth of Christ being in the dead of winter is ludicrous, and thus far is merely erroneous.

However, the culmination of errors from this point on evolves into heresy! Most of the rest of Christmas is derived from pagan religions, welded together by Roman Catholicism. Most any reference book or encyclopedia can cite the history of how the Roman Catholic Church and a host of pagan religions joined together to originate "*Christ Mass.*"

In the long haul, Christmas has to fall into the category of blasphemy. Christmas has impacted Christianity and personal relationships with Jesus so negatively that it is incalculable! What effects have the fables of a Santa Claus had in the minds of children when they hear of the real Christ? *Santa Claus' bribing presents far outweigh the mere stories of a so-called Christ-child!* Can children distinguish between the real Savior with the phony Santa? *After getting all those goodies, who cares?*

When the fallacy of Santa Claus appears to the children, will they then not subconsciously question the reality of the Savior, His birth, His death, His conquest of death and His Redemption of fallen man? (The latter three items are seldom ever mentioned in the Christmas story!) *It makes it all sound mystical!*

How can anyone with clear conscience risk mixing the fictitious with the real and not expect some permanent negative reaction to Jesus in the minds of the people, especially the children? The taint of the secular gifts connected with Santa Claus and the accompanying avarice makes it even harder to objectively consider the reality of Christ and salvation through Him.

The final objection to Christmas comes to a head when people celebrate an event that the Lord never instructed should be celebrated and then ignore so many things that He did instruct His people to do and be.

People are in a metal brake: A set of jaws consisting of biblical ignorance and tradition grip the people while the bending force of personal avarice with a very obvious secularism twists the people into a warped mass of confusion and contradiction. When people see and hear stories, fables and songs that incorporate a fact, incident or name smeared together with an unholy alliance of talking and walking snowmen, navigating flying reindeer with nose-lights, wonderful snow, poor drummer boys, and a long list of other ridiculous truth-sapping but emotional images, it is no wonder Christ is lost in Christmas.

The lubricant for the brake is apathy and the torque on it is avarice! Again, if tradition holds sway over the truth about the birth of Christ, how botched up will the story get when we study His life-changing roles in Scripture, and there are plenty of them?

The Way to Calvary

Which direction was Jesus going when he fell under the weight of the cross? Was He going east west, north, south, uphill, downhill or in little tight circles?

Who knows! Who cares? There is no mention of the direction He was going. As a matter of fact, there is no scriptural reference that Jesus fell at all, not under the cross or any other time.

The so-called Bible-scholars developed the idea that Jesus fell because a by-stander was drafted to carry Jesus' cross part of the way to Calvary for Him. Jesus having fallen is only someone's idea of why Simon was drafted to carry Jesus' cross. It may have been that Simon was bad-mouthing a soldier when the soldier made him take up Jesus' cross. Maybe the soldier already knew Simon and wanted to be mean to him. Who knows? But Scripture does not record Jesus falling!

When you consider that Jesus was Who He said He was, the concept of His having fallen and come into the need of assistance from a mortal is not only ridiculous, but blasphemous, too.

Easter—The Resurrection

This topic is best handled with questions and answers:

> What time of day did Jesus die? Evening (Matthew 27: 57–61).
>
> How long was Jesus to be buried? Three days and three nights, approximately 72 hours, by Jesus' own prophecy (Matthew 12: 38–41).
>
> If Jesus was crucified on Friday, and buried Friday afternoon, how can He arise on Sunday morning, only 36 hours later?

Tradition has stated He was crucified on Friday because the so-called scholars of the Bible saw that He was crucified the day before the Sabbath. Many reference books and Bible commentaries print and document this nonsense in their "Harmony of the Gospels" and biblical chronologies. These so-called Bible scholars show no evidence that they know that the Day of Passover was also called the Sabbath—the High Sabbath (John 19: 31).

The High Sabbath could fall on any day of the week. In this case it had to have been on Thursday. Thus, Jesus was crucified on an afternoon and buried on that afternoon (and He was), He would also of necessity arise on an afternoon! That sums up to three days and three nights. That is the only way it sums up to three days and three nights! Then it had to be this way or Jesus Himself goofed!

Jesus had to have been crucified on Wednesday, buried on Wednesday evening, remained in His grave through the High Sabbath, arose victoriously on Saturday evening and was not discovered arisen until Sunday morning. That accounts for approximately 72 hours and does not conflict with any Scripture. The traditional accounts of the resurrection have a problem with the timing element.

The Body would not be disturbed between Thursday and Saturday evening after sunset because of the Old Testament Law. Anyone who touched a dead body was considered unclean for a week (Leviticus 19: 11-13). There would not be time enough to further treat the Body for burial after sundown on Saturday. Hence, when the task was to be taken on come early Sunday morning, there was Jesus alive and victorious!

What we have amounts to traditions based on incorrectly perceived history regarding the detailed facts as Scripture records it. There are some who teach that there was a cultural expression of time that made it possible to count only a portion of a day as a full day. Therefore, if

Jesus had been crucified on Friday and Friday evening was counted as a full day, plus Saturday (a full day) and then the early part of Sunday was counted as a full day, the total would be three days. However, the words Jesus chose to repeat were "Three days and three nights," not the cultural length of time, "Three days" (the one where only portions of days count as full days).

If so-called Bible scholars go along with tradition, disregarding Jesus' prophecy, what will they do to the subtle things in Scripture that turn lives around? The subtle things I speak of are the things that identify believers—things of which most believers have absolutely no knowledge. These are some of the many things taught in churches that confuse ordinary believers who hear these things. Again, the idea that Jesus accomplished only half of what He said He would accomplish moves from ridiculous to blasphemous.

Long Time Trends

There are a couple of teachings that are worth a quick mention, and they are related to each other. They are "The Universal Brotherhood of Man" and "The Universal Fatherhood of God" dogmas. Both concepts are so far removed from God's Word that anyone who knows anything about the purpose of Jesus can quickly dismiss either dogma as satanic nonsense. The foundation of these teachings was crushed flat when Jesus told Nicodemus that one must be born again (John 3).

Mixing the Old with the New:
Legalism, Pseudo-legalism and Appeasement

Because of the use of the following terms in various circumstances and by several different groups, some definitions are in order.

The first term is *Legalism*. For our usage, *Legalism* refers to the scriptural terms that mean exactly what they appear to mean: *Adopt, Adoption, Redemption. Redeem, Plea, Plead, Witness, Testify, Confess (Profess), Forgive, Pardon, Cleanse, Remit, Create and Re-create, Servant and Slave, Heir, Child, Children, Wages, Gift, Justice, Judge, Judgment, Intercede, Intercession, Propitiate* and *Propitiation.*

These are all scriptural, legal terms that relate to our salvation by the grace and mercy of God the Father.

Pseudo-legalism, one the other hand, refers to the tendency for some believers and pseudo-believers (those who claim to be believers, but aren't and don't) to adhere to the Old Testament Law, or some part(s) thereof. This could mean abstinence from eating pork for religious reasons, seventh day (or Sabbath) religious functions, a system of works or deeds to please God, tithing, and other Old Testament based concepts. These first two topics lead directly to the next term: *Appeasement.*

Appeasement refers to the attempt to do something that will mollify an irritated or angry God or to keep an easily irritated God from becoming irritated. Rather than recognize that the Father has accepted, forgiven and recreated them by His grace, some folks try to live in such a manner that He can find no fault in them or their behavior. They attempt to live a "holy life" by their own efforts and in their own strength. Having said this, look at the chapters regarding the bondage of appeasement: Romans, Chapters 14 and 15 and realize that the issue is really more than the days of the week or the meat sacrificed to idols. Read Galatians 4: 8–10 and 4: 19–5: 16. The problem lies in *why people are attempting to hold onto Old Testament traditions (laws).*

> Galatians 4: 8 Howbeit at that time, not knowing God, <u>you were in bondage to what by nature are not gods</u>: but now that you have come to know God, or rather to be known by God<u>, how can you turn back to the weak and beggarly rudiments, wherein you desire to be in bondage over again?</u> You observe days, and months, and seasons, and years. I am afraid for you, lest by any means I have bestowed labor upon you in vain.

This returning to the functions and conduct of the Law is often a pattern of conduct called *Galatianism*. Paul wrote Galatians to a church that was contending with those who were attempting to return to the Old Testament Law from which Christ had redeemed them.

In this passage in Galatians 4: 8—10, Paul reminds them that they had been servants of idols and they had met God and He had delivered them from the elements of the world. Paul cites how they were observing the days, months, times and years (probably the Old Testament feasts and year of jubilee). Then he said he was afraid for them because of the possibility that he had wasted his time on preaching to them.

In Verse 19, Paul says he was in travail for them again because of this tendency to return to the Law, and he wanted to be with them to clear things up.

My little children, of whom I am again in travail until Christ be formed in you, but I could wish to be present with you now, and to change my tone; for I am perplexed about you.

In Verse 21, he addresses in particular those who wanted to return to the Law and asks them:

Tell me, you who desire to be under the Law, do you not hear the Law? For it is written, that Abraham had two sons, one by the handmaid, and one by the freewoman. Howbeit the *son* by the handmaid is born after the flesh; but the *son* by the freewoman *is born* through promise.

He explains that Abraham had two sons: One by a handmaid (Sarah's suggestion to have a son vicariously by one of her maids), and one by the freewoman (Sarah, Abraham's wife). Sarah's suggested method of helping the LORD keep His promise to Abraham brought forth Ishmael. Later, after all else failed and Abraham and Sarah were well beyond child-bearing age, Isaac was born to them (miraculously, as God often does things). Isaac was the promised one. Ishmael was the attempt.

> An Aside: Because Sarah—and then Abraham—tried to help God out by their activity to bring an heir into the family, it set up a foundation that the enemy uses to this day to cause strife and war between the nations that descended from Ishmael (the Arabs) and the nation that descended from Isaac, Israel.

Paul goes on to explain the allegory. Each woman represented a covenant; one woman, Hagar, represented the Law (Sinai), and bondage. The other, Sarah, the wife, the freewoman, represented the Promise. The woman Hagar connects to Sinai and is involved with the Jews and their Law. And these people who try to hold on to the Law are putting themselves in bondage to the Law. Verse 24 continues the lecture:

Which things contain an allegory: for these *women* are two covenants; one from Mount Sinai, bearing children to bondage, which is Hagar. Now this Hagar is Mount Sinai in Arabia and answers to the Jerusalem that now is: for she is in bondage with her children.

Paul explains that Jerusalem that is above is free, and asserts that it is their mother Sarah. He confirms that by referring to the Scripture in Isaiah 54: 1. Galatians 4: 26 and 27:

> But the Jerusalem that is above is free, which is our mother. For it is written, "Rejoice, you barren who bears not; Break forth and cry, you who travail not: For more are the children of the desolate than of her who has a husband."

Paul continues to explain that the spiritual, as Isaac was, are the children of the Promise. He also parallels the persecution that Ishmael perpetrated on Isaac with the current persecution Paul and the other believers suffered for their stand regarding the Law. Because of Ishmael having abused Isaac, Sarah moved on Abraham to have the bondwoman and her son thrown out, and that without an inheritance. Paul identifies the Galatians and himself with the children of the freewoman, because Christ made them free. In that freedom they were not to get entangled again with the bondage of the Law. Verse 31:

> Wherefore, brethren, we are not children of a handmaid, but of the freewoman. For freedom did Christ set us free: stand fast therefore, and be not entangled again in a yoke of bondage.

Paul is so dogmatic that he asserts that even circumcision is of no real value unless one intends to keep the whole Law. One would have to make animal sacrifices again, and God would never accept them because Jesus was the ultimate sacrifice, fulfilling the Law. So it was and is evident that keeping the whole Law was and is out of the question.

Therefore, it is absurd to try to keep any portion of the Law for keeping the Law's sake. Further, you will sever fellowship with the Redeemer if you try to live by the Law. Paul continues in Chapter 5 of Galatians, Verses 2–4:

> Behold, I Paul say to you, that, if you receive circumcision, Christ will profit you nothing. Yea, I testify again to every man that receives circumcision, that he is a debtor to do the whole Law. You are severed from Christ, you who would be justified by the Law; you have fallen away from grace. For we through the spirit by faith wait for the hope of righteousness.

Paul goes so far as to say that circumcision is nothing. The whole answer is summed up in the last of Verse 6: Faith that works through Love. Verse 6:

> For in Christ Jesus neither circumcision avails anything, nor un-circumcision; but faith working through love.

Paul turns his attention on the promoter of the disruption. Who bothered you with this? It wasn't by Jesus. A little yeast raises the whole batch of dough. Paul gives a statement of faith to the Galatians, "I have confidence in you, but the one who troubled you will answer for it." Verses 7–10:

> You were running well; who hindered you that you should not obey the truth? This persuasion *came* not of him who calls you. A little leaven leavens the whole lump. I have confidence toward you in the Lord, that you will be none otherwise minded: but he who troubles you shall bear his judgment, whoever he might be.

Paul reminds the Galatians that he was also being persecuted for the stand against the practice of keeping the Law. He goes on telling the Galatians that they are called to freedom. But they are to refuse to use that freedom as a license. He sums up the whole Law, just like he did in the letter to the Romans, "You shall love your neighbor as yourself." Don't judge one another, or badmouth each other because what goes around comes around. Finally Paul ends the matter: Walk in the spirit, and you shall not fulfill the lust of the flesh. Galatians 5: 11–16:

> 11 But I, brethren, if I still preach circumcision, why am I still persecuted? Then has the stumbling-block of the cross been done away. I would that they who unsettle you would even go beyond circumcision. For you, brethren, were called for freedom; only *use* not your freedom for an occasion to the flesh, but through love be servants one to another. For the whole law is fulfilled in one word, *even* in this: You shall love your neighbor as yourself. But if you bite and devour one another, take heed that you are not consumed one of another.
>
> 16 But I say, <u>walk in the spirit, and you shall not fulfill the lust of the flesh.</u>

Regardless then, whether we speak of tithing, eating certain foods, attending church on certain days, or even a manner of dress, if it is done absolutely to the Lord, it is perfect for Him. If it is done to keep up appearances or to keep the Law or some other tradition of men, it is not acceptable to the Lord, nor will it ever be. Whatever you do, do all to the glory of God (I Corinthians 10: 31).

Seventh Day or First?

This is a topic of almost irrelevance because of the conclusion that the Scriptures come to regarding it as discussed in the previous section. The argument is over the selecting of a certain day of the week on which to worship. Some folks believe the day to worship above all others is Saturday, the Sabbath. Others believe Sunday should be used. Some people on both sides of the question are upset at those on the other side of the fence. Therefore we will address the issue specifically in spite of the previous resolution.

There are some folks who allege that the Seventh Day is the day that God wants His people to come together to worship Him. One bunch of these folks also abstains from pork and they cling to other Old Testament traditions.

Opponents claim that the days of worship were changed from the Seventh to the First Day. They base their stand on several alleged reasons.

> First, Jesus was discovered to have arisen on the first day of the week (Mark 16).
>
> Second, Jesus once visited His disciples on the first day of the week (John 20: 19).
>
> Third, Paul told the Corinthian believers to bring their offerings for Jerusalem together on the first day of the week (I Corinthians 16: 2).

It may be of note that the first day was somewhat prominent, but there is no command to celebrate church services on a particular day in the New Testament, and there is no word to change the primary day of worship from one day to another. So it appears that some folks like one day and other folks like a different day.

Paul wrote in Romans 14: 5 that it is not important whether one day is preferred or if all days are alike, but to be convinced in one's own mind about the issue. In other words, the days do not matter; the relationship with the Lord is what matters (Galatians 4: 10). The previous topic ("Appeasement") in this composition should have settled the "day of worship" issue, too.

Pork or No Pork?

Another aspect of the controversy about conduct pertains to certain foods, especially meat (and in the Word it is the meat that is sacrificed to idols that is in question). Peter had a rough time when he had the vision of the sheet lowered and the Lord bidding him to kill and eat (Acts 10: 9—22). Remember that Peter was reared with the concept that some meats were unclean and others were acceptable. The Lord was teaching him to accept the Gentiles as clean people once they were saved.

The Scriptures are very clear on this matter. Paul tells the Romans (14: 1–23) that we should avoid doubtful disputes about food choices and preferences of days. Some, according to Paul, are weak in faith. Maybe they were recently saved or perhaps they were isolated from sound teachings, but nonetheless they were weak in faith. The relationship between those who are strong enough in faith to tolerate eating meats that were sacrificed to idols without any condemnation and those who cannot eat meat sacrificed to idols without conviction for it should be harmonious in spite of these differences.

There should be no condemnation from either direction (Romans 8: 1). People on both sides of the issue are to respect the folks on the other side. Paul asserts that while some eat whatever they want to and some see every day as every other day, they are not isolated and should consider their conduct in front of those who abstain from certain foods and hold some days in higher regard than others.

The whole argument is settled before the Lord. Every man is to settle the issue in his own mind; whether eating what he may want or seeing the days alike, do it as to the Lord. If abstaining from some foods or holding one day apart from the others, it is done before the Lord, too. Romans 14: 6 says that either way, the regarding the day or not is to be done as to the Lord.

The issue is laid out flat when Paul addressed the very issue in Colossians. First Paul says following the traditions of men robs people. Then he points out that believers are made complete in Christ who is the Head of the Body of Christ, the Church (the real Church). The next point Paul makes is that believers are identified with Christ through baptism—the death of the flesh and the resurrected spiritual life in conjunction with Christ's baptism and subsequent acts of redemption.

> Colossians 2: 8—12: Take heed lest there shall be anyone who makes spoil of you through his philosophy and vain deceit, after the tradition of men, after the rudiments of the world, and not after Christ: for in Him [Christ] dwells all the fullness of the Godhead bodily, and in Him you are made full, who is the Head of all principality and power: in whom you were also circumcised with a circumcision not made with hands, in the putting off of the body of the flesh, in the circumcision of Christ; having been buried with Him in baptism, wherein you were also raised with Him through faith in the working of God, who raised Him from the dead.

Thus, believers were once dead by and in their sins, but Christ made them alive with Him, having forgiven the believers of all their sins. The ordinances and commandments were thus all removed—having been nailed to His cross!

It was through these commandments that the principalities and powers got their teeth to demand justice for transgressors before the Father-God. But when Christ fulfilled the Law and set it aside, He made a demonstration of His defeat of these principalities and powers. All these principalities and powers had remaining after Christ got through with them was bare gums—no teeth!

> Colossians 2: 13 And you, being dead through your trespasses and the un-circumcision of your flesh, you, *I say*, He made alive together with Him, having forgiven us all our trespasses; having blotted out the bond written in ordinances that was against us, which was contrary to us: and He has taken it out of the way, nailing it to the cross; having despoiled the principalities and the powers, He made a show of them openly, triumphing over them in it.

Based on these new conditions for the believers, Paul discourages believers from allowing themselves to be robbed of their reward by being judged for things that no longer matter—food, drink, days or nights, what is to be eaten or not eaten, handled or not handled, or touched or not touched.

There are some Messianic Jews who celebrate the Old Testament feasts even in this modern era. While they realize that Jesus Christ is the fulfillment of these symbolic pictures, they still go through all of the feasts. Because they are celebrating these feasts from the Old Testament in honor of Him who fulfilled all, they are demonstrating who Christ is and how He affects those He redeems.

Believers are to be free of all ordinances. Obeying ordinances satisfy the flesh, but that is all it accomplishes! Of course it follows that believers are not to subject each other to such judgment or condemnation! The bottom line is to avoid judging each other whether one celebrates the feasts or not, or how he or she may do it! Colossians 2: 16–23:

> Let no man therefore judge you in meat, or in drink, or in respect of a feast day or a new moon or a Sabbath day: which are a shadow of the things to come; but the body is Christ's. Let no man rob you of your prize by a voluntary humility and worshipping of the angels, dwelling in the things which he has seen, vainly puffed up by his fleshly mind, and not holding fast the Head, from whom all the body, being supplied

and knit together through the joints and bands, increasing with the increase of God.

20 If you died with Christ from the rudiments of the world, why, as though living in the world, do you subject yourselves to ordinances, handle not, nor taste, nor touch (all which things are to perish with the using), after the precepts and doctrines of men? Which things have indeed a show of wisdom in will-worship, and humility, and severity to the body; *but are* not of any value against the indulgence of the flesh.

Once the matter of satisfaction of the flesh through obedience to ordinances is settled, Paul reminds believers that once they have been raised with Christ from the dead through baptism, they are dead (having been buried)! It would only be logical then to seek those things that are alive (having been raised from the dead)—therefore, seeking spiritual things. After all, when you died in Christ, your life was hidden with Christ in the Father-God!

Colossians 3: 1–3: If then ye were raised together with Christ, seek the things that are above, where Christ is, seated on the right hand of God. Set your mind on the things that are above, not on the things that are upon the earth. For you died, and your life is hid with Christ in God.

So, once you are united with Christ in His redemption of you, nothing else matters—especially the traditions of men.

The High Priest's Rope

Some people teach that the high priest had a rope around his waist when he went into the Holy of Holies to make the annual blood sacrifice. Some people teach that the high priest had a rope around his ankle when he went into the Holy of Holies to make the annual blood sacrifice. Which was it? Was it the waist or the ankle? Who is correct?
Which teaching is correct? Neither!!

<u>An Aside</u>: The alleged rope was to be used to pull the dead priest out of the Holy of Holies if the offering he was presenting to the LORD did not please the LORD and the LORD killed him there. Because the sacrifice the high priest was presenting was an annual one and only the high priest was ever allowed to do it and no one was ever to go into the Holy of Holies except the high priest, no one could go in to get the dead priest if he was slain. So they

allegedly put a rope on him with which to drag his dead body out of the Holy of Holies.

The instructions for the High Priest's apparel are found in Exodus 28: 31–35 and Exodus 39: 22–26. If there were instructions about a rope, it would be in these passages. Mention is made of the bells and the pomegranates that were on the hem of the high priest's robe. The bells were to make a tinkle to show that the priest was not dead, a positive sign. Only bells and pomegranates were mentioned—no rope! You see, God is a God of Faith, even in the Old Testament (Hebrews, Chapter 11). The instructions were that the High Priest was to make the offering once a year. He had instructions on how to do it. When the high priest entered the Holy of Holies, he was entering in believing he was doing things according to God's instructions.

In other words, he was going in by faith. If he had a rope to pull his dead body out, he was not going in by faith. Three thoughts address the rope and its fallacy:

1. Romans 3:30 tells us that the LORD'S acceptance of the Israelites was *by faith*, and having a rope was not a sign of faith. It showed doubt and fear.

2. The bells were for a sign to the listeners that all was well because the priest lived, just as we believers hear the Word and know our Great High Priest still lives!

3. Everything in the Tabernacle in the Wilderness and in the ordinances of the priests and the sacrifices were pictures of things in the New Testament and our redemption. If there had been a rope, the only thing that the rope could possibly represent was the potential of Jesus' failure! That concept is unacceptable, to say the least!

Those who use the High Priest's rope to show God's dealings with His people should look at the Word to substantiate their teachings.

Pleading the Blood of Jesus

Another modern practice that some folks have adopted is *pleading the blood of Jesus*. The foundation for this practice is the misconception of Revelation 12: 11. Someone in the early twentieth century assumed that "*by the blood of the Lamb and by the word of their testimony*" meant <u>pleading the blood</u>.

There are several things wrong with this idea. First, look at the problem from the legal standpoint. Proponents of pleading the blood of Jesus admit that *pleading* is a legal term. The Scripture they allude to in creating the idea of pleading the blood uses the term *testimony*. A *testimony* is given by a *witness*. A *plea* is brought forth by a *defendant*.

These are two roles—two different roles (one witness and one litigant) in a legal situation—two actions—two meanings. A witness does not plead or make a plea—he gives a testimony. A defendant has one of several options: He can plead "guilty," "not guilty," or "no contest;" or he can add to his plea of "not guilty" with another plea—"by reason of insanity," "ignorance" or something to explain or re-enforce his plea of not guilty. The latter pleas would be considered excuses for the action of the charges against him. In all likelihood such additions would be ignored because of the necessity of making such additions valid, which is usually a waste of time.

In any case, the defendant does not plead "$50." or "Five years at hard labor!" One would never plead the amount of the fine or the length of time for the penalty for the alleged crime, or any other arbitrary amount for a price of fine or ransom. And certainly, because it is Jesus' Blood and not belonging to the one making the plea, no one has the right to plead it in any case.

Then in the same verses of Scripture in Revelation 12, notice the word *by*. That word indicates that the blood of the Lamb is one thing, and their testimony is another—two different things. These two unlike things cannot logically be added together and come up with only one thing. An apple plus a tricycle do not equal a granite statue! The *Blood of the Lamb* is one thing and the *Word of their Testimony* is another. No matter how one may chop up these terms and recombine them, no intelligence will come forth.

The phrase, *pleading the blood*, is not scriptural. No one in Scripture, especially the Lord, ever pleaded the blood. The terms *plead* and *blood* are never used in the same passage of Scripture. The term *plead,* or any term related to or derived from it, is not even used in the New Testament. When mentioned in the Old Testament, *plead* is usually used when someone is imploring the Lord to plead a case or cause. For someone to plead a case or cause is understandable because there are factors involved that could be used as talking points. On the other hand, how would someone plead the name of something—a single noun?

Because we are Children of God (assuming that you know Jesus as your personal Savior), we have already been redeemed by the Blood of Christ, and we need not plead the blood. Jesus has already taken His blood to the Father to pay for our redemption. Jesus is the propitiation for our sins. Why would we want to plead His blood or Him again?

This is not to say that the Blood does not have an important role in our relationship with Jesus. Read I Peter 1: 18–21:

> Forasmuch as you know that you were not redeemed with corruptible things, as silver and gold, from your vain conversation received by tradition from your fathers, but by the precious blood of Christ, as of a lamb without blemish and without spot, who verily was foreordained before the foundation of the world, but was manifest in these last times for you, who by Him do believe in God, who raised Him from the dead and gave Him glory, that your faith and hope might be in God.

You can readily see how important the blood is, being the price of your redemption. It was important enough to have been planned out before the foundation of the world was laid. It is obviously more precious than the wealth of silver or gold. So there is agreement that the Blood of Jesus, the Lamb of God, is of the utmost importance.

The Blood is not only important, IT'S VITAL!! It is blasphemy, foolish, and unscriptural to plead the Blood. If we are already redeemed by the Blood, it is ludicrous for us to try to re-redeem ourselves by pleading the Blood. What a pitiful concept! If we do plead the Blood of Jesus, we are subconsciously saying that when Christ redeemed us with His Blood, "He didn't do it good enough for me, therefore I have to do it myself. Jesus needs my help to complete and maintain my redemption!"

Hebrews 9: 1—14 and 11: 14 completely destroys the idea of pleading the Blood.

> But Christ becoming a high priest of good things to come, by a greater and more perfect tabernacle, not made with hands, that is to say, not of this building, neither by the blood of goats and calves, <u>but by His Own Blood He entered in once into the holy place, having obtained eternal redemption for us</u>. For if the blood of bulls and of goats, and the ashes of a heifer sprinkling the unclean, sanctified to the purifying of the flesh, how much more shall the Blood of Christ, who through he Eternal Spirit offered Himself without spot to God, purge your conscience from dead works to serve the living God? <u>For by one offering He has perfected forever those who are sanctified</u>.

Jesus did it. He entered into the presence of the Eternal Judge and with His Own Blood obtained the eternal redemption for us! He did it well and forever. If I attempt to re-do it, it is a slap in the Savior's face. The great Court of Justice has declared believers innocent of all charges of wrongdoing that the enemy may accuse them of, and a believer's miserable pleadings of Christ's Blood are not only pitiful, but blasphemous to say the least.

Also if I do my own pleading, it takes my case out of the hands of my Advocate and High Priest. In I John 2: 1 and 2 the Word declares that if we sin we have an Advocate with the Father. Hebrews 7: 25 says that He ever lives to make intercession for us.

There is a great deal of difference between being redeemed by the Blood and pleading the Blood. Redeemed by the Blood is a sound truth that we should never forget, but it is a completed transaction that we come into by God's grace. We can add nothing to it and we can take nothing from it. "It is a done deal!" If we attempt to alter it by adding a phrase here or there, we question and subliminally insult the validity of the transaction in our own cases.

Those who teach pleading the Blood use this phraseology: *In the Name of Jesus, I plead the Blood of Jesus*. We are told several times that when we pray we are to use the name of Jesus (John 14: 13; 16: 23, 24; Mark 16: 17 and 18), but nowhere are we ever told to do any pleading in any form for any reason to anybody!

The promises come through using the name of Jesus. When a prayer is answered—whether a combative, intercessory, supplicating or any other kind of prayer—the answer comes by, and only by, our use of the name of Jesus. You cannot add to the efficacy nor can you add to the authority of the name of Jesus by pleading the Blood of Jesus.

Pleading the Blood of Jesus can only cause problems because of the insult to the Father, the Son and Their work in the believer. One poor missionary lady recounted passing through a village in desperate poverty. She said she looked in pity at the town and pled the Blood of Jesus over it. Another missionary pled the Blood of Jesus over our military in the Middle East. They could have just as easily lit a candle or spun a prayer wheel for all the good it would do. If there is a need for prayer, pray and do it in Jesus' name. The Lord will honor such, but pleading the Blood of Jesus over something is . . . . well, you know what's next!

> Don't bother to plead the Blood or you will insult God's integrity
> and grace.

Today's Trends

Meanwhile, look at some other destructive extra-scriptural teachings that are making the Christian circuit these days.

Free-moral Agency

There seems to be a tendency in some circles that unless one believes and teaches free-moral agency as a doctrine, the rest of whatever one has to say is of little consequence. This is one of the strongest indications that a church, group or individual has turned toward becoming a cult. (See <u>Cocooning,</u> "Appendix 2," *Book 1*)

No doctrine should be held in such regard, especially one that is not mentioned in Scripture. The concept of man's absolute control of his own destiny is so absurd that it is hard to believe so many people have been fooled into believing it.

What do we mean by *free-moral agency*? Because the expression is not mentioned in Scripture, we must make sure we are talking about the same thing.

There are two possible meanings:

1. *Free-moral agency* is the privilege that someone has of being able to choose to either obey or disobey God, yet knowing of the consequences of disobedience: Discipline for any disobedience.

2. *Free-moral agency* is the ability and right that someone has of being able to choose to either obey or disobey God with the consequences of disobedience: Loss of identification as a believer (i.e., becoming lost).

The first definition has merit because God's Justice will see to it. We may not see what we think is justice, but in the end, God's Justice will absolutely prevail! The second definition is the one that is heard altogether too often. Look at what the Scriptures say about man. Remember, these people were all writing under the anointing of the Holy Spirit!

The Psalmist said man is born in sin (Psalm 51: 5; 58: 3). No one can change that fact or condition.

Isaiah said men were all gone astray like sheep (Isaiah 53: 6). No one can change that, either.

Paul said all are sinners and repeated that none are righteous (Romans 3: 9–23). No one can change this condition.

Paul also referred to the un-regenerated as servants or slaves to sin, as well as dead in them (Romans 6: 16–20; Romans 5: 15; Ephesians 2: 1–7). (*Servant* and *slave* are the same words in Greek [*doulos*]). No one can change that.

Do any of these statements make it sound like we have a choice of who or what we are?

Sure, Joshua gave the call, "Choose you this day whom you will serve." But does that mean we as human beings have the ability to become someone or something that we are not. Joshua gave that call to un-regenerated people long before Jesus made anyone free.

> <u>Notice:</u> Joshua's challenge was based on an action: To serve. There was no identification or re-identification of those who either followed Joshua's challenge or those who did not follow Joshua's challenge. No one was to receive a new life, especially an everlasting life or a new identity. They could only do or not do a series of acts. There was no change available to them.

To prove that there was no real change, look how long it took those who had responded to Joshua's challenge to revert to their misconduct before Jehovah! It did not take long!

One should not make a doctrine based on one call by one leader to one group of people who were not believers without a logical link between that group and born-again believers.

A person cannot choose his lineage, and certainly cannot change the nature he or she was born with. Jesus said "Whom the Son sets free is free indeed," but that still does not mean that we have the ability to change our nature or our identities in God's (or Satan's) eyes. Upon maturity, the person cannot change his or her nature with conscious effort independent of spiritual forces. Only the Father-God can make such a change and He won't reverse what the Son has already done!

That is where the mistake occurs. People look at salvation as a possession, something we have and can handle almost in our hands, to either hold and maintain or lay down, ignore or abandon. They treat the topic of salvation like they would a cheap ball-point pen—use it and lay it down and later pick it up again.

People often do not realize that when we accept Christ as Savior, we take on a new identity and become a new creation. We are Sons of God, not mere men. We have been re-created in God's image. We are not merely revamped, over-hauled or cleaned-up same old selves. Salvation is not only part of us like appendages, but it is us in our totality! We are new creations in Christ (II Corinthians 5: 17)!

Sure, we have the choice to either obey our new nature or follow the old habits that we were saved from. In our new creation, we have the ability to say "No!" to the lure and demands of sin on our life-styles. This is what we are free to do. This freedom comes with the re-birth through Jesus Christ; He has set us free. But freedom of choice of actions does not change who we are or where we owe our allegiance in the eternal grand scale.

If you go to the bank and obtain a loan of $10,000, you may choose to not repay, but because you have signed on the line, you are a debtor for the $10,000 plus interest. That is a legal transaction that you approved of and for which you are legally responsible. Regardless of how you may try, you either repay the loan or lose whatever you have placed as security against the loan.

When you accepted Jesus Christ as your Savior, you made a legal transaction. There are no provisions for a reversal of that decision. Regardless of any will on your part after the deed is done, you owe Him yourself! Regardless! You are not your own, for you have been bought with a price (I Corinthians 6: 19, 20; 7: 22, 23)! Because you are a member of the Body of Christ, you cannot legally be cut off (I Corinthians 6: 15; 12: 27)! No man can pluck you out of His hand, and you do not have the right to pluck yourself out (John 10: 27–30). You are legally redeemed (Galatians 3: 13). There isn't anything you can do about it, even if you are stupid enough to want to.

Although many Christians have been taught the truth about free-moral agency, few have ever received the real understanding of our new relationship with our Father through the rebirth without revelation knowledge by the Holy Spirit through the Word of God. In other words this information is no mere doctrine but it is the cornerstone upon which we maintain a living relationship with the Lord.

The Word of God is that revelation knowledge and one has to be a-tuned to the Holy Spirit to receive the revelation. It is not received according to reason. One may be taught the doctrine, and the verses of Scripture, but the real truth of it comes only as the Lord reveals it by His Word as directed by the Holy Spirit. This is why some who have been taught that redemption is complete have gone astray in their conduct before the Lord. They have allowed selfish or worldly ways to enter into their lives.

A real understanding of the substitutionary work of Christ in our redemption would not allow such things to happen. The faith that is made manifest in such an understanding generates a love that produces obedience to His Word (John 14: 23, 24; 15: 10–15).

Human reason says, "Unless you live the life, the life will cease." But the recreated spirit says, "Eternal life cannot cease." The former idea sounds good (not only logical, but religious), being based on human reason; but the latter is based on the Word of God.

Now, allow the new life, the eternal life, to manifest itself by walking in it. Indeed, the work of Christ in your life is the only true freedom of choice that you have. You are redeemed from the absolute slavery to sin in which you used to be in bondage as a slave!

If you do not understand this truth, there are only two things you need to do:

> First, recognize the fact that you and others who do not see the truth of the rebirth and all it means may be ill-informed. Just admit that you need more understanding.

> Second, ask the Holy Spirit to reveal the truth to you. Simply be willing to accept it when you see it in the Scriptures. If you will honestly do these two things, the Holy Spirit will accommodate you.

Regardless of whether you receive the revelation of the fullness of the substitutionary work of Christ in your life or not, the only thing that will lead you to live the way you think Jesus would have you live is LOVE. Jesus said "If a man loves Me, he will keep My words" (John 14: 15–24).

Only Love leads us to live our lives as the Lord desires, regardless of what we may or may not have been taught or what we may or may not believe.

Modesty

Modern concepts of style (or not) have almost obliterated the notion of modesty. Even the daily news on TV has almost become a flesh-show. Flesh has been used to sell almost everything, regardless of any connection with what someone may look like or not.

I Timothy 2: 9 In like manner also, that women should adorn themselves in modest apparel, with shamefacedness and sober-mindedness, not with braided hair or gold or pearls or costly array,

The terms that accompany "modest apparel" mean "properly" and "discreetly." The people who dress like early twentieth century (or earlier) people are often making a spectacle of themselves, trying to obey what they perceive as a law, even though they may perceive it as from the New Testament. They are doing what Paul wanted to avoid—becoming a spectacle. One may be modest without being embarrassed in public, wearing out-of-style clothing that serve most of the time to draw attention to the wearer.

What does *modest* mean? It does not mean to get out a ruler and attempt to establish a standard: Not a standard for length of hair, sleeves or hemline. Such standards constantly change. If a person is an honest believer before the LORD, he or she will not want to become a one-person exhibition. In no way, neither positively nor negatively, does he or she want to become a spectacle.

Modesty is a relative word. Long (as hair, sleeves or hemlines) is also relative. On some of the islands of the South Pacific and some areas of Africa the native women wear nothing above the waist. Complete nudity is acceptable in some tribes of South America, New Guinea and the Philippines. To these various peoples, they themselves are modest! No doubt such modesty would serve as a culture shock for many believers and it would be a true task for them to make the transition between the extremes of our modesty and theirs! So modesty is where you find it—inside the believer, not in their dress—or lack thereof!

One more thing: Did you notice that the vast majority (something close to all!) of these clothing and appearance standards promoted by churches and cults are addressed toward women and girls? Once in a while something will address the men, but most of the "rules of dress" apply only to the womenfolk.

If the rules exist in order to eliminate lust, as some allege, the rule is a spit into the wind. Lust has been around for centuries and it never made any difference how the victim was dressed or appeared. The lust, as modesty, comes from the heart, not outward appearances.

Those who dress a certain style in their religious culture are marking just that, their religious culture. If they like it and are comfortable with it, and if they are doing it as to the LORD without being dogmatic, self-righteous, or stretching Scriptures to do it, then by all means do it to it.

However, no one should throw rocks of condemnation over this topic from either direction.

If the attire is an attempt to appease the LORD as if they were in a servant-master relationship, there is a need to read and study Galatians.

Religious Clichés

Sometimes someone will say something that sounds so wonderful, but it is really something false from the very first. For instance, *"I'm just a sinner saved by grace."* (Or *"We are all sinners saved by grace."*) Absolutely not! One is either a saint by grace or he is still a sinner, having never known the Savior. No one can be both a sinner and saved at the same time (II Corinthians 5: 17). This concept was discussed and hopefully destroyed in Two Natures, under "Guidepost 7" in Chapter 1, *Book 1.*

> An Aside: Regarding the plight of most people, believers or not, false humility is a robbing spirit that engenders defeat, lack, depression, panic and every other foul attitude that the enemy can get to embrace it!
>
> It is absolutely beneath words what many believing Christians do to themselves by false humility. People who have accepted Christ as Savior are <u>new creations in Christ</u> (II Corinthians 5: 17); they are <u>members of His very Body</u> (I Corinthians 6: 17; 10: 17 and 12: 27); they are <u>one spirit with the Lord</u> (John 14: 20) and there are literally dozens of wonderful things that can be said of a believer regarding who he or she is in the Lord. (See Appendix 4).
>
> For that person to insult himself, herself and the Lord's Substitutionary Work in that person's re-creation by saying something that relates them to being yet unsaved, unworthy, insignificant, or some other vile insult to who and what the Father-God created in him or her as a believer is below words!
>
> False humility is a diabolical force   a demon or stronghold—that sets out to rob, kill and destroy by means of one's own mouth! Many clichés have False Humility as a source and none should ever be repeated—not even in jest! One of the main sources for this vileness is the acceptance of the myth of the believer's dual-nature. (See <u>Two Natures</u>, Guidepost 7, Chapter 1, *Book 1.*)

Another cliché that is rank, usually smacking with self-righteousness: *"My Bible tells me . . . !"*

The best way to handle this is to ignore the statement. However, if the statement is to be challenged, here is how to do it. Ask the person who makes the statement where the Bible makes that exact statement, whatever it may be.

Most likely the person will not know where any such statement is. Often it will be something misquoted, if it is scriptural at all, and, if found, will not apply to believers. Test the passage with the Bible-study guidelines.

Do not allow someone to sweep you away with idioms and clichés that the Scriptures do not bear out.

Misguided by Song

Another realm where error thrives is in music—even in, and often especially in, church-music! When you hear (whether you sing along or not) lyrics that lift up a relationship with the Lord based on future events—such as death, heaven, "after a while," or some other event that is in everyone's future, consider them nonsense!

When you hear lyrics that mention the past conditions that may be lodged in someone's memories—such as mothers calling to you, seeing mothers again, long-since buried revival meetings, verbal scenes of long-ago splendor full of imageries that stir the emotions, recognize that these emotional-based lyrics are empty of any real and genuine spiritual qualities whatsoever! The tears (or other indicators of emotions) are of no value—not to you or anyone else!

More importantly, do not assume that a song or hymn that mentions something "biblical" is actually biblical at all! The alleged "Cabins in the Corner of Glory-land," or the cabins that someone is building (in Heaven), or, worse yet, the mountain someone is working on—all of these and things like them are poetic imageries that someone has created to bring out emotionalism.

What we need to do, the only thing we need to do, is to accept the things that the Lord has already done! The vain cries for more of God's blessings are worthless because people have not yet taken advantage of all the Father-God has already provided!

Some church music plays on ignorance by mentioning other non-scriptural events or conditions. One very popular hymn mentions a cross that everyone carries through life that they will eventually get to lay down at the feet of Jesus. Another one mentions that Jesus fell under the weight of His cross. Yet another one (a chorus) mentions that Jesus, the Light of the World, is located somewhere in some dark shadows, abandoned and alone. These are emotional concepts that throttle the identity of the Lord and shunt His work of grace in people's lives.

These are all very emotional songs and choruses, having great tunes and often loved by people who really love the Lord, but the singers and listeners have never evaluated the lyrics to see the truth or non-truth of them. These "doctrines" lodge in their minds and before long, these errors are seen as fact. These bits of error add up to a mistaken relationship, one that often fails to function as the Father would like it to!

Then there are those songs that slap the Father, the Son and the Holy Spirit across their collective faces by the lyrics that deny the acts of redemption and the results of those acts. These lyrics habitually beg "God" (not the Father) for something that He has already provided through the Substitutionary Acts of Christ, i.e., Redemption and its fruitage.

When in song people seek the Lord for a closer walk with Him, holding His hand (or vice versa), or better knowledge of Him or some other link in fellowship, or for Him to make them into a better person, these folks are implying that He has not yet done enough for them. They imply that He has failed in His mission to redeem them, to save them, to keep them, to supply for them or otherwise completely perform for them every human whim they may desire! Some of these lyric make Calvary a mere roll of dice!

These so-called prayer songs or praise songs are more emotionalism from people who have not looked into the Word to see who they are, what they are and what their real potentials are in the Lord! Their whole existence after their regeneration (if even that) is wound up in emotionalism. The writers of such songs may be musicians first, and believers (maybe) second. But if these composers really knew the Lord or His Word, they would vest their time in something else—or at least in more fundamentally and scripturally sound music.

So do not listen to or sing music and the lyrics of music that are not sound scripturally. These subtle teachings will subvert a real and viable relationship with the Father because of the embedded error (and often blasphemies) in those lyrics.

Christian music should celebrate the things that the Father has already done, worshipping, praising and honoring Him. He has already done all for us He will ever do. It is up to us to find in His Word what those things are and how to manifest them. Sure, He will give us the miracles we need in our futures, but it is because He has already provided them for us through the faith He gave us in order to redeem us. Outside His Word, He will not go the extra mile for us. He did it already when He saved us! All we need to do is bring our relationship with Him and His miracles to manifestation through the Word!

The top of the line music of the Lord is His Word put to music—rhythm, tune, melody! There are many of them and they are very edifying, too.

Public Ministries

What can one say of the televangelists, radio broadcasters and writers, both of books and articles? We'll just address them collectively as *media ministers* (MM). We must recognize that all of them are people just like us. They are from the same molds as the preacher on the platform and the teacher behind the lectern in the local churches. Most of whatever can be said of any ordinary messenger in any ordinary church can be said of the MM—and vice-versa. However, there are some differences.

The differences between the ordinary messenger and the MM are mostly based on attitude and scope. The attitude that puts these MM and their ministries on pedestals is not appropriate. MM are often held there higher and longer and by more people than the minister of the local church. Most ministers, whether media based or local, have an inflated opinion regarding the importance of their ministry to begin with. The ministry is most important to those doing the ministry—whether it is a real ministry as done for and to the Lord or a business-based ministry designed to make someone a living—honest or otherwise.

Regarding the importance of the MM, real or imagined, the MM claim that they do not exist to replace local churches and other ministries. They are there to enhance and aid the locals.

However, in spite of the claim, the MM still vie for the "tithes and offerings" (or portions of them) that would normally be donated primarily to the local churches. (We discussed the matter of tithes in Chapter 1, *Book 1.*)

Meanwhile, the audience of the electronic and published ministers should realize that these are mere men and women and they are just as likely to err as anyone else is. Not only that, but if someone in the audience needs to speak with one of the MM, forget it. To speak with one of these almost untouchable voices, be prepared to spend much time, effort and money to do it. Pastors of large congregations are often so busy that they are unapproachable to many of the congregants. MM are worse. Of course MM often get over-inflated with their own self-importance.

There is a lot of money involved with them, and the way some of these ministers use the money is quite questionable, to say the least. If you haven't been completely isolated, you've heard of the monumental scandals that have rocked several electronic ministries in recent years. Some ministries have even terminated because the leader was jailed and some others should have been. Meanwhile others got caught with embarrassing items in embarrassing places, and many others have tampered with projects and programs that have not turned out well in the long term.

The reasons are vague regarding the psychology of the rise and fall of the MM. It seems that they surround themselves with "Yes" people who are influenced by either the power of the name of the MM or the MM's money. It may be the MM's money, or ability to dispense money, that leads to their branching out into areas of ministry of which they know absolutely nothing.

Look at the way many of these ministers have arisen to fame and fortune. Typically the minister has one message (or series of messages), maybe two, but seldom any more than that. They get on the air or are published and in comes the money, the accolades, the "Yes" people, the new projects, programs and new messages (many of them empty) and of course the "power!" Then of all things, often these MM are viewed as authorities on subjects relating to things they never mentioned before!

After the substance of the MM and their messages are boiled down, the emptiness of their ministry often becomes evident. Then down goes the ministry. The MM may not go down in TV or radio ratings or readership, but the real ministry and its messages do! (There may never have been God-life there in the first place. Some of the MM were never born of God and except for help from someone who dug deeply into money-filled pockets to get the ministry going, the ministers never would have been heard of.)

Meanwhile, the typical MM has left his one or two messages that the Lord has blessed him or her with and he or she starts going beyond the area of God's calling, if there ever was one. An evangelist starts a school or college, or he starts teaching topics that he or she knows little or nothing about. When MM try to spread out their ministry, they often spread themselves into foolishness as far as that one ministry is concerned. If one's ministry is evangelism, that person should evangelize and do nothing more. Evangelists should leave the teaching to teachers. Teachers should teach and leave the missionary work and evangelism to others.

The scope of these ministries is a factor that makes it hard to justify their existence when they make errors. When the MM branch out into areas other than what he or she has been blessed to do, they leave themselves open to the errors of a novice. And they make those errors, too. They make the same errors that the local ministers do, get the same misinformation, break the same Bible-study principles, and muddle things up the same ways.

This is where a small error can become gigantic. While the local minister may make an error, he reaches one congregation in one town. In a single service, a correction could be announced and the error corrected. But if an MM makes the same error, that error reaches farther and faster than he or she can easily recall and mend.

One modernist preacher had preached on the air for years and had had books published, but when he was born-again, he had a problem. He had to start refuting the things he had taught on the air and in those books published when he was a modernist.

With the elevated attitude that many folks hold of these MM, any error can be devastating. Like the modernist cited above, many make some of the most ignorant and arrogant claims and boasts that can be imagined. Audiences should recognize that MM are altogether too human sometimes and apt to teach something less than a wholesome doctrine.

There are MM who have wonderful messages regarding healing of the body and prosperity of the believer. But they often have a dim view of God's ability to heal a mind or spirit. They will apply the Word to one's body for healing regardless of what circumstances look like, and they will apply the Word to one's finances to bring believers to prosperity, but turn right around and void out the Word that refers to the believer's mind, soul or eternal spirit and their welfare.

Second generation ministers (electronic, published and local) are usually occupations rather than callings from the Lord and the messages and ministries reflect it.

Why do these MM stretch themselves out to other areas, or delve into things they know nothing about? Why will they compromise their integrity before the Father to do these things? Is it desire for more power? More money? More fame? More relevance? Will they change their message in order to stretch their outreach? Is it pressure from their contributors? Is it fear of the loss of followers? Is it that they do not see the revelation of the substitutionary work of Christ? Is it that they never had a real calling to begin with? Is it something just to allow the ministers(?) an income?

All of these factors influence a man or woman's thoughts, some more than others and not necessarily in any particular order. But then to be a real minister, one should teach what one knows to be in the Word, regardless of what others may or may not think or do in response to that teaching. When a minister reaches millions in a single broadcast or publication, the failure to teach, preach and practice the truth of the Scriptures becomes a real downer.

There are some very "successful (commercially)" MM whose message is flat and not worth a second glance from anyone, saint or sinner. There is nothing to their message but noise, but because they have reached donors aplenty, their income indicates that they are successful.

At any rate, keep an even keel regarding the MM and their ministries because, after all, they are people too and just as likely to make the same errors as anyone else.

Bible Editors, Commentators and Researchers

Many Bible printers, editors, commentators, and publishers design and sell their wares to people of certain leanings. There is no doubt that many comments and references are biased toward a particular leaning, whichever leaning it may be. In this section we will look at how two well-respected Bible teachers handle a common scriptural topic and each makes mistakes in how they come to their conclusions.

The first one, a well-known Bible-commentator stoops to outright fabrication to prove a point that the Scriptures in their totality refute. People of other leanings practice some of the things that this commentator claims do not exist any more.

Regarding the prophecy in Isaiah 53: 4 where Isaiah wrote the following:

Surely He [Jesus] has borne our griefs and carried our sorrows; yet we did esteem Him stricken, smitten of God, and afflicted.

Other translations note that the word <u>griefs</u> should be <u>infirmities</u> and the word <u>sorrows</u> should be <u>sickness</u>. The commentator in our discussion makes his first error in judgment: He does not mention these alternate definitions as found in some other translations. He makes no mention that other words could have been used.

Other translations read that passage something like this:

Surely He has borne our infirmities and carried our sicknesses; yet we did esteem Him stricken, smitten of God, and afflicted.

Matthew refers to this passage in Isaiah when he tells of Jesus healing people and casting demons out of them (Matthew 8: 17).

That it might be fulfilled what was spoken by Isaiah, the prophet, saying, He Himself took our infirmities and bore our sicknesses.

Matthew saw the Scripture in Isaiah as it really is—the text using <u>infirmities</u> and <u>sicknesses</u>. But this particular commentator who shall be nameless wrote this in reference to Isaiah 53: 4:

> "Because Matthew quotes this passage and applies it to physical disease (cp. Mt. 8: 17 with context) it has been conjectured by some that disease as well as sin was included in the atoning death of Christ. But Matthew asserts that the Lord fulfilled the first part of Isaiah 53: 4 during His healing ministry of His service on earth. Matthew 8: 17 makes no reference to Christ's atoning death for sin.

> "The Lord took away the diseases of men by healing them. He died for our sins, not for our diseases. For physical disease in itself is not sin; it is merely one of the results of sin. Thus Isa. 53: 5–6 prophesies that Christ would bear our sins on the cross(cp. I Peter 2: 24–25). His death was substitutionary and atoning."

To read Matthew 8: 17 closely enough to say Matthew "asserts that Jesus fulfilled that portion of Scripture," one thing is overlooked: The timing. If He had fulfilled the passage completely, as our commentator implied, He would not have continued to heal and deliver. Christ would have fulfilled the passage, quit doing those things, and got on with other things. But instead He not only continued to heal and deliver in His earthly ministry, but commissioned others to do it, too. The reason Matthew said that Jesus was fulfilling that Scripture was to convince the gainsaying

Children of Israel that Jesus was indeed the Messiah. He did not mean that Christ's healing ministry was all over with at that point in time.

And His commission continues today because of His promise in Mark 16 and John 14. Mark 16: 17–20 [Jesus is speaking]

"These signs shall follow those who believe, In My Name they shall cast out demons, they shall speak with new tongues, they shall take up serpents, and if they drink any deadly thing, it shall not hurt them; they shall lay hands on the sick, and they shall recover."

So then, after the Lord had spoken to them, He was received up into heaven, and sat at the right hand of God. And they went forth, and preached everywhere, the Lord working with *them*, and confirming the Word with signs following. Amen.

If one is a believer, then these signs should follow (or accompany him or her): In His Name they shall

Speak in New Tongues,

Cast out demons,

Take up serpents,

Be unharmed if drinking something deadly, and

Lay hands on and heal the sick.

The errant Bible-commentator on the verse in Matthew also forgot what Jesus said in John 14: 12:

Verily, verily, I say to you, he who believes on Me, the works that I do shall he do also; and greater *works* than these shall he do; because I go to the Father.

Jesus promised that His followers would also do these and greater works than these because He was going to the Father to authorize them to do it, and the Holy Spirit was coming to empower them to do it.

This Bible-commentator strained so hard to make his teaching and general practice scriptural that he distorted the truth in what he alleged Matthew meant.

He not only strained to make him and his followers conform to Scripture by distorting what Matthew said, but he overlooked one more little problem: No one in the New Testament used the word atonement but once. It is in the KJV in Romans 5: 11. Every other translation uses the word reconciliation. There is a vast difference between being "*atoned for*" and being "*reconciled with.*"

Atone means *to cover* while *reconciliation* means to *restore to fellowship*. Indeed, in the case of our reconciliation, it is a recreation in His image, a joining together into one spirit, gaining membership into His very Body!

Atoning death? No! We New Testament believers are not merely atoned for; we are not merely covered. Instead, <u>we are gloriously recreated in Christ</u>. Jesus' reconciling death makes us sons of God, heirs and joint heirs with Christ and many other things above and beyond mere servants!

The second teacher in our discussion, was asked if the stripes Jesus suffered, as mentioned in Isaiah 53: 5, were provision for physical healing? The portion says this: "and with His stripes we are healed." The teacher related what it says in Isaiah 53: 5 to what it says in I Peter 2: 24:

> Who his own self bore our sins in His own Body on the tree, that we, being dead to sins, should live to righteousness; <u>by whose stripes we were healed</u>.

The teacher did it right when he put the I Peter phrase in context with Christ having taken our sins in His Body as He was being crucified, thus saving us spiritually. However, he incorrectly concluded that the stripes were for our spiritual healing only.

If Christ saved us by dying in our place, making us new creations (and He did), how and why will that new creation be sick, infirm or any other negative condition? Did not the Lord's salvation for us do a complete job therefore necessitating the stripes to go with His redemptive death?

This second teacher did put the I Peter quote in its context, rightly so. But he erred by not putting the related verse in Isaiah in its context, too. Isaiah 53: 4 and 5:

> Surely He has borne our <u>infirmities</u> and carried our <u>sicknesses</u>; yet we did esteem Him stricken, smitten of God, and afflicted. But He was wounded for our transgressions, He was bruised for our iniquities; the chastisement of (for) our peace was upon Him, and with His stripes we are healed.

When the context of Isaiah 53: 5 was omitted by the second teacher, the connection with <u>infirmities</u> and <u>sickness</u> was lost. He did not even consider the reality that the spiritual healing could and would manifest itself in the physical-material world!

Everything from creation forward has a spiritual source. The Father (Spirit) spoke and material, tangible, physical things appeared; He spoke and things changed. It's been that way from day one! Psalm 107: 20 says He (the LORD) sent His Word and healed them.

In context, this is only one phase of four where the LORD delivered man from the errors of his own misguided ways. How did He do anything? He (the LORD) is a spirit and therefore everything He does is spiritual. Everything that He does, He does spiritually but when we see it, it is because He has made it manifest in our world—in our natural. It is essential for us to realize that what He does naturally for us, He has first done spiritually.

However, that is not the end of His spiritual influence. Just as in creation, His Word still has creative power. If His Word brought forth the whole of creation, His Word can certainly heal physically as well as spiritually.

Christ's spiritual death made it possible for us to have spiritual life; His suffering the stripes before his death makes it possible for us to have physical healing!

Both teachers came to the same conclusion: Christ's substitutionary work did not provide for physical healing. One made one set of mistakes and the other made another set of mistakes.

Neither teacher considered the fact that other people of other denominations were experiencing the very things that these men said was not available to modern believers. The second teacher has made remarks condemning "faith healers" for being in error because the Lord forbade some of His healed subject from telling others about their healing (Matthew 8: 4; Luke 5: 14, as examples), and therefore they were not properly putting forth the message of salvation. He also claimed that these "faith healers," once aged, got sick and died.

Human frailty exists for all men. Just because a person gets old and dies, it does not mean what he practiced as led by the Lord was not valid and real. Jesus' disciples who spread the Gospel with signs following also all got old and died. But these conditions do not invalidate what the Lord does, what He provided or what His Word says to us today.

The connection between what Matthew said of the Isaiah 53 passage far outweighs what either teacher proposed as their conclusion. Matthew was there, witnessing what Jesus did and hearing why He did those things. If these teachers had been correct in their conclusions, especially the second one who was so judgmental with "faith healers," then Matthew was wrong in his conclusion regarding Christ healing physical and moral sickness and infirmities! That in turn meant that the Holy Spirit, who was guiding Matthew in recording these things, also messed up!

So you can make a choice: Do you believe these two teachers or do you believe Matthew?

Any topic studied must include <u>all angles</u> and perspectives of the Word as well as <u>all angles</u> of what is going on around us. If the Lord is moving somewhere and He is not moving in your surroundings, find out why! Don't brand something as either good or bad without at least examining it! These men closed their minds to an angle of the Lord's Word and an angle of the Lord's work. It would be nice to think they were both honest in their conclusion, but it is hard to believe so. They appeared to have cocooned themselves to some extent.

As you research biblical topics, be thorough with your information, be honest with your conclusion, and be willing to accept your own change!

Bias

Previous teaching, whether well known teaching or not, usually contains bias and causes bias. Most Christians do not even know that they have bias—and many will never admit it, even if they do find they have it. Let's look at brother So-n-so.

Brother S. received the Lord several years ago and has been faithful to attend his church meetings ever since. He knows what he believes, but he has never examined another church's teachings in a positive light. He heard what they believe, how it is different (what is wrong with it!), but he knows what he has is real and does not think it is important to seek anything different. His pastor has taught him well and completely!

More subtly, *what he has is as good as anyone else's and he can prove it!* His preacher is a real man of God and he knows the Lord and His Truth. He loves his preacher and the preacher loves him and the preacher will never deceive him! Their church, their experience, and their relationship with God are the absolute best, and no one can show him differently!

This attitude is the result of cocooning. The cocoon syndrome often results in putting confidence in man, church, education or some other arm of flesh (See Cocooning, Appendix 2). Those fibers of incomplete information or misinformation, placed so lovingly, so innocently, around the new convert, entangle the convert there and growth either ceases altogether or deformation and distortion occur—resulting in religion!

Growth ceases, not necessarily because of the preacher or the church, but because of the bias that the enemy has sown in their hearts—to make them satisfied with one truth or part of one truth, then to close the mind to any other truths of God's Word.

The loss of blessings brought by unknown truths may literally cut one's life short. People's well-being is often disrupted by their ignorance of the Word and what it really means. No one really likes to be shown that there are better things than what they already have, especially when it comes to one's politics, one's religion or one's Christianity.

Too often, when one is shown that their relationship with their Heavenly Father could be improved upon, a violent reaction occurs. It may be anger, bitterness, resentment, hate and a whole range of other negative reactions that can take place. It takes either a revelation from the Father along with His intervention or a lot of subtleness and friendly persuasion to keep the revelation on an even keel.

Sometimes, however, there is joy and relief, followed by reception of the new truths. These are the people who grab the new truths and hold them firmly!

On another plane, one regarding a public manifestation, it is embarrassing for a church to have a minister or Sunday-school teacher to be born-again after several years of ministry or teaching. It happens, though, and other blessings remain for victims of cocooning if they will receive them.

Fear of Demons

Here is another weak and groundless teaching—one that the name of Jesus dispels at a whisper! Some people teach that Satan and demons have powers beyond what we believers can deal with. One such notion teaches that a believer should always pray with his or her eyes closed lest a demon come into that person while praying.

Another line teaches that a believer should not attempt to cast a demon out of a host for fear that the demon will come onto the one casting it out or someone else nearby.

Both of these teachings are groundless and are lies from the enemy! Demons should never be ignored. If a demon manifests itself, or if someone discerns the presence or intentions of a demon, immediately bind them up and cast them out in the name of Jesus.

While one of these loose doctrines promotes the idea of demonic superiority to our wills even while we pray, the other plants fear so that we will not resist the devils and watch them flee. Only the enemy stands to profit from such lies. Scripture teaches that we are masters over our satanic enemies, and we are to resist Satan and his forces using the name of Jesus.

There is the case of the vagabond Jewish exorcists who tried to cast out a demon and the demon and its host turned on those men and overcame them (Acts 19: 13–16). Those men were not believers. Neither the host nor the would-be deliverers were believers. They could not perform the acts of the believers because they knew not, nor did they have, the Savior within. If you are a believer, you do!

James said, "Submit yourselves to God, resist the devil and he will flee from you" (James 4: 7).

Paul wrote in Ephesians 1: 18–23:

The eyes of your understanding being enlightened; that you may know the hope of His calling, and what are the riches of the glory of His inheritance in the saints, and what is the exceeding greatness of His Power toward us who believe, according to the working of His Mighty

Power that He wrought in Christ when He raised Him from the dead, and set Him at His own right hand in the heavenlies, far above all principalities and power, and might, and dominion, and every name that is named, not only in this age, but also in that which is to come; and has put all things under His feet, and gave Him to be the head over all things to **the church, which is His Body,** the fullness of Him who fills all in all.

Paul points out the believer's position in the Body of Christ as above all principalities, power, might, dominion and name. How will a demon (or even Satan himself) challenge such authority?

Jesus said in Mark 16: 17:

And these signs shall follow those who believe; "In My name they shall cast out demons;"

If there were a danger in following Jesus' words, surely He would have warned us! But there is no warning!

And in John 15: 7 and 8 He said:

If you abide in Me, and My Words abide in you, you shall ask what you will, and it shall be done to you. In this is My Father glorified, that you bear much fruit; so shall you be My disciples.

How will you bear fruit if you are fearful of doing what Jesus said? How will the Father receive His glory from such an event if one of His redeemed ones ends up possessed by a demon?

In light of these Scriptures (and many others), when you use the name of Jesus to cast out demons, there is no doubt about what the demons are to do! They must leave their host and they sure won't go into the person who cast them out! They can't, unless they are invited. They cannot come into a believer unless the believer unwittingly allows them to enter by his own will.

Demons must obey the Name of Jesus.

Demons cannot invade the Body of Christ.

If you are believer, you may use the name of Jesus and be the masters of demons, and as a member of the Body of Christ, they must do what you say and cannot come into you unless you invite them.

More Groundless Beliefs and Practices
Poverty

Some folks who are so blinded to the truth of the Father's good will toward believers believe that everything that happens and everything encountered in life are God's will, even the bad things.

The argument rages regarding healing being in the atonement or not. It also fits then, wondering if prosperity is in the atonement of not. Who cares? Atonement is an Old Testament word that does not pertain to believers at all. So let some believe that healing and prosperity are in the atonement and some disbelieve it. It doesn't matter.

We do not get our sins atoned for in the New Covenant. We are redeemed, and by Christ having done that for us, our sins have already been paid for. That is what redemption does. No atonement is needed because Christ Himself is the propitiation for our sins!

Some people will say that God wants us to be poor. Others will say that He wants us to be sick because that's the way things happen on earth.

Now, let's look at these groundless remarks. "We should be poor" is probably based on one of the Beatitudes (Blessed are the poor . . . . [Matthew 5: 3—12]). Jesus said this to the un-regenerated Jews of His day. Read the rest of it:

Blessed are the poor in spirit, for theirs is the Kingdom of Heaven.

Blessed are they who mourn, for they shall be comforted . . .

To whom was He referring? He was speaking of and to those present, those whose spirits were lost, dead, and separated from their God. As the discourse continued, it becomes more evident that He was talking to them as the lost sheep of the House of Israel and because they were hearing Him, their lot and roles were about to change, continually improving.

It is not possible that Jesus was addressing the role of the believers when He said "Blessed are the poor" because the born-again person is never poor in spirit. He's been born-again and can't possibly be poor in spirit! His spirit is part of the Body of Christ! The believer's body is the temple of the Holy Spirit! And to think that believers are to be poor is an excuse to not reflect God's prosperity that He wants us to live in! This is where the Church at Smyrna erred (Revelation 2). They thought they were poor when they weren't.

If it were true that Jesus meant that believers are to be poor, why will a believer ever hold down a job? There's no better way to be poor than to be unemployed! The last person I heard say that God wanted Christians to be poor was a man who was working 14 to 18 hours a day to be out of God's will! If that is what he actually believed, he was sure a rebellious Christian working all those hours so he wouldn't be poor!

Illness

And the same rationale holds true to those who say God wants them sick for some reason or another. How will being sick ever bring glory to the Father? Does God use sickness to teach us something? Perhaps compassion? Or the understanding of others? Hardly! That's why He gave us His Word and the Holy Spirit. Some people will say that the Lord wants them sick, then they'll rebel and go to a doctor to get well. Such rationale is ignorant, not to mention blasphemous!

The Scriptures plainly teach that the will of the Father is for us to be in both health and prosperity. John wrote in III John, Verse 2:

Beloved, I wish above all things that you may prosper and be in health, even as your soul prospers.

So it doesn't matter if healing and prosperity are in the atonement or not. It's plain to see both are in our redemption because the Father loves His children.

Here are a few Scriptures that promise what the Father has provided for you as a believer. A little study on your part should convince you that the idea of the Father's ill-will toward us is ludicrous.

You may have enough for all your needs and to share with others by Christ's substitution (II Corinthians 9: 8, 10)

The LORD supplies *all your needs* (Philippians 4: 19).

The LORD has good thoughts for you (Psalm 139: 1-18).

Whatever you ask in Jesus' name, He will do it (John 14: 13, 14).

Whatever you ask the Father in Jesus' name, the Father will give you (John 16: 23, 24).

By Jesus' stripes you are (were) healed (I Pet. 2: 24; Isaiah 53: 5).

Jesus came to heal the broken hearted (Luke 4: 18).

The LORD withholds nothing good from you (Psalm 84: 11; Romans 8: 32; I John 3: 22, 23; James 1: 17–25).

God wants us to be ill or poor? RIDICULOUS!!!

God's Punishment

This is another concept of the Father that is so far removed from Scripture that it is hard to deal with. There are some folks who believe that the hard times that they have fallen into are punishment for sins that they have done. Their own conscience is not clear, and they believe that the Father is angry with them.

But in reality, it is the enemy who is accusing them, and they've believed his lies and accusations. Even if they have done something bad or evil, there isn't anything that a believer can do that the Father will not forgive (I John 1: 9).

In the Old Testament there are instances of God punishing people. On the other hand, there are instances of people doing things that God did not approve of that there is no evidence that God ever punished the perpetrator for. The prophet who lied to another prophet and got him killed was one example (I Kings 13). The adventures of the selfish and disobedient Samson serve as another example (Judges 13–16).

On the other hand, when someone is warned to not do something and the person does it anyway, what would any God or Father do? It is His responsibility to teach the offender that He is still the One who is in control! Look for example at David, the man after God's own heart (I Samuel 13: 14). He disobeyed the Lord when he took a census of the people of Israel. Although David was warned through Joab to not bother with it, David insisted that Joab count the people. The LORD spoke by the prophet Gad that David had a choice of three punishments to endure for his egotistical effort (II Samuel 24). The difference between each episode is dependant completely on the LORD as Judge who knows all the various factors by which to evaluate the individual circumstance or situation.

> <u>An Aside</u>: The reason David held a census was the same reason people post church and Sunday-school attendance and church-membership numbers for the public to see: Ego—self-promotion—Pride! That is why the LORD looked so dimly on David's deed (besides the fact that the LORD was not happy with the people of Israel, as indicated in the first verse of that chapter).

In the New Testament things are a little different! First, it is true that open sin or rebellion can sever the fellowship with the Father, hence, cut off the blessings that would normally flow.

But look at the situation. It is not God Who did the cutting. It is the rebellion of the one who holds on to the rebellious attitude, action or lifestyle. As that person repents, thus discontinuing the rebellion, its action, reaction and attitude, the fellowship returns and so do the blessings. (Read Psalm 107.)

It may be true that the rebellious one has dug a financial, psychological, or physiological hole for himself or herself, and it may take time, effort and means to get out of that hole. But it wasn't the Lord who dug it and it may be that the Lord will allow the natural course of events to get that wayward believer out of his or her hole. If the Lord should suddenly and miraculously deliver the returning prodigal every time he or she returns, that would amount to enabling. No one, not the Lord of one's life, wife, husband, father, mother, sibling or anyone else should enable anyone. Enabling is detrimental to anyone who is enabled.

The Lord certainly won't do it. Digging one's self out of one's own hole is good therapy, as well as a means of teaching. Yet God's hands-off approach should not be considered punishment. Discipline? Yes. Punishment? No. Once the lesson of living is comprehended, the fellowship can be healed with no restrictions, with no remembrances.

For instance, look at the prodigal in Luke 15. He was the one who wanted to squander his inheritance, not his father. It was the son who blew the wealth he'd been given, not his father. Then it was the son who lived with and like the pigs, not his father. His father did nothing wrong, and he did nothing to enable or correct his errant son. But when the son returned to his father on his own volition, there was great rejoicing (Luke 15: 11–24)!

While punishment deals out justice, discipline changes the heart. The Father knows how to discipline His Children to bring them back into fellowship, and He will. As soon as repentance comes, then there will again be a wholesome relationship. Punishment is not on the Father's agenda for the believer.

Jesus was already judged for our sin—all of our sins, past, present and future. That's why He went to the cross—as a propitiation for our sins. If Jesus already paid the penalty for our sin, it is unjust of God to make us suffer punishment for the sins again.

> An Aside: Jesus redemption of man is timeless—being all inclusive of past, present and future. He died for all of our sins. Sins of those before Christ were covered (atoned for) by the animal sacrifices as set forth in Moses' Law until Christ would come and be a propitiation for them. The sins of those who rejected Christ and crucified Him were included as He forgave them at his crucifixion, again as the propitiation for them. And finally, all the sins that His redeemed ones would commit were in the future when He became the propitiation for them. So Christ's offering for sin was timeless.

Therefore sin is not what keeps people from having eternal life. What keeps people from having eternal life is not having Jesus as Lord and Savior. Sin is not the problem. The problem is not accepting Christ as personal Savior!

Returning to the topic of God's punishment, there is no better response to the concept of God's punishment then Romans, Chapter 8:

1 There is therefore now no condemnation to them that are in Christ Jesus.

33 Who shall lay anything to the charge of God's elect? It is God who justifies.

34 Who is he who condemns? It is Christ Jesus who died, yea rather, who was raised from the dead, who is at the right hand of God, who also makes intercession for us.

This information is not the only answer to such tripe as God's punishment, but look at what the Word is saying: There is no condemnation to those who are in Christ!

Who will charge those who are in Christ? Satan!

What is the Father's response to such charges? Christ died to be a propitiation for sins—all sins and He was raised from the dead to seal that propitiation and He now sits interceding for the redeemed ones.

Where in this plan is there any room for punishment? If you believe that your life is reflecting God's punishment for something you do or did, quit whatever that something is and renew the fellowship that you want to return, only make it better.

If you think God is punishing you for past sins, prayerfully and carefully study Romans, Chapters 2–8. You've only seen a portion of it in this book. The passage is too long to deal with here. There in those chapters you will see that Jesus was your substitute and propitiation for sin and that He saved you from anything or anyone who can legally or psychologically condemn you.

If you believe God is punishing you, know that it is the enemy using your own conscience to condemn you. Know that the Lord has forgiven you as soon as you repent of the action(s) or attitude(s). All you need to do is bind the enemy and his lies out of your face and forgive yourself—the Lord has already forgiven you upon your apology. Read and study those chapters in Romans and allow them to prove this to you.

Remember:

I John 1: 9: If we confess our sins, He is faithful and just to forgive our sins and to cleanse us of all unrighteousness.

Mary, Mary, Mary, etc.

When presented with the observation that Catholics pray to Mary and other so-called saints, the denial comes forth they are not praying to them. They are merely that seeking the assistance of these other persons to pray for and with the person who is praying. Their rationale is this:

Because Mary (or Joseph or Peter or Whoever) was close to Jesus, they could persuade Jesus to answer their prayer sooner, better, or at all.

That is what the world calls "Political pull." First of all, the Scripture plainly says there is only one Mediator between God and man, and that is Jesus Christ (I Tim. 2: 5). If we go against the message of the Word, we go against the LORD Himself. If we were to use other mediators, the Word would have said we could. But it says plainly that there is only One.

The reverence for the dearly departed Mary and others in her category is idolatry. To bow before an image of someone—anyone—is not following the Word of God in obedience.

You shall have no other Gods before Me (Exodus 20).

Nor shall you bow down before them (Exodus 23: 24).

Although these Scriptures are Old Testament, they reflect the Father-God's attitude toward idolatry and His views never change. If idolatry didn't please Him then, it certainly won't please Him now! (By the way, idolatry is one of the 50 abominations mentioned in the Scriptures [Deuteronomy 17: 4; Isaiah 66: 17; II Kings 23: 24; Ezekiel 18: 10–13].)

Second, there is no Scripture that favorably teaches such mediation as one person seeking the appeasement or blessing of another person via a third person. However, there is an example in Scripture where someone went to a third party to intercede for him. I Kings 2: 12–32:

And Solomon sat upon the throne of David his father; and his kingdom was established greatly. Then Adonijah the son of Haggith came to Bath-sheba the mother of Solomon. And she said, "Do you come in peace?"

And he said, "Peaceably." He said moreover, "I have somewhat to say to you."

And she said, "Say on."

And he said, "You know that the kingdom was mine, and that all Israel set their faces on me, and that I should reign. Howbeit the kingdom is turned about, and has become my brother's, for it was his from Jehovah. And now I ask one petition of you; deny me not."

And she said to him, "Say on."

And he said, "Speak, I pray you, to Solomon the king (for he will not say you 'Nay'), that he give me Abishag the Shunammite to wife."

This scene takes place just after the death of King David, and after the struggle for his throne. Obviously Solomon won and Adonijah lost. Later, Adonijah went to Bath-sheba, Solomon's mother, to seek her mediation for the benefit of his request. Notice that the request seemed innocent enough. There was no threat to the King or to the Kingdom. Adonijah was acknowledging that the LORD had assigned the role of king to Solomon. But see Solomon's reaction!

And Bath-sheba said, "Well. I will speak for you to the king." Bath-sheba therefore went to King Solomon, to speak to him for Adonijah.

And the king rose up to meet her, and bowed himself to her, and sat down on his throne, and caused a throne to be set for the king's mother; and she sat on his right hand.

Although there is no record of how Jesus and the Father greeted Mary upon her demise, but for argument's sake, let's assume that Mary was as well received into Heaven.

Then she said, "I ask one small petition of you; deny me not."

And the king said to her, "Ask on, my mother; for I will not deny you."

And she said, "Let Abishag the Shunammite be given to Adonijah your brother to wife."

And King Solomon answered and said to his mother, "And why do you ask Abishag the Shunammite for Adonijah? Ask for him the kingdom also; for he is my older brother; even for him, and for Abiathar the priest, and for Joab the son of Zeruiah."

Then King Solomon swore by Jehovah, saying, "God do so to me, and more also, if Adonijah has not spoken this word against his own life. Now therefore as Jehovah lives, who has established me, and set me on the throne of David my father, and who has made me a house, as

He promised, surely Adonijah shall be put to death this day."

Solomon appears to have actually gone back on his word and denied his mother her request, but he didn't. Remember, it was Adonijah's request that was denied, and Solomon apparently denied it in a rage! This event so set Solomon off that he acted on all the things that David had commissioned him to do just before David died.

It may appear that Solomon went back on his word to Bath-sheba, but Our Father won't go back on His Word to us. He never established but One Mediator between Himself and man—the Lord Jesus Christ!

The story continued and ended with Solomon's reprisals against David's enemies. The mediation request was denied in spite of the messenger, Bath-sheba, Solomon's mother. Solomon could see through the smoke and mirrors; the Father-God has even better eye-sight!

The manner of the request brought down the wrath of the king onto the heads of his and his father's former enemies who might never have been actually punished except for the ignition sparked by this attempt at mediation.

Likewise, when the Lord returns to earth in all His glory, there will be some slow marching and sad singing when those who have abused His grace must face Him in all their disobedience. He, as Righteous Judge, will do some big-time attitude re-alignment!

Let's look at this mediation from another perspective. Hammers are used to drive nails. On some occasions the nail that is driven is one of those attached to a finger or thumb! Now, let's suppose that due to some error in judgment something caused the hammer to miss the right nail and the thumbnail was hit instead. There it is! A thumb, let's say the left one, mashed, split, bloody, numb and soon to be throbbing, is in dire need. The left thumb realizes the right thumb is more favored because it is on the dominant side of the body, asks the right thumb to go to the head and the heart to get some relief from the soon to be throbbing thumb, and to get it cleaned up!

The right thumb first goes to the brain and says, "Honored Head-thing, please be aware that your own precious left thumb is wounded and in need."

Then the right thumb gets hold of himself and goes to the heart. He, the right thumb, knows that the nearest and dearest thing to the heart is the left lung. So the right thumb says to the left lung, "Hey, L. Lung, my friend, please go the wonderful heart and see if you can get some help for left thumb . . ."

You can readily see what a ridiculous scenario this becomes. One believer asking another believer, who is dead and gone and not in any position to help anyway, for assistance is equally ridiculous.

The Scriptures teach us to bear one another's burdens but that is a charge from the Lord for one believer to help another in prayer—both believers being yet alive! It is also acceptable to request someone to pray for someone else, and better yet to agree in prayer regarding a need as specified in Matthew 18: 18 and 19.

But believers who are dead are not in any position to receive a prayer request from a living mortal. If they are with the Lord (and they are if they were believers), we should not interrupt them, even if we could. It would be rude, even if we could. Here is yet another scenario that illustrates how erroneous it is to use the so called saints for intercessors.

What do you think the saints do when they get to heaven? Are they not to live in a peaceful, restful and altogether lovely place in the presence of the Lord? Just what are they to do?

So here comes a low-ranking angel. He drops a large bag down beside where Mary is sitting. "Here's the morning mail. Requests are down. There are only three quarters of a million requests for intercession in this delivery. Peter only got three hundred thousand and John got fewer than that. Requests are really down. Everyone is way short now. But this is only the first delivery of the day!"

Mary looks at the angel over her reading glasses. "That's good. We're either doing things right or everyone is doubting our ability to perform. Anyway, I haven't seen my Son for a week and a half because of all these miserable requests. I'm so tired of people who are unwilling to take on their own responsibilities. After I finish here, I think I'll take a nap."

"Okay, Mary," said the angel as he made a move toward the door. "I'll see you in a couple of hours with the mid-day delivery."

Oh, sure, Mary wouldn't use reading glasses, nor would an angel serve as mail carrier. But neither of these misrepresentations is as ludicrous as the whole concept of a saint in heaven interceding at all.

The whole concept is rank in the nose of the Father. First, if you have accepted Jesus Christ as your personal Savior, you are a member of His Body, much like the previously mentioned thumbs and other body parts (I Corinthians 6: 15). You have as much pull with the Head as anyone in the Body does. You need not be as stupid as the thumbs in their attempt at mediation.

Secondly and thirdly, Jesus said whatever you would ask the Father in His name the Father would give to you (John 16: 23—28). It also says in the same passage that the Father loves you Himself!

Fourth, Jesus said that if in His presence any two should agree on earth as touching anything that they should ask, it would be done for them (Matthew 18: 18, 19).

Fifth, Jesus said that if you abide in Him and His Word abides in you, you can ask whatever you will, and it will be done (John 15: 7, 8).

Sixth, you are the one who has been charged to do as the Lord instructed. He never said for you to ask someone else to do what you were told to do, not even Himself. He did not say to ask Jesus to tell the mountain to be removed. The charge is for you to tell the mountain to go (Matthew 17: 20). You tell the mountain to go in Jesus' name, and it must do it.

Seventh, read Chapter 8 of Romans and see who and what you are in relation to any problem, and not once is any mention made of former saints being in a better position than you are! These are seven sound reasons why intercession through and / or by saints is error!

Speaking of Mary

There is absolutely no doubt that Mary was blessed among women. The Word says she was (Luke 1: 28, 42). The Word said she was highly favored. And no doubt she was a very nice lady, but the Word did say "among," not above or over women. The idea of people addressing Mary as the Mother of God has as much validity as saying John the Baptist was the inventor and creator of the Holy Spirit.

Mary was pure enough and sincere enough that the Father chose her as the vessel for the birth of Jesus. After her role as surrogate mother, which included her heartbreak at Calvary, and her subsequent role as a believer in the early Church, her ministry was ended. She was an egg donor, and a surrogate: Not the Mother of God!

Jesus was Son of God and Son of Man. She, Mary, was the contributor of the "Man—Side" of Jesus' identity. Besides, Mary was born of a woman, just like John Baptist was, and Jesus said no one born of woman was greater than John Baptist! (Matthew 11: 11)

These traditional things began to be taught almost two millennia ago, but that longevity does not make any of them truth. If there are Scriptures to contradict the traditional teaching (and there are usually many of them), the light of the Scriptures should dispel the darkness of the traditional teachings. If people continue to follow the traditions, they are walking in darkness, practicing idolatry, blasphemy and disrespect to the Father, the Son and the Holy Spirit and Their work in and for man!

If their walk in darkness continues, the fellowship between the believer and the Father, which is already in jeopardy, could come to a very grave conclusion!

If you're not at peace, or your prayers are not being answered, or you've lost fellowship with the Father, these relationships with traditions may be the problem. Turn to the Word of God for your instructions and leave off the traditions of men!

Your reverence should be reserved for the Lord. Bowing, praying to, at or toward any other being is not acceptable in the eyes of the Father. *He loves you in your own position in the Son.* You pray to the Father in the name of Jesus. It is to the name of Jesus that every knee shall bow and every tongue shall confess that He is Lord (Philippians 2: 10). There is no other. The promises are to you; not to them, regardless of whom we are speaking.

To Whom Should We Pray?

The Scriptures plainly teach, not only those things in the previous paragraphs, but Jesus consistently taught by lesson and by example that we are to pray to God the Father. In the first place, there was no one else to whom Jesus could pray. He could not very well pray to Himself! Therefore He always prayed to the Father.

Besides that, Jesus always taught His followers to pray to the Father. The so-called Lord's Prayer is addressed to the Father. He included all who prayed to Him as equal to Jesus Himself by saying "Our Father" in the address of the prayer.

In John 16: 23–28 Jesus transferred the responsibility of prayer from Himself to His followers. He said of the immediate future that they (His disciples) would not ask or demand anything of Jesus. He further instructed them to pray to the Father in His (Jesus') name and that the Father would fulfill their needs to the glory of the Father. Jesus even removed Himself from the intercession scene because believers would go directly to the Father with their needs.

THE FATHER WOULD RESPOND TO THEIR PRAYERS BECAUSE THE FATHER HIMSELF LOVES THEM!!

John 16: 23 [Jesus is speaking] "And in that day you shall ask Me nothing. Verily, verily, I say to you, <u>if you shall ask anything of the Father, He will give it you in My name.</u>

Hitherto have you asked nothing in My name: <u>Ask, and you shall receive, that your joy may be made full.</u>

25 "These things have I spoken to you in dark sayings. The hour comes, when I shall no more speak to you in dark sayings, but shall tell you plainly of the Father. <u>In that day you shall ask in My name: and I say not to you, that I will pray the Father for you;</u>

27 <u>**for the Father himself loves you,**</u> because you have loved me, and have believed that I came forth from the Father. I came out from the Father, and am come into the world: again, I leave the world, and go to the Father."

The saying goes: "If at first you don't succeed, follow the directions" So it is in the world of relations with the Divine: "If at first you don't get through to Him, follow His directions!" Prayers are obviously to be addressed to the Father, and to Him alone.

The Makeup of Church Government

As has already been discussed (See <u>Religious Titles</u>, Guidepost 6, Chapter 1), Catholics were taught that Peter was the first Pope. Because the topic of the Pope has already been concluded, look past the Pope to other religious titles.

Cardinals are also unscriptural, as well as the politics that attend to the head organizations of many non-Catholic Churches. All these things are based on self-proliferating traditions. And if you do not believe this, look open-mindedly at the current situation in the Roman Catholic Church regarding the criminal activities of the pedophilic and homosexual priests, and the cover-ups and musical ministries played to avoid their prosecution.

A debate exists regarding the role of these alleged priestly criminals. Are they pedophiles or only homosexuals? The "modern church" (being "sensitive") evidently wants to set aside the sin of homosexuality and its practices (Romans 1: 32). Many church officials (both Catholic and otherwise) have yielded to political correctness and have quit condemning homosexuality. The Word still says it is wrong along with these (Romans 1. 23 – 25).

Idolatry,	Unrighteousness,
Fornication,	Wickedness,
Covetousness,	Maliciousness,
Envy,	Murder,
Strife,	Deceit,
Malignity,	Whispering,
Backbiting,	Hating God,
Invention of evil things,	Boasting,
Disobedience to parents,	Insolence,
W/O Understanding,	Covenant Breaking,
W/O Natural Affection,	Implacableness,
W/O Mercy, Pride,	etc. (vv. 29–31).

So what is the difference? If the priest is only a homosexual rather than a pedophile, who cares? Both are abominations to God! Both are absolutely evil in the sight of God and neither a homosexual nor a pedophile should be a priest or any other minister of God (Leviticus 18: 22; Romans 1: 27; Proverbs 3: 22; 11: 20). Furthermore, those who practice these other vices should not even be considered believers, much less ministers of God!

So when the church officials play musical chairs with and for these criminals in the clergy, it is absolutely wrong. That makes the church leadership share equally in their vileness! They go along with what they should be condemning. And being a party to the crimes and their aiding the criminals should bring charges of aiding and abetting. So some of the so-called church leaders should do their churching in the slammer!

In 2002 in Rome the Pope told the church leaders in the United States to install a Zero Tolerance Policy on these clergy-criminals.

After the leaders got back to the U. S., they decided that that policy was too strict and some of their buddies would be out of a career if the policy were enforced. They modified it.

One church leader (a Cardinal) has been in so much trouble with public opinion that he is out of office. He got re-assigned! One more note for the musical assignments!

One priest was re-assigned when he became a suspect in the murder of a nun. After years of being unavailable for questioning, the law enforcement agencies got enough proof to seek a warrant, arrested and eventually tried and convicted him. He died in jail.

Authorities are arresting and prosecuting many priests that the church had put into the musical job cycles in order to protect them from prosecution. This protection is wrong, pure and simple. Early in '07 the total payout to cover the losses in court for the civil suits for alleged pedophilia and homosexual activities of Roman Catholic priests exceeded $1,000,000,000 (one billion dollars) for all those lawsuits from all those victims for all those years this nonsense has been going on.

In January of '08 it was announced that the diocese of Los Angeles was selling buildings to pay for settlements for this clergy-criminal activities to the amount of an additional $660,000,000.

That means the total payout is approaching $2B. (Some of the cases have not been fought in court and the church is merely paying on demand. It may be that some people are taking improper advantage of the church. On the other hand, the unchallenged settlements are being paid to avoid embarrassment due to the probability or likelihood of proof of the criminal accusations.)

Why the Catholic membership will continue to attend and support a church that practices these things is mind-boggling. Recently some well-known people have converted to Catholicism. That is even more mind-boggling! It is obvious that the practices that the church has engaged in are immoral. Yet the faithful to that church are still faithful to that church in spite of its vileness. They love the church and its rituals and trappings more than they love God. If they love God more than the church and its traditions, they will come out of it, regardless of how difficult it may seem.

It takes a lot of fortitude to give up one's life-long religious practices. Just as difficult, it is hard to work up enough courage to change one's political party affiliation: Once a Democrat (or Republican) always a Democrat (or Republican). One's political philosophy may be opposite from the philosophy of their party, but the person often does not change his or her political affiliation.

Believers should be exceptions to this general observation! So it is with a church affiliation. Sometimes it takes a real shocker to make someone give up all that tradition and leave it lie dead. But by their fruit you shall know them. Look at the fruit.

If the fruit is sinful, abandon it! If the fruit is love, follow it. (For more on this topic, see Appendix 2, "Cocooning.") Please take note of this: <u>Christianity is not a religion. Christianity is the living relationship between the Father God and the believer by the work of the Son as anointed by the Holy Spirit.</u>

Regardless of the name on the church, Catholic or otherwise, the practices and teachings beyond pure Christianity are only religious ideas and ideals. They are also changeable. They can also be abandoned with impunity!

And most certainly, these organizations have absolutely no positive bearing on a believer's status with the Heavenly Father—NONE! The only affects that the organization's relationships have on true believers are restrictive, impairing and debilitating. Having established that, the true believer should not support an evil organization.

Go ahead and be faithful to God your Savior, but make sure any religious activities you actually practice or support are endorsed by the Father-God and His Word.

> <u>An Aside</u>: The criminal activities mentioned above that relate to the Catholic priests and bishops should not be considered as Catholic-bashing. The problem is with the Catholic Church leadership—its base. Many Catholic followers know the Lord and love Him, but many of the members are blinded by religion and not following

Christ. The latter remain an open field, ripe for harvest. May the Father-God have His harvest among them.

Catholics are not the only church leaders who go afoul of law, order and decency. Many others do, too. But the church involved with any such illegal, immoral or unethical conducts should not protect the person who commits the activity. Most other churches do not protect their members regardless of their standing. Many of them assist the authorities with investigations and get out of the way of prosecutors. Only cults will protect their illegal allies.

Confessionals

When the Bible mentions confessions of one's faults or sins (James 5: 16), it says to confess them to one another. That is, one to another, not one to a clergyman of any type. Also, accompanying those confessions is prayer—mutual prayer! There is no mention of penances—neither by a clergyman nor by a brother or sister!

James 5: 16: Confess therefore your sins one to another, and pray one for another, that you may be healed. The supplication of a righteous man avails much in its working.

This is not grounds for a confession booth! You are talking to one another, praying for and with one another. There is no mention of meting out penalties for those faults or sins, but praying and conquering them. Look at the promise! "The supplication of a righteous man avails much in its working." Righteousness follows the confession, not a penance or penalty! Your prayer together as brothers or sisters in the Lord brings up I John 1: 9:

If we confess our sins, He is faithful and righteous to forgive us our sins, and to cleanse us from all unrighteousness.

This promise is why James reports that the prayers of a righteous person are so productive—because he (or she) has been cleansed.

Pseudo-Catholicism

In recent times some so-called prophets have set out to show themselves off by displaying wonderful (NOT) signs. They present messages from Mary. They allege to have bleeding hands like Jesus' hands after His crucifixion.

They claim to have holy oil to anoint someone with. They spew out vague and mysterious predictions and promises to various ones, blessings if they will do something or other. Mary is the so-called messenger who allegedly speaks through some of these phonies.

Don't waste your time. Watch TV or something. Read a comic strip. Work a cross-word puzzle. Take a nap. Don't bother with this type of drivel.

5

Independence

Study the Word Independently

If you are serious about your own well-being and spiritual welfare (and I'm sure you are at this point), one more thing you need to do: Independently study the Scriptures. Study away from everyone else, using reference sources and commentary from other churches, ministries, denominations, and factions of Christianity.

No church or ministry has a monopoly on the Truth! Some of the cults have found nuggets of truth that mainstream churches have long-since overlooked or abandoned.

Open your mind to see what the Father-God is really saying. Ask Him to help you, and study for yourself. By relying on Scriptures as your final authority and as you are led by the Holy Spirit, you can always reject something that isn't God's Truth. Lean heavily on the Holy Spirit!

On the other hand, there are many really foul publications that are circulating through religious circles these days. If you will ask the questions relating to their claims that you are to ask when considering Scripture, you can readily see how to lay aside any false information. Consider any information that does not improve your relationship with your Savior as false and get rid of it!

Remember the questions:

Who said it?

To whom was it said?

What were the circumstances under which it was said?

Does it apply to me?

Many times you will find that people have an agenda: Relevance (Self promotion), sales of literature, promotion of a church, doctrine or cult, political leanings and so forth for their own benefit. On the other hand, when you find something scriptural that you believe to be especially precious, do your best to keep it to yourself long enough to substantiate it with other Scriptures—still all by yourself with the Holy Spirit's input.

Then, if you need help, turn to the LORD and find a Christian with whom you may share, but proceed slowly. If no one is available, you may have to find Christian literature about the topic to study and to write your responses to the literature in a journal or letter. You may have to resort to the internet. But be patient with how you handle the information. It is the enemy (Satan) who desires rapid decisions, actions and impulsiveness. He will use your emotions to urge you into a hurry mode that he can use to exploit you in your situation.

Regrettably, you cannot depend on Bible commentaries, commentators, Bible-translators, teachers, ministers, churches, those emotions or any other source as completely as you can the Holy Spirit and your relationship with Him. He, the Holy Spirit, is your teacher; He will lead you into all Truth (John 16: 13). Trying to fully depend on men and women for all of your spiritual food is counterproductive.

A Short Defense

So far you have received instructions on how to deal with the Bible's text and those who present it to you from a defensive stance. All of the "guideposts" and other hints to this point have been time consuming, at least. However, this next topic takes less time to do than it does to write about.

For an adequate defense in any war, game, or sport, the participants need to put on the correct uniform and associated gear. Christians should do the same thing. Here is the armor of God. Look at Ephesians 6: 13 17:

> Wherefore, take the whole <u>Armor of God</u>, so that you may be able to withstand in the evil day, and having done all, to stand. Stand, therefore, having <u>your loins girded about with Truth</u>, and <u>having on the Breastplate of Righteousness</u>, And your <u>feet shod with the Preparation of the Gospel of Peace</u>; Above all, <u>taking the Shield of Faith</u>, with which you shall be able to quench all the fiery darts of the wicked. And <u>take the Helmet of Salvation, and the Sword of the Spirit</u>, which is the Word

of God; Praying always with all prayer and supplication in the spirit, and watching thereunto with all perseverance and supplication for all saints; And for me . . . .

Notice that the list of items that the believer should put on or take:

Truth,

Breastplate of Righteousness,

Shoes of the Preparation of the Gospel of Peace,

Shield of Faith,

Helmet of Salvation,

Sword of the Spirit, which is the Word of God.

Every item on the list is spiritual—that is you will never see them with your physical eyes. You may very well see the direct results of these armaments; they are real and essential for every believer. However, the only way to manifest them is directly from the Lord Jesus Christ by His Word. (Every believer actually has these armaments, but they may be only in seed form—in the spiritual DNA.)

The Lord wants you to not only have these things, but to manifest and use them. However, you must be willing to use them before you will ever really manifest them.

So, your instructions are to first call on the Lord for salvation if you have not already done so (Romans 10: 13). The basic instructions are under "Audience and Purpose" in the "Introduction." Recognize that these issues are all settled as you have accepted Christ personally:

1. Your sins are forgiven

2. You have eternal life with its divine nature and attributes

3. Jesus is now both Savior and Lord of your life.

If you need to renew your commitment, simply pray to your Father-God in Jesus' name re-affirming at least these three items, and then ask for the whole armor of God. Read the list to the Lord if you want to; but be specific and deliberate in what you say and how you say it. God will honor your request and the more deliberate you are, the more quickly you will see the results of your prayer.

On the other hand, do not be afraid to ask in any words you may find In your mouth. God knows the thoughts and intents of your heart. So you are in a win-win situation. You call and He does!

As you read this, you are likely hearing a voice in the background saying that this advice is "Okay for those other people, but it will not work for me," or "What about all those evil things I've done? God will never listen to a person like me." DO NOT HEAR THAT VOICE! Read Romans 10: 13:

For whoever shall call upon the Name of the Lord shall be saved.

The word *whoever* (*whosoever*) eliminates all those accusations that the voice puts in your head. It is a life decision to do it; so do it in spite of the voice.

To verify that you receive what you have asked the Lord for in your salvation, read these Scriptures: Isaiah 43: 25, 26:

I, *even* I, *am* He Who blots out your transgressions for my own sake, and will not remember your sins. Put Me in remembrance; let us plead together; you declare, that you may be justified.

Know that your sins are blotted out. He will not remember them against you any more, and He wants you to communicate with Him regarding your justification. (Romans 4: 8; 8: 33, 34, and 37)

Blessed is the man to whom the Lord will not impute sin.

You are blessed in that God will not impute sin to you because you are His.

Who shall lay any thing to the charge of God's elect? Shall God, Who justified? Who is he who condemns? Shall Christ, Who died, yes rather, Who is risen again, Who is even at the right hand of God, Who also makes intercession for us?

No, in all these things we are more than conquerors through Him who loved us.

"There is therefore now no condemnation to those who are in Christ Jesus," is how Paul started out that 8th Chapter of Romans. And then he comments on that bold declaration by challenging with these thoughts:

Who will charge you before the Lord? Satan would love to. He's the accuser of the brethren (Revelation 12: 10).

After dying for you and in your place, will Jesus now condemn you? Hardly! It is Christ who has redeemed you.

How ludicrous that He would then turn against you!!

Look what the Father-God has said regarding this challenge! I John 4: 4:

> You are of God, Little Children, and have overcome them [the spirit of antichrist] because greater in He who is in you [Jesus] than he who is in the world [Satan].

You have the Greater One indwelling you. No matter what the circumstances are or who the enemy is or what he's up to, how can you lose with the knowledge that the Greater One lives in you?

> I Corinthians 6: 17: But he who is joined to the Lord is one spirit.

Being a believer, you and the Lord are one being in spirit. II Peter 1: 3, 4:

> According as His divine power <u>has given to us all things that pertain to life and godliness</u>, through the knowledge of Him Who called us to glory and virtue; by which are given to us exceedingly great and precious promises, that by these [the great and precious promises] <u>you might be partakers of the divine nature</u>, having <u>escaped the corruption that is in the world </u>through lust.

You, as a believer, are now a partaker of the divine nature. You receive the promises of God, and these things and these promises lead to the fulfillment of the divine nature in you.

> II Corinthians 5: 17, 21: Therefore if any man be in Christ, he is a new creation; old things have passed away; behold, all things have become new.
>
> For He [God] has made Him [Jesus], who knew no sin, to be sin for us, that we might be made the righteousness of God in Him.

These two verses are the cornerstone of your faith in the Father-God and His dealing with you. You are a new creation, and that new creation is the personification of the Father-God's own righteousness!! Being aware of these facts, move on in your Bible study as you proceed to *Reaching Forth*!

The End of *Book 1.*

Proceed to *Book 2.*

Appendices

The appendices contain information that will lead you to further your relationship with your Heavenly Father. Browse through them to see what is there and take advantage of the information as you proceed in your fellowship with the Father.

Appendix 1

REASONS TO STUDY GOD'S WORD
FROM EIGHT PERSPECTIVES

A well-known TV judge said something like this: The best contract is a handshake between two honest men. No amount of written contracts can be better or more reliable.

It is for this reason that contracts have become so arbitrary and necessary in our society. Men have often forsaken the role of honesty! Contracts must almost always be written and even then many people attempt to alter them, ignore them or otherwise break them. Men have stooped to moral lows almost beyond imagination!

Another idiom says that man is no better or worse than the words of his mouth. Putting these two formulas together means that untruthful man is not one who holds truth very dear. Then when men like these read the Bible, it is no wonder they often call it a collection of myths, fables and moral stories. Academia, if allowed to speak of God's Word at all, often brands the Book as a collection of fairy tales and myths. Indeed, these over-educated academians often cast doubt regarding God, His nature and even His existence!

Why is that so hard to understand? A man reads a message and evaluates that message, regardless of who sent the message, against his own set of values. If he has no values, then neither will the message have any value regardless of who sent it. So this negative trend seems to be established in these last days.

But it need not be! You, dear reader, may be an exception to the tide. You may see that the Word of the Lord is good, sweeter than honey in the honeycomb. The two men you are about to meet thought so and one of them said so (Psalm 19)!

The LORD God, our Heavenly Father, established David as King of Israel and identified David as a man after His own heart (I Samuel 13: 14; Acts 13: 22). It doesn't take a knowledgeable person to know that David was not sinless. David and his scurrilous conduct regarding Bath Sheba was proof enough for that, not to mention his inability to be a loyal husband to his wife (wives) and father to his many children. Why then did Jehovah decide to say that David was the one man who was after His heart?

Before we answer that, let's look at another well-received man in Jehovah's eyes: Abraham. We can answer why Abraham, according to James, was called the "Friend of God" (James 2: 23).

In the context of the passage in his epistle, James mentioned that Abraham believed God and it was counted to him for righteousness. Paul, in his various epistles, especially the one to the Romans (Chapter 4), dwells on the topic of Abraham believing God and having that belief establish Abraham's righteousness, too.

Here, then, are two people, one after God's own heart and the other identified as a friend of God, who had done something (or were something!) that made the LORD pay them special, favorable attention. One was obvious: He believed God and even though decades passed and he perpetrated more than one act of deceit, he still clung to God's promise of a son to him. Yet after all those decades of waiting, Abraham was willing to make a sacrifice of that son, Isaac. In spite of all the love Abraham had for Isaac, he was willing to sacrifice him to Jehovah. His belief was strong enough that he maintained that Jehovah would restore and keep His promise to Abraham. Read the story. It is delightful (Chapters 18, 21 and 22 of Genesis).

It's easy enough to understand about Abraham who was not to be moved from the LORD's promises to him and thus receive such an acknowledgement from Jehovah. But what did David do to merit such a title as one who was after God's heart?

Let's look at some of what David had to say and we will discern why the LORD held him in such high regard. It is David who is accredited with writing 73 of the 150 Psalms, while additionally about 27 more were attributed to him but without absolute knowledge of every one of them. One of those attributed to David is the 19th Psalm.

The heavens declare the glory of God; and the firmament shows His handiwork. Day to day utters speech, and night to night shows knowledge. There is no speech nor language, where their voice is not heard. Their line is gone out through all the earth, and their words to the end of the world. In them He has set a tabernacle for the sun, which is as a bridegroom coming out of his chamber, and rejoices as a strong man to run a race. His going forth is from the end of the heaven, and his circuit to the ends of it; and there is nothing hid from the heat thereof.

<u>The Law of the Lord is perfect, converting the soul: The Testimony of the Lord is sure, making wise the simple. The Statutes of the Lord are right, rejoicing the heart; the Commandment of the Lord is pure, enlightening the eyes. The Fear of the Lord is clean, enduring for ever: the Judgments of the Lord are true and righteous altogether. More to be desired are they than gold, yea, than much fine gold; sweeter also than honey and the honeycomb.</u>

Moreover by them is Your servant warned; and in keeping of them there is great reward. Who can understand his errors? You cleanse me from secret faults. Keep back Your servant also from presumptuous sins; let them not have dominion over me: then I shall be upright, and I shall be innocent from the great transgression. Let the words of my mouth, and the meditation of my heart, be acceptable in Your sight, O Lord, my strength, and my redeemer.

Examine the vocabulary and the tone and see if that is not a precursor for the 119th Psalm. Psalm 119 is unique in that it is not only the longest chapter of the Bible, but the entire poem is an acrostic. An acrostic is composed of lines of verses that start with the same letter in stanzas named after a letter of the Hebrew alphabet.

For instance, the lines of verse in the stanza *Aleph* all start with the letter *Aleph*; the lines under *Beth* all start with *Beth*; etc. All 22 letters in the Hebrew alphabet are in this poem and each letter is followed by eight lines—all beginning with that letter. The topic of the Poem is God's Word, whether it is called His Word or any one of these terms: Words, Law, Testimonies, Precepts, Statutes, Commandments, Judgments, Ordinances, or Way, (the latter is used synonymously for any of the other terms). All except four verses contain at least one of these terms that refer to God's Word.

All the pleadings and prayers that David prayed and wrote addressing Jehovah, and all the things David had to do to avoid the hostilities with Saul, yet refusing to take Saul's life because it had once been anointed by the LORD, bear witness that the LORD and His Word were central in David's mind. This Psalm 119 is then the culmination of David's attitude toward his source of strength and the abilities with which he had been endowed.

Furthermore, in all the chaos and convolutions of David's confrontations and fellowships with Saul and his children, especially the conflict with Saul and his jealousy and rebellion against Jehovah, David always remembered what the LORD had said about Saul. What the Lord had said about Saul was all that kept David from taking Saul's life more than once. That is how highly David esteemed the LORD's Word!

Allow Abraham, who believed God and it was accounted to him for righteousness, and David, who won the key to God's heart through acknowledging His Word and its manifold roles in his life, speak to our generation in this 21st Century to inspire us to depend and rely on the Eternal Word for ourselves.

The Perspectives

There are eight sound reasons why people, whether believers or not, whether seeking anything in particular or not, should learn enough about the Word of God to at least avoid the deception of those who want to exploit people's ignorance of the Scriptures.

So beginning with the most basic reason to study the Word, look what the aim of the Word is in the first perspective.

Perspective One—What Paul Said

Many people who will read this document will not ask the question "Why study the Bible?" They will remember what Paul wrote in II Timothy 3:16 as an answer to the deceivers that have to come into the world. He states that the Word was and is inspired by God Himself, just as if the Father-God is speaking directly to the reader, and that the message addresses four areas:

> For doctrine (manner of living as it was meant in Scripture);
>
> For establishing the Truths of God when a doubt arises;
>
> For correction when one is either in error or considering getting involved with error; and
>
> For showing us how to live for and in the Lord in honor, righteousness and victory.

All Scripture is given by inspiration of God and is profitable for doctrine, for reproof, for correction, for instruction in righteousness, that the man of God may be perfect, thoroughly furnished to all good works. (II Timothy 3: 16)

And then they will remember what else Paul wrote in II Timothy 2: 15. The second most common Scripture regarding the topic of studying it, further warrants that it shows us how to meet the Father's approval, becoming a workman who is productive (having nothing to be ashamed of).

> **Give diligence to present yourself approved to God, a workman who needs not to be ashamed, rightly dividing the word of truth.**

Here is a clue that many people overlook regarding "How to study the Word." One should "rightly divide the Word of Truth." Briefly said, "Rightly dividing" does not mean "Picking and Choosing" or "Selecting verses at random and using them accordingly." Rightly dividing the Word means to see what Scriptures apply to you in your situation and use them for your benefit only if they address you. You see God's Word addresses many different people, and a particular passage may address someone other than the reader at that moment. (See Guidepost 2, Chapter 1, *Book 1* for more on this topic.)

Though these two verses are true and important, they are only two reasons to study the Bible. Many more verses put even more emphasis on the importance of studying, really studying, God's Word.

There are warnings for those who do not take time for the Word, as well as innumerable blessings and rewards promised to those who stand firm on the Word. For example, read carefully Mark 4: 1–20. The sower sowed the Word, and the four kinds of ground represent the four kinds of reception the Word receives in the hearts of the hearers.

The first group was immediately robbed by Satan.

The second lacked enduring depth (personal commitment).

The third was overcome in worldliness (too busy).

The fourth was divided into thirty, sixty, and one hundred-fold fruit-bearers (victorious disciples).

Thus you can see the effect of the Word on Its hearers, progressing from those who were immediately robbed, all the way to those who were most productive.

Perspective Two—What Hebrews Said

Another perspective contradicts the way some people perceive and present the Word. This may come as a surprise, or even a shock, but the way some people teach the Bible, it is not delivered as the Word of God. There are some Bible scholars who know the text of the Bible very well, but have no knowledge of what it means, because they do not know its Author. Many may have studies about the Bible, but often these same people do not study what the Bible really says!

This may be the most valid of all reasons to absorb the Word. Hebrews 4:12 declares The Word of God is alive, and powerful, and sharper than any two-edged sword . . . .

Many Bible scholars are not alive (not having eternal life that is brought by the Lord Jesus Christ) and the real Word of God is a mystery to them. Yet they know the text of the Bible.

The natural [un-regenerated] man does not receive the things of the Spirit of God; for they are foolishness to him, neither can he know them, for they are spiritually discerned (I Corinthians 2: 14).

In other words, when one reads the Bible, he or she is reading a living text. Unless the reader is alive also, the text is alien or foreign to him or her. The Bible to that reader is just so many words until the Holy Spirit makes the words alive in the reader and the reader takes on the Life of the Father-God that is in His Word. It is then that the Bible becomes the Living Word of God to that person.

Because the Word of God is the main foundation of the Christian Faith, it is essential that every believer have as nearly perfect understanding of Scripture as possible. If you are not a believer, then it is through the message in the Word of God that you may become one.

Perspective Three—God's Own Opinion

What does the Father-God say about His Word? There are many people who have an odd evaluation of God's Word. They claim that they believe it, yet when it comes to acting on what it says, they hedge saying that they are not sure that it means just what it says.

And there are those who say the Word of God is only a general idea of what God wants us to know, and that not every word is really His—just the general idea is His.

Look briefly at the Father-God's opinion of His Word. As you read, ask yourself if God meant what He said or not and if you should hold the Truth of God in uncertainty. Again in *Hebrews*:

Therefore, we ought to give the more earnest heed to the things we have heard [words], lest at any time we let them slip. For if the word spoken by angels was steadfast, and every transgression and disobedience received a just recompense of reward,

How shall we escape, if we neglect so great salvation, which at first began to be spoken by the Lord, and was confirmed to us by those who heard Him, God also bearing them witness, both with signs and wonders, and with various miracles and gifts of the Holy Spirit, according to His own will? (Hebrews 2: 1–4)

Look at what you've read: First, really listen to what you Heard—the Word! If the message of angels was valid, how shall we be able to shrug off what the Lord Himself is saying to us?

Second, that message we heard from the Lord Himself was confirmed as truth by those who heard Him first hand, and that God Himself bore record with them that what they were communicating about salvation was true by miracles and the gifts of the Holy Spirit.

The signs and wonders spoken of here are not manifested through those who either hold God's Word in uncertainty or deny the inspiration of the words of the Bible. No, the signs, miracles, and gifts of the Holy Spirit are present to confirm the message of salvation as presented in the Truth of the Word.

Perspective Four—The Word Vs Experience

Here is a little background regarding what Peter wrote. Matthew, Chapter 17 records Jesus' transfiguration. Jesus took Peter, James and John with Him to go pray on a high mountain. While there, Jesus was transfigured before them and was visited by Moses and Elijah.

In II Peter, Chapter 1, Peter alludes to this event when he says that he wants us to remember the great promises he had just written about (Vv. 2-8) and that we are not following cunningly devised fables in regard to the power and coming of the Lord Jesus Christ. He concludes (from the last half of V. 16 and continuing through V. 18):

but [we] were eyewitnesses of His [Jesus'] majesty. For He received honor from God the Father, honor and glory, when there came such a voice to Him from the Excellent Glory, "This is My Beloved Son in Whom I am well pleased." And this voice that came from Heaven we heard when we were with Him in the holy mount.

Would not this be one blessed experience to witness such a marvelous thing! Many people would give their eye teeth to see such a wonderful thing! But wait, Peter continues! Verses 19–21:

> We have also a more sure word of prophecy, to which you do well that you take heed, like a light that shines in a dark place until the day dawns and the Day Star arises in your hearts; knowing this first, that no prophecy of the Scripture is of any private interpretation. <u>For the prophecy came not at any time by the will of man, but holy men of God spoke as they were moved by the Holy Spirit</u>.

What Peter is saying is that no experience, regardless of how wonderful, is equal to the message of the Word of God. He used the reference to the prophecies because there was no written New Testament in those days, but the New Testament message has the same Author as the Old Testament. The audience is different and so is the message, but the authorship is the same and so is the reality and power of it.

Regardless of what a blessing the experience is, the Word of God surpasses it. An experience will fade, not only in memory, but in impact. The written Word will not change, cannot change, because it is God's Word and He does not change.

Some experiences can deceive. Look at the history of the cults and cultists. Have not many of them had visions and conversations with what they thought were divine beings? Absolutely!! And they were deceived. They did not compare what the so-called "divine one" told them with what the Scriptures say. And if they did, the Scriptures were removed from their context, misappropriated, or the meanings of the words were altered—breaking at least one of several essential Bible-study principles.

Perspective Five—Did You Know . . .?

Here are several things the average person may not know about the Word of God. They are things that God has said about His Word as He speaks to His people through the ages. Without comment, you may look them over and may be pleasantly surprised at what you may find out from His perspective.

Although Philippians 2: 11 tells us that "at the Name of Jesus, every knee shall bow . . . and every tongue shall confess," there is something esteemed yet higher in God's eyes: His Word!

> Psalm 138:2: I will worship toward Your holy temple and praise Your Name for Your loving-kindness and for Your Truth; for You have magnified Your Word above all Your Name.

Further, the psalmist said he would worship the Word of God. Psalm 56: 4, 10:

In God (I will praise His word), In God have I put my trust, I will not be afraid; What can flesh do to me?

In God (I will praise *His* word), In Jehovah (I will praise *His* word),

Part of the reason that it is not possible to separate the Person of Jesus from the Living Word of God is because the Word is the force behind all of creation. John tells us this:

In the beginning was the Word, the Word was with God, and the Word was God. The same was in the beginning with God. All things were made by Him . . . , and the Word was made flesh, and dwelled among us . . . . (John 1: 1–3, 14).

Peter says it, too, that the Word of God was the creator. II Peter 3: 5, 6:

For this they are willingly ignorant of, that by the Word of God the heavens were of old, and the earth standing out of the water and in the water, by which the world that was, being overflowed with water perished. (See also Hebrews 11:3; Psalm 33: 6)

When the Word of God is applied to something, It gets results. Isaiah 55: 10-13:

So does My [God's] Word that goes forth out of My mouth: It does not return to Me void, but It accomplishes that which I purpose, and It prospers in the thing whereunto I send It. (See also I Thessalonians 2:13)

The Lord has put such store in His Word that He personally stands behind it to make sure it's good. Jeremiah 1: 12:

Then said Jehovah to me, "You have well seen: for I watch over My Word to perform it." [Amplified Bible, Zondervan Publishing House, 1965] (See also II Peter 3: 9; Ezekiel 12: 23 and Isaiah 45: 26.)

For with God nothing is impossible, and no Word of God shall be without power or possibility. (Luke 1: 37) These verses could continue for some time. Here are a few main ideas that you may look them up in your Bible to see the exact wording.

The Word will judge its rejecters. John 12: 48

The Word is a daily sustenance. Matthew 4: 4; Psalm 19: 7–11, 14

The Word's source is divine. John 1: 1-14; II Peter 1: 21

The Truth of the Word frees us. John 8: 31, 32

The Word enhances our relationship with God. John 14: 23; Romans 15: 4; Psalm 119: 105

The Word is our source of new life. John 6: 63, 68; I Peter 1: 23; James 1: 18

The Word cleanses us. John 15: 3; Ephesians 5: 26

The Word heals us. Psalm 107:20; Proverbs 4:20-22

Meditating on the Word makes us prosperous. Joshua 1:8

There are many others still. (See Appendix 4.)

Perspective Six— Surveying the Enemy

The enemy has a litany of names that give us clues to his real nature: *Thief, murderer, tempter, accuser of the brethren, deceiver, god of this world, imitator of a roaring lion,* and most prominently, *liar,* and many, many more.

> <u>An Aside</u>: Isn't it a peculiar twist that Satan will deceive us (or try to) about something, tempt us to do something, or intimidate us into doing something, then he will accuse us when we have fallen into the trap? Yet if we don't fall for his lies or his threats, he ridicules us for having missed out on something or other! Well, these are the things Satan does best.

Paul presents a bird's-eye view of the enemy's spiritual, yet very real, organization in Ephesians 6: 12:

> **For we wrestle not against flesh and blood, but against principalities, against powers, against the rulers of the darkness of this world, against spiritual wickedness in high places.**

Look at the arrangement Paul presented of the enemy's forces:

Principalities,

Powers,

Rulers of Darkness of this World, and

Spiritual Wickedness in High Places.

These are the four levels of Satan's Kingdom, against which we believers are to wrestle. The top level, Satan himself, is not listed because he is already defeated. Jesus did that at Calvary (Genesis 3: 16; I John 2: 13; 3: 8; Colossians 2: 15; Hebrews 2: 14).

Another level is not mentioned because It Is demon activities in consort with man's cooperation to some extent: Strongholds. Strongholds are resisted by intercessory and combative prayers as led by the Holy Spirit because of the human attachments to the problems. The lowest level, demons, also is not mentioned here because we have been authorized to be their masters by using Jesus' Name (Mark 16: 17, 18; James 4: 7; I John 2: 13; and 4: 4).

Some of the manifestations that the enemy displays in our society are cited in II Timothy 3: 2-5:

> For men will be <u>lovers of themselves</u>, *lovers of money*, **boasters**, <u>proud</u>, *blasphemers*, **disobedient to parents**, <u>unthankful</u>, *unholy*, **unloving, unforgiving**, *slanderers*, **without self-control**, <u>brutal</u>, *despisers of good*, **traitors**, <u>headstrong</u>, *haughty*, **lovers of pleasure rather than lovers of God**, having a form of godliness but denying its power.

Is it any wonder that Paul urges us to wrestle against these forces? These are the forces that wield power over their subjects, the people. People, in turn, manifest the leadings and persuasions of these over-lording spirits. These are the people that do evil and allow evil things to happen to and in society. Why do you think many crimes go unpunished? Even when the perpetrator is known, a plea bargain or technicality will allow the perpetrator to go free to do his or her act again. No individual is to be blamed for these foul conditions because the problems come from the evil influences of these satanic spirits that have infiltrated our society from top to bottom. We know these spirits exist because we see their fruit continually.

We not only see these types of fruit continually, but we rub elbows with the people who cooperate with them wherever we go. They're in the media and entertainment industries. They're running our local, state, national and international governments.

They're in our social structures—education systems, government agencies, morals, mores, and economies. No facet of our lives is free from them or their influence. They are even manifested in so-called Christian Churches and Assemblies across our alleged Christian nation.

> Notice: We do not struggle against human beings as our enemies, but we should and do resist the forces that influence (even control) some people.

Perspective Seven—What Jesus Said

In John 15: 7, 8 Jesus made an astounding promise. He said,

> "If you abide in Me, and My words abide in you, you shall ask what you will, and it shall be done to you. In this is My Father glorified, that you bear much fruit; so shall you be My disciples."

This means that we are to become completely involved with the Word, absorbing it and retaining it like a sponge, and when pressed, releasing it to allow its life and powers to alter us and our situation.

Jesus Himself is the Word Incarnate (the Word made flesh—alive in a physical body) and to attempt to separate the Person of Jesus from His role as Word is not possible. "I am the Way, the Truth [the Word] and the Life," He said (John 14: 6).

"In the beginning was the Word" according to John (the first chapter) and the Word as Creator turned out to be the Redeemer as well. So we see that Jesus as Word, alive in us, and His Words alive in us, become the means by which our needs, both inside and outside, are met.

Perspective Eight—Our Part

Man continually tries to get us to believe God's Word, but God doesn't attempt to convince us to believe His Word at all. He simply gives us His Truth of Life and tells us to act on whatever that particular portion of Scripture teaches or instructs. Here is James 1: 22-25:

> But you <u>be doers of the Word, and not hearers only</u>, deceiving your own selves. For if anyone be a hearer of the word, and not a doer, he is like a man beholding his natural face in a glass: For he beholds himself, and goes straightway forgetting what manner of man he was. But <u>whoever looks into the perfect Law of Liberty, and continues in it, he being not a forgetful hearer but a doer of the work, this man shall be blessed in all his deed.</u>

The key to scriptural success is *acting* on the Word. The translators put in the word *work* in the Book of James, but *action* would have been better. *Act* on the Word. What the Word says to do, *do*. It's a hands-on relationship. If you read instructions, you'll probably not remember them long, but if you do them, you can learn them faster and keep them longer than by merely reading them. It is this type of application that is successful in the Word of God. It's a Hands-on learning process, and you are blessed by it.

But no one can act on the Word if he or she does not know what the Word says. This is the goal of this composition: To show you how to find out what the Word really means to you. Then you will know *how* to ACT on His Word.

You can act on His Word to not only fulfill your expectations in your spiritual life, but maintain your physical and material life by the Word, as well.

Appendix 2

COCOONING—THE CULTS AT WORK

The Definition

Because this is a brand new topic from the perspective of deliverance, you need to know the meaning and use of a new term: *Cocooning*— or the *cocoon syndrome*. *Cocooning* refers to the way people attempt to change other people. People changing people is very seldom Christianity. When people try to change other people in order to make Christians out of them, they are reducing Christianity to a mere religion.

> An Aside: The changing of people by someone leads to "Control." This control is facilitated by one person dominating another person. This system of domination or control fits the description of and definition of *Nicolaitanism* as mentioned in the Lord's Letters to the Seven Churches of Asia. This definition is important here to establish the fact that Jesus hates Nicolaitanism (Revelation 2). Nicolaitanism is the life-blood of cults!

> Definition: **Christianity is not a religion. Christianity is a living relationship between the Father-God and His believer(s) through His Son Jesus Christ by the Holy Spirit.**

This process of people-changing people could have been called *mummifying*. However, people usually visualize the mummy as someone dead all bound up with strands of cloth. But people usually try to change other people while the subjects are young and ignorant. They do not often deal with adults. Therefore the word *cocooning* better fits the current definition. This is exactly what religions do, all religions! (You can readily see why the Lord hates Nicolaitanism!)

The cocoon fibers are teachings, doctrines or practices that the leaders (whether church, cult, or other group) created to allegedly help the new convert to identify with the group. The leaders establish doctrinal standards, guidelines and dogmas to set the new convert out on the road that the leaders think is for the convert's best interest (or their own!). Nearly always these edicts depart from the standards of the Word of God, and religion (or a cult) is the result.

They spin a web around the convert to ostensibly protect him or her from outside harm. But instead of the cocoon fibers protecting the convert, the convert often gets entangled with the fibers so that growth, progress and maturity are stifled. Thus, the convert becomes a victim, suffocated by religion, or worse. What man thinks is right is not always so.

There is a way that seems right to a man, but its end is the way of death. (Proverbs 14: 12; 16: 25)

> <u>Note</u>: The problem surfaces when a group first contacts the convert-victim and persuades him or her to label themselves as a member of that group. Once that is accomplished, the group starts teaching and training that person to be whatever it is that the group represents. Often the group is CINO—Christian in Name Only!

You saw the example of attempted cocooning cited in the "Introduction" to *Book 1* when Jesus was speaking to Peter about John. Peter wanted to know what John would do or what would happen to John. There is no telling why Peter thought he needed to know, but too often the reason people want to know what others are about is to control them. This desire for controlling others is the beginning of Nicolaitanism, of which the Lord had nothing good to say (Revelation 2: 6). (Often a cocooner's objective is best started like this: *Numbers have power, and if we can make a league with someone, we can have their support—or at least their money!*)

Degrees of Cocooning

Cocooning comes in degrees, or levels of intensity, ranging from the gentle (dead-pan types), through the moderate (the active, often enthusiastic pseudo-evangelical types), and finally to the radical (the fanatic, hyper, maybe psychotic types). Always remember, many churches, cults and ministries are only businesses trying to gain and maintain a profit—at the expense of their congregation.

Gentle Cocooning

The gentle cocooners are the beginning of changing Christianity to a religion. They do it by adding rules, words, customs, habits, rituals and such—or by not following what the Scriptures plainly teach. They may be gentle, but they are no less dangerous from an eternal perspective than any other cocooner. Cocooners at every level are used of the enemy to rob, kill, and destroy.

The gentle cocooners are less aggressive because they have less to promise. Their Lullaby simply puts folks to sleep and they never wake up. Some of the gentle cocooners are so ignorant of what God's Word teaches that they could even promote such ridiculous teachings as the universal fatherhood of God or the universal brotherhood of man. (See Long-Time Trends, Chapter 4, *Book 1*.)

The gentle cocooners sometimes have a genuine desire to help the new convert, but because they hold Bible understanding in error (if they hold it at all), these people only repeat those errors.

A real experience in Christ offers the believer some definite benefits that the Lord manifests immediately (the fruit of the spirit, Galatians 5; the gifts of the spirit, Romans 8; I Corinthians 11–13, signs following, Mark 16; and others), but many churches and groups have little outward benefits to offer. Little, for these people, ranges from absolutely zero to some vague promises about the future, or maybe a social program. *After all, something too exciting may end the Lullaby!*

Since there are no manifestations immediately available, when asked about the difference between them and the New Testament Church, the group can only offer excuses. For the gentle cocooners, the excuses are usually mistakes, and just that, mistakes. However, these mistakes could cause someone to miss out on what the Father- God would have them experience.

Their biggest mistake is the almost complete neglect of Scriptures in their lives and/or in their church services. The gentle cocooners tend to have a set order to their meetings: A prayer, three songs, announcements, offering and another song (or a number by the choir) and a sermon about

C. L. Chapman

"Someday up Yonder." They may even have a responsive reading, but that would be a Psalm or something non-committal, and even that would be without comment or explanation. (The message and the songs usually have the same theme—"Someday up Yonder")! Of course there is always the possibility of a political or social topic to preach about. But there is seldom anything designed to activate or change one's life or lifestyle. (*We can't afford to disturb anyone. They may leave! Maintain the Lullaby! They won't leave unless they sleepwalk!*)

These are sometimes the same politically correct or sensitive churches that will avoid social pressures from outside the church by going along with society's demands for change. They may adopt an open stance to evil—such as homosexuality or abortion rights. Right away arguments supporting either abortion rights or homosexuality, along with "private decisions or life-styles," win over any moral stand against these immoral movements. There is no fiber in them to resist any worldly teachings whatsoever! These are the folks who split their churches when the pastor becomes an open gay!

Most any controversial political topic will affect the gentle cocooning church. These are the ones who follow political party dictates without looking at either the issues or the Word for guidance. If the issue they decide to support contradicts the Word or vice-versa, they will never know it because they look at neither.

If someone draws their attention to the differences between the Word and the party line, they simply shrug it off as a biblical error. Their prayers are general prayers, "Lord, Bless everybody everywhere. Amen." Maybe everyone will shake hands with everyone else and they will then go home and watch television.

The formats for their services vary from group to group, but seldom vary within the groups. About all they can offer a convert is membership into their group.

Once a person commits to the gentle cocooners, the cocooners attempt to control the person by use of fear, guilt, or obligation, feelings of benevolence, duty, or loyalty, any of which can be associated with the whole group or individuals within the group. *All this while maintaining the sleep-walk.*

The fear would be typical of linking one of the emotions with each other; such as telling someone that he or she should be regular attendees of the meetings or hurt the pastor's feelings or disappoint the pastor. Thus

176

the threat of guilt of disappointing someone would engender fear, because of the failure of loyalty or neglect of duty.

A Universal Torque-wrench—Tithing

Nearly every church distorts the truth of Scriptures somewhere. In a cocooning church, even the gentle ones, one particular truth is exploited. The Verse in Malachi 3: 10 says to the descendants of Jacob:

> Bring all the tithes into the storehouse, that there may be food in My house . . . .

Because we have well-discussed this topic earlier (Guidepost 3, Chapter 1, *Book 1*), this section will be edited for the sake of brevity. A cocooning church will ride the topic of tithing to the maximum and place that obligatory guilt-trip on everyone in sight in order to glean every dime out their audience!

While we have explained that there may be a logical claim to a portion of someone's tithe (if that person wishes to believe in and practice tithing) if the group supplies some portion of the follower's spiritual food, there are no grounds for a cocooning organization to have any real attachment to anyone's money or property for any reason to any extent! A cocooning organization will not—it cannot—provide any spiritual food to a true believer!

The same rationale that would allow a snake to suckle a baby rabbit! In the first place there is nothing on a snake's belly for a baby rabbit to nurse, and in the second place, the baby rabbit would simply be a quick meal for the snake!

There will be no spiritual food supplied by the cocooning church unless it happens accidentally! The best they will do is supply placebos. (*Placebos* are mental-level lessons about biblical topics that should be spirit-level lessons. For *placebos*, see Moderate Cocooners, Next Section, This Appendix.)

And If the church does feed them spiritual food, does it feed the people all the spiritual food they receive? A person who depends on a church, an organization, a ministry or a person for their spiritual food will starve spiritually. Believers must feed themselves on the Word of God with the aid and guidance of the Holy Spirit or they will not prosper in the Lord. No church can supplant that basic relationship between the Lord and the believer by the Word! A cocooning church is even less qualified to feed the spiritual food to believers!

Spiritual food is the Bread of Life. A church is not. The church cannot feed its followers the Bread of Life! Only Christ Himself can feed His own! A cocooning organization, which the Lord hates, will never be able to nurture a believer. They simply do not have the wherewithal to do it!

Every church that cocoons its followers wants to obligate that follower to give all tithes and offerings to that church. Even the most gentle of cocooners do it. The more extreme the cocooners, the more extreme the demands for tithes and offerings!

Moderate Cocooning

The Moderate Cocooner types increase the pressure of changing Christianity to a religion. Nicolaitanism becomes even more evident—and stronger! They simply have more activity in their corner, and more rules, rituals and customs, as well as programs. Therefore they have more persuasive power. Once the control over a convert is established, the cocooner has gained mastery and overthrows the will of the cocoonee.

The moderate cocooners are usually just as honest in their attempts to aid others, but they are a little more aggressive about it. They use some Scriptures and will put up good defenses for their views, although they probably violate the Bible-study principles. The moderate cocooners mention God's manifestations, but are as likely to oppose them as teach them. Some may manifest God's presence or His gifts in some physical sense such as healings or utterance gifts, while others never manifest any semblance of God.

If there is a political topic that activates these folks, they are apt to raise money or to put on a march or demonstration to support or oppose the political stand.

The Gifts of the Holy Spirit

The Moderate Cocooners often abandon good Bible-study practices; sometimes the errors are honest errors; sometimes not. One of their favorite and often seen errors is the breaking of lists, as described in <u>Guidepost 1</u>, Chapter 1, *Book 1*. The moderate cocooners hold onto the new-comer by using the same tactics as the gentle cocooners, except more extreme guilt trips, heavier obligation and then harsher criticism, thus more fear of rejection and/or condemnation. The threats may become a real load of life-changing duties, and time-consuming tasks. *If one neglects or slacks in these chores, the person has sinned against God, the group, the group-leaders, or all of the above.*

Moderate cocooners go heavier into tithing and/or giving than the gentle cocooners do. They have programs, projects, and operations to finance and they "need your money!" They spend much time pleading for money and even putting people into guilt in an attempt to get the last possible penny from the followers.

Placebos

Moderate cocooners are the masters of presenting placebos rather than spiritual food although all cocooners do it to some degree. If a church is supposed to feed its parishioners spiritually, these are the folks who are most apt to serve up a plate of placebos. They will research a topic in Scripture, history and/or science, render it out, then teach it to the congregation and call it spiritual food.

In the real world, the church is not commissioned to feed the followers. The Lord is the source, not the church. If the person is depending on the church (any church) for his or her spiritual food, the person will starve. An individual may feed another individual or group occasionally, but it will be the Holy Spirit who feeds the believer as He uses the other party or parties.

Feeding the congregation is not the function of a church. Also, even if the Holy Spirit is using someone else to provide spiritual food for another person, that person should never be dependant on the provider as a sole source. It would only be an occasional tidbit or feast—not the complete and sole diet.

Here's what I mean. My wife and I heard one radio preacher who spent about 8 to 10 minutes of his half-hour raising money for his broadcast. Typical. Then he spent the rest of his time talking about the mustard plant, the source of the mustard seed that Jesus compared to the Kingdom of God in Matthew 13: 31 and other passages. He spoke of the botanical qualities and traditional/historical roles mustard played and a lot of other stuff. Whoop-de-do!

When he finished, my wife and I looked at each other and wondered what his point was. So the plant was popular, widely used, grew tall from a small seed, and all the other wonderful and essential things the man told us. So what? If someone is in need, is that knowledge going to help? If someone wants to change his or her life, will that provide them with knowing how? Just what did he expect that knowledge would do for anyone! The bottom line is—WHO CARES?

That was a placebo and many ministries feed this kind of information (???) for spiritual food. It is not spiritual food! It's swill! It may be interesting, or even educational to an extent, but it's still swill! If the message does not have a positive affect on someone's life (initiating or enhancing a relationship with the Lord), it's a placebo. **Swill!**

Moderate cocooners often thrive on this type of worthless message, convincing their followers that the source of this information is someone who needs that follower's support (money!). If this sounds like someone you know, quietly bow out and find another place to fellowship and another group to do it with. Any group you choose should have the Word of God as its center, not some one's education or opinions.

Radical Cocooning

Finally and unfortunately, there are the radical cocooners. They set out to obtain a following and they do not seem to care about the means of doing it—the end will justify their means (any means, regardless). While gentle and moderate cocooners often have little or no signs following, or outward manifestation of God's blessings, the radical cocooners often go to extremes to show God's manifestations. However, they are quite likely to abuse them (or fake them) for the benefit of self-promotion.

Their goal is not to prove the Word of God by the signs, but to prove their own godliness. They know people will follow a godly person and they set out to show that they are godly and deserve a following.

Proving that they are godly may be unreal. They must have a following, regardless of how phony the evidence of godliness is. Many of the radical Cocooners leave Christianity out of their teachings and practices altogether. They play on peoples' emotions, linking them to biblical characters, ideas or themes. But underneath the biblical character, idea or theme is a diabolical, pagan religion.

One such cult uses an alleged Mary as a so-called medium to deliver prophecies and to show signs. While the appeal is to follow her, the signs are nothing beneficial. The prophecies are general, and the signs or temporary. They are nothing at all like the signs in Mark 16: 17, 18:

> These signs shall follow those who believe: In My Name shall they cast out devils; they shall speak with new tongues; They shall take up serpents; and if they drink any deadly thing, it shall not hurt them; they shall lay hands on the sick, and they shall recover.

The signs mentioned in Mark, along with the gifts of the Holy Spirit as mentioned in I Corinthians 11 and Romans 12 are beneficial both to those who receive of the ministry and those who administer the ministry.

Many Radical Cocooners like to refer to themselves as "God's servant," especially in connection with those proving signs. Some Christians have developed the idea that "signs following" endorse the person through whom the sign came as something more than a believer. More devastatingly, they cling to the idea that the signs following endorse all of what the person is teaching, some of which could be something right straight from the pits of hell.

A believer is someone who believes in the Lord Jesus Christ. Everyone who believes in the Lord Jesus Christ should have the signs following (Mark 16), but the signs following do not necessarily endorse all of what that person does or says.

The Message vs. the Messenger

There is a fine line distinguishing the message from the messenger. The LORD honors His Word, from whatever the source. He watches over His Word to make it good (Jeremiah. 1: 12). But the messenger could misunderstand or be ignorant of what portion of God's Word he is presenting that the accompanying signs are attesting to.

For instance, there used to be a radio minister who, when he was anointed by the Holy Spirit, preached one line of doctrine, but when he was asked about what he had said, he would deny saying it. His rationale was that he didn't believe that particular doctrine as he had preached it. He did this consistently for a number of years. He preached doctrines from his re-created spirit by the Holy Spirit that he didn't believe in his head.

Under the true anointing of the Holy Spirit, ministers frequently preach something they do not understand. Often a minister who is anointed by the Holy Spirit will learn something from his own ministry. So signs following do not necessarily endorse or condone the messenger, nor does it necessarily condone or endorse every portion of the messenger's teaching. The manifestations of the Lord become manifest at the presentation of the Word of God; all else could possibly be amounting to zero!

No one can say Samson lived a Godly life—filled with temptation, lust and selfishness. Yet God honored Samson's prayer, even when Samson was committing suicide (Judges 13-16).

Another example is in I Kings 13 where an old prophet lied to a man of God, leading him to disobey the LORD, which resulted in the man of God's death. After the old prophet deceived the man of God, he prophesied to him, foretelling his doom. Was the deceptive prophet worthy of his office? Would you want to be taught by him? Or preached to by him? Yet there is no record of God punishing him for his sin. It would be and is foolish, therefore, to swallow every word that every "signs-following" person has to say. Many are inflated with their own self-importance and their words are as useless as the old prophet's were.

Emotions, Feelings

The radical cocooners more often than not resemble the second prophet in their means. They usually emphasize feelings (of which the Scriptures are absolutely silent). There is no reference to or about feelings, emotions or anything of the like in Scripture. Yet the radical cocooners want to make someone *feel* something or other. *(You need to feeeeeel gooooood!)*

These same feelings emphasized by the radical cocooners change from moment to moment in an individual or group, and so does any relationship that may depend on those emotions. Thus, a person may "be saved" one moment, and "lost" the next—or vice-versa. Both the cocoonee (one who has been cocooned) and cocooner (one who cocoons others) often suffer sudden mood changes. They may feel happy if they "*feel godly*" or they may feel depressed if "*God is no longer there.*" Simply put, they are living on their emotions!

Besides being moody, these people are often very aggressive, argumentative and forceful. Some are even violent enough to be dangerous (Jonestown and Waco, for examples**). These people do much speaking, but they use little, if any, Scripture. When they do use the Bible, they use it as if it were a bludgeon to knock others down and force their views onto their target (victim).

Not only are cocooners usually moody and over-aggressive, they are often self-righteous, loud, and hyper. They often use money or other wealth as a tool to gain their goals. They will also use sex, any kind of sex (straight or homosexual), as a lure, threat or other device to control their followers. Some have even used narcotics as levers on their followers.

They will also use abstinence as a tool to control their followers— or to have their own sexual urges readily gratified. Some cult leaders have been known to force celibacy onto their followers except for the one(s) the leader chooses for a partner. They ignore the fact that Scriptures plainly condemn homosexuality and fornication, as well as deceit, greed and materialism.

Their doctrine consists of only a few select verses of Scripture that they have twisted and distorted into saying exactly what they need them to say. They could have an isolated truth that they are emphasizing to an extreme—thus making everyone else wrong. When a potential cocoonee encounters a cocooner who uses the Scriptures to justify doctrines that the cocoonee does not agree with, the cocooner will often forsake any mantle of love or concern, and attack the cocoonee's character, pointing out the cocoonee's alleged error and condemning them for it. Verbal personal attacks are common, calling the cocoonee names, judging them for alleged failures, and insulting their education, intelligence, appearance and/or their demeanor.

The cocooners attempt, and often succeed, to isolate their victim from all outside sources of information or help. Thus, they can heap their mind-twisting tactics onto the victim, often causing permanent damage. The hold on the victim follows all the typical strategies of fear and torment. Guilt, criticism, threat of rejection and condemnation are the starting tools, followed by threats of ostracism, hell, dismemberment and/or death. Thus the torture can be mental, physical or both. Sometimes the threats are based on potential reality—again Jonestown and Waco serve as examples.

> An Aside: ** Waco and Jonestown refer to two cults. The first one, the Branch Davidians of Waco, Texas, led by Vernon Howell, alias David Koresh, were attacked by governmental agencies that led to the deaths of 82 people, including Koresh, in 1993. The cult was well armed, gunfire broke out; and the government moved against the Davidians, many of whom were burned to death.

Jonestown refers to another cult, the People's Temple, a semi-political-semi religious group, led by Jim Jones. He led his group to Guyana where they built Jonestown. In the late 1970's about 1000 people followed him there to start a new life free from oppression, but relatives in the US sought help from the US Government to investigate their activities. As the investigators were leaving the area, no doubt with negative reports about the set-up, Jim Jones led his followers to drink Kool Aid laced with poison. In all, 913 died; some who refused to drink were shot; only a few (85) survived.

Definition: *Stronghold*

A *stronghold* is a spiritual force caused by demonic forces and the lies they tell in conjunction with the victim's belief of those lies and, hence, the victim's cooperation with the demons and their lies. Many strongholds involve more than one person—sometimes whole communities (Waco and Jonestown serve as small examples while political parties or religions serve as larger examples).

Once the cocoon is securely around the victim, a defensive attitude almost always develops. This defensive stance to protect the cocoonee along with the cocoon itself amount to a stronghold. These are things that restrict people by allowing them to imagine things that are presented to them by demons as if they were true and because they have affections for these demonic things, they protect them.

These things consist of anything and everything that raises itself against the knowledge of Christ and His redemption. Although the stronghold may appear more prevalent and stronger in radical cocooners and cocoonees, they are common in all religious circles and most political circles, as well an individuals, both the unsaved and saved. They are destroyed by spiritual warfare tactics, not human means (II Corinthians 6: 12; 10: 3–9).

Radical cocooners really ride the tithing-giving bandwagon. They want money, property, businesses, physical bodies, and even ask to be beneficiaries in the followers' wills! They hesitate at nothing to say or do to get a follower to give anything of value to them and their causes, which may be anything from a new car to a paradise on earth.

The cocoon syndrome sufferers' aggression may not be right, but it is understandable because the leader is usually a tyrant. He often has others cater to his every whim. Typical cocoonees act the same way as their cocooners. When they do not get what they want, they become the same ugly person as the cocooner.

Cocooning Symptoms

Like a disease in the body or malfunction in a machine, cocooning has several symptoms.

A) Separation: The tendency for members of a group to separate from other groups varies from a modest separation (subtle superiority but a continuance of socializing with and recognition of others) to complete isolation from others (downright hostility with no avoidable contact).

If a convert speaks of having talked to someone of another leaning, the convert's fellow cocoonees may deliver anything from a cold response and a quick change of subject to a stern lecture on the ills and faults of the other group mentioned. The stronger one feels or responds negatively about fellowshipping with another church or group not in that person's own group, the more that person has been cocooned.

(B) Zeal or Pride: The cocoonee may show zeal or pride (or both) to one or more of the following:

1. Their leader(s): Whatever the leader says or does is law. The followers place the leader(s) on a pedestal where the followers view him, her or them as anything from respected teacher(s) to another Messiah. The followers accept without question all of the leader(s)' words and actions as the ultimate answer to a any given situation. The leader may break all rules, laws, mores, and ordinances existing, but the followers, too often, do not question the leader's identity, credibility or authority to do as they do.

Many congregations place their ministers in this Position— on the pedestal. Members will say, "I just love my pastor and I would do anything for him (her). He (she) is the . . (superlatives)." To love is one thing; to idolize is another. It is cocooning that makes someone idolize a man or woman.

2. A church, sect or denomination: The minister and his or her ministry are often together on their pedestal, but sometimes cocooners place whole groups on a pedestal rather than placing just one or two persons there. The group may be a denomination or fellowship—which includes the whole assembly or assemblies with all their trappings. If a member does not even consider attending another church or fellowship with a different group than those who he or she is with, he or she has been cocooned.

3. Doctrines, dogmas, ordinances, or practices: Very closely akin to the church, sect or denomination, the church's followers may hold zeal and pride for one or more of the group's doctrinal elements. If another person or group of outsiders will accept all of these doctrinal elements, then, and only then, will they be accepted into the circle of the friends. Certain doctrines, or the mention of certain doctrines, will cause a cocoonee to react (usually negatively) toward someone who holds to that doctrine.

4. Code of conduct: The cocoonees may direct their zeal and pride to the "poor and humble" (or other) lifestyles taught by the leaders. Not often do the leaders practice the lifestyle of humility and poverty, although they may teach those things. But their followers do not see the leader in his accustomed surroundings. Many ministers have plenty while their parishioners do without. Less obvious cocooners are those who shun others who do not "live the life" as the cocooners think they should.

C) Exclusive Literature, CD's and Other Electronic Media: Separation and isolation extends to the reading and study material the group uses. This selection of literature ranges from choosing a particular publishing house that specializes in one type of literature to private Bible translations by and for that group. Those who use their own translations often have whole series of publications, including Bible lessons, stories, and hymnals.

They will sometimes change the words of traditional hymns to fit their doctrines and purposes. Some have even published books that they equate with the Bible as revelations from God. Of course when words come into consideration, so do special vocabularies.

For example, one group will not use the term *millennium* because they do not find the term in the Scriptures. The term "a thousand years," which means *millennium*, is used, however, so there is no real difference in meaning. But the group still will not use the term *millennium*.

Another example is a group who realizes that the Christians comprise the real Church (Romans 12: 4, 5: Ephesians 1: 22, 23) and they refuse to recognize the use of the term *church* as meaning a place for believers to assemble, or as the service in the church building. They do not go to church; they *meet*.

Regardless of the selection of literature, the more cocooned a group is, the more they depart from good Bible-study practices. After all, that is why and how they exist.

Cocooning robs people of blessings that God intended Christians to have. Cocooning promotes a sense of having attained all that there is in the Lord for Christians, and it simply is not true. The promise to Abraham and his descendants (an allegory of the Christian's relationship with the Lord) was to receive and possess the land as far as the feet trod (Genesis 17: 8 and Joshua 14: 9).

Because some have been cocooned, they drive their tent-stakes down too early—when they could and should have gone further. Instead of going into the heart of the Promised Land, they set up camp by the very border, if indeed, they are on the inside at all!

WARNING

Cocooning is dangerous—either from the perpetrator's position (that one will be accountable to God for it) and from the standpoint of the cocoonee (restrictive doctrines and practices hamper any new life that may exist, as well as restricting that new life's blessings).

Cocooning is subtle, often glossed over by apparently real concern, love, and benevolence. You must exercise caution with everyone, even those you think you know best, and make sure they teach and preach Scriptural Truth—not their own. Most of *Book 1* is related directly or at least indirectly to cocooning. Even though it may not be mentioned often, realize that this information can help set you free from error—thus establishing a better relationship with your Savior.

The Assault

A documentary presented the accounts of several college age young people who had allegedly been brainwashed by some cultists who relieved the victims of their worldly goods and twisted their minds almost to the point of dehumanizing them. It seems that youth in general are seeking something spiritual to satisfy them. To be satisfied spiritually is a natural craving. Only God can really satisfy this craving.

These partly-recovered victims of brainwashing accused their captors of continually assaulting them with Scriptures, sermons, lectures and lessons. They said the information came at them so fast and so continually that they could not deal with it and they lost their identities in the maze.

We are talking here about radical cocooning. This is what happens to young victims:

Progression to Cocooning

(A) Ignorance of the Word

The victims never had a real understanding of the Scriptures or who the Scriptures represent (though several of them claimed they were born-again Christians before the experience with the mind-bending cultists).

(B) Targeted

The cultists recognize these naive, inexperienced, un-scriptured, church-goers as the types that are ripe for the picking as convert-victims!

(C) Bombarded

The cultists bombard the victim with so much, so fast, that there is no way that the victim can process all that information, and warping follows. The information is not the Word of God; it is Bible verses out of context, re-defined terms, broken up passages all thrown into the faces of the victims.

Is it any wonder the victims are obsessed with what they are taught? The cultists themselves are either religious sociopaths, or have themselves been deceived by their own previous leaders (or both). If they know better than to deceive and lead others astray, they hide it well. The cocooners themselves need deliverance from the powers that bind and enslave them.

Slow Them Down, Check Them Out

Cocooning comes in all forms, from the extreme, mind-twisting cultists to loving, gentle, honest but mistaken Christian leaders. I used to be cocooned. A church that borders somewhere between the moderate and the radical cocooners had enshrouded me with much misinformation. Thank God, I was at least born-again when it all happened. It took the Lord and a revelation of Scripture to start my deliverance. I had been convinced that I had had the Truth, all the Truth, but when the Holy Spirit showed me I was following some erroneous teachings, it turned around my whole concept of Christianity, the Lord, and my relationship with Him.

The Holy Spirit showed me one Scripture, and I checked it out to make sure I wasn't losing my mind, and the freedom I received! The bonds of cocooned-based restrictions are still falling off (and that first revelation came more than a half-century ago). *So I know from experience what I am telling you. You must be careful who and what you follow.* Trust no one enough to accept everything that he or she may tell you without searching the Word of God for confirmation. *If the leader or teacher is taking you too fast, slow him or her down. If he or she does not slow down for you, leave and take your belongings with you! The Father-God is never in a hurry; only the enemy tries to rush things.*

If you find yourself in need of leaving a group and the other person or persons will not allow you to leave, turn to the LORD immediately. Do it while you read this book if necessary. Call on the Name of the Lord. "Jesus, save me, help me and deliver me from my oppressors!"

Look under the headings <u>Identity</u>, Chapter 3, *Book 1* and <u>The Battle</u>, at the end of This Appendix. There you find instructions on what to do and how to do it. Read and start to follow those instructions right now. Remember, II Timothy 1: 7 says "For God has not given us a spirit of fear, but of power and of love and of a sound mind."

Shepherd or Hireling?

I have loved every pastor (shepherd) or Bible teacher I ever had. But since my deliverance, I also checked up on them for errors. If I thought I found an error, I would later find a way to ask about it. They knew I was watching them and they respected me for it. I have learned many things from these questions—and so have they. An honest minister (shepherd) does not mind being checked up on. Only a hireling (one who wants something other than what he/she claims he/she wants) will get upset with your cautious measures.

If that person gets upset at your questions, break free and go your way, finding another group—one that promotes and teaches the Scriptures as they should be. Call 911 if you have to, but leave and take your belongings with you. Check up on every message you hear.

The Battle

> <u>Notice</u>: Because a reader sees the word *you* in the text, there may be a tendency to identify with the content of the message. This must not happen. Therefore in this section, the main topic will not be *you*, but will be the *victim*. In this case the victim is one who has believed a false teaching or is involved with a cult or cultish church.

This is the pattern of the battle from the victim's perspective. When the victim sees that he or she is indeed following error at whatever level—whether a false teaching that might encumber the relationship with the Father-God, or an outrageous lie from the pits of hell—remember that the error is designed to kill, rob and destroy the victim. That is the intent of the enemy when he designed the error in the beginning. It worked in the Garden of Eden and it works today if someone will swallow his lies. So, not only does the lie and its opposing truth need to be revealed, but the spiritual powers that gave credence to the lie need to be bound up, and the destruction the lie did needs to be repaired.

Once the lie is unveiled, it is imperative that the victim be recovered:

> Delivered of the lie and its power;
>
> Healed of the effects of the error for the victim, the victim's relationships and material standing; and
>
> Restored (or made whole) of the damages done.
>
> Act on what you know:
>
> Pray: Come to the Father-God boldly (Hebrews 4:16) in the name of Jesus; Address Him as Father, reaffirming the decision to be His, if need be;
>
> Repent of the error(s) (naming it or them as best you can);
>
> Seek deliverance, healing and restoration, all in Jesus' name.

Bind the enemy and cast out his lies: Focus on the enemy.

Address the enemy (Satan, or demon) and tell him (it) that the victim binds him up IN JESUS' NAME; Still addressing the enemy, tell him to go and to take his lies with him IN JESUS' NAME!

Worship and thank the Father for the victim's deliverance, healing and restoration.

It is likely that the victim will instantly know in his or her spirit that the prayer (in whatever words) and subsequent rebuke of the enemy (in whatever words) have been answered, resulting in the victim's deliverance.

It may be that the enemy wants to linger or return, but by the victim reminding himself or herself and the Lord of this prayer, the enemy's attempts will be thwarted.

It may be a good idea for the victim to write down the terms of the prayer and subsequent rebuke of the enemy, date it, and read it aloud from time to time as needed.

The victim should be careful to study the verses of Scripture that tell who and what he or she is in the Lord and grow thereby, free of the former lies he or she had believed.

Appendix 3

SPECIAL TRANSLATIONAL PROBLEMS

There are a few cases in the Scriptures themselves that deserve a quick comment about what either translators or editors have done with the Word. It is not readily known who is responsible for the additions and other changes to Scripture that are being published in Bibles. Some areas of the Word that man has tampered with are relatively important. Some of these additions are noted by being printed in italics, as well as noted in reference columns or footnotes. Some are not noted and believers must root these problems out for themselves as they study the Word.

Mark 16

The first area is in the last chapter of Mark, verses 9-20. As a matter of fact, some of these Scriptures have already been discussed in this book (Guidepost One, "Breaking Lists," Chapter 1, *Book 1*).

Some Bible editors or translators have rejected these verses as part of the Bible because the oldest manuscripts did not contain these verses. The oldest, the Sinaitic Manuscript, was being used as fuel when it was discovered—thus part of it could have been burned. In the other ancient manuscript (the Vatican), Mark was not complete, but a space for those verses was present, although empty. There remains only conjecture regarding why these verses were not inserted in the text with the rest of Mark.

All the other manuscripts contain these verses and most Bibles have them in their texts in normal font. As you have seen, these verses contain some valuable information for believers. Some of those who reject these verses are doing it, not because of the historical questions of the verses' absence, but because they do not manifest the "signs following."

Romans 8: 1

The next passage that contains relevant altered information is in Romans 8: 1.

> There is therefore now no condemnation to those who are in Christ Jesus.

That's the whole verse; all of it. But many translations have copied the words in the fourth verse and inserted them into the first, making the text read like this:

> There is therefore now no condemnation to those who are in Christ Jesus, who walk not after the flesh, but after the Spirit.

The original manuscripts did not have these ten added words in the first verse, but someone changed the text and its meaning by copying these words from verse four and inserting them in verse one. Some Bibles have these words in their text in normal font; others will have them in italics, as they should be if they are present at all; and some Bibles do not have these words in that verse at all.

You can see the change in the meaning of this passage. It is not known who made the change, but most new editions of the Word have removed the addition.

I John 2: 23

There is an example in I John 2: 23 where nine words are italicized in many Bibles and not in others. The verse reads

> Whoever denies the Son, the same has not the Father; *he who acknowledges the Son has the Father also.*

A statement revealing one truth should not automatically authorize the use of the opposite concept. Usually it may be true, but not always. Does merely acknowledging Jesus mean that the person has the Father in his being? Reading the conversation Jesus had with His disciples in the 14th through 17th Chapters of John, you would believe that this statement in I John is absolutely correct. But does it belong right here? You recall the verse where Jesus said "Not everyone who says, 'Lord, Lord' shall enter into the kingdom of heaven" (Matthew 7: 21). So, in final analysis, do those nine words belong or not?

I John 5: 7

In First John someone inserted a whole verse. In I John 5: 6–8 the text reads like this in one translation:

6 This is He Who came by water and blood, *even* Jesus Christ; not with the water only, but with the water and with the blood. And it is the Spirit Who bears witness, because the Spirit is the truth.

7 For there are three who bear record in heaven, the Father, the Word, and the Holy Spirit; and these three are One.

8 For there are three who bear witness in earth, the Spirit, and the water, and the blood: and the three agree in one.

If Verse 7 is removed as the original manuscripts would have the text read, you would have this:

6 This is He Who came by water and blood, *even* Jesus Christ; not with the water only, but with the water and with the blood.

7 And it is the Spirit Who bears witness, because the Spirit is the truth.

8 For there are three who bear witness, the Spirit, and the water, and the blood: and the three agree in one.

Someone who evidently wanted to reinforce the doctrine of the Trinity inserted this verse (Verse 8 of the first version presented) to make that argument. These added words should also be in italics, but there would also need to be a footnote explaining the shift in versification of the text. Here, too, you can readily see the differences in the text and its meaning.

I John 5: 13

Another change is right next door: I John 5: 13. The words "and that you may believe on the Name of the Son of God" have been added although they are not in the original manuscripts.

These things have I written to you who believe on the name of the Son of God that you may know that you have eternal life.

With the words added, the text would read like this:

These things have I written to you who believe on the name of the Son of God that you may know that you have eternal life, and that you may believe on the name of the Son of God.

It does look a little confusing and redundant, doesn't it? Why were those words added or who added them? Who knows? Who really cares? The main thing is to become aware of these changes and respond accordingly.

Revelation 22: 19

There is another change that you should know about. And if any man shall take away from the words of the book of this prophecy, God shall take away his part from the tree of life, and out of the holy city, which are written in this book.

Some Bibles (KJV) have the "*book of life*" where this translation has "*tree of life.*" A reference should also be in place to point out the differences. Why someone put *book* for *tree* is unknown, but the difference is the subtle point of eternal life, either being presented as in the book or sustained as by the fruit of a tree.

John 5: 3 and 4

Yet another addition is in the account of the healing at the Pool Bethesda. The last few words in Verse 3, "Waiting for the movement of the water" along with the entire 4th Verse were added at some time to explain why the impotent man answered Jesus as he did. "Sir, I have no one to put me in the pool after the water is troubled." (V. 7)

It may be evident that a local superstition was being followed to make the man wait all that time for someone to help him get into the water before someone else entered before he could gain the one-time healing affects of the water.

There is a noted absence of scriptural comment regarding any alleged special healing affects from this practice as portrayed in this passage. It is highly suspect that it was all empty promises based on a local legend of some sort.

There are probably other instances of omissions and additions that occur in the Bible's text. When you find them, pray about them and study them out and respond accordingly.

Rightly Dividing the Word of Truth

Book 2

Reaching Forth

Becoming Fruitful and Victorious in Christ

Introduction

Anyone who has ever played (or observed) a sport has heard the old cliché "The best defense is a good offense." Because *Book 1* portrays an almost exclusively defensive stance, this book will show you some offensive Bible-study/Word-ingesting tactics.

The one problem that most people have and seldom overcome is procrastination. The vast majority make little progress because they will not prepare themselves. Even if you know what to do and how to do it, it isn't enough. You must act on what you know.

Realize this:

YOU CANNOT BUILD A HOUSE

IN A THUNDERSTORM!

The time to build a house is when things are going well. Don't wait until the wind and hail come down on you before you start to put your house up. The time is now!

Don't wait until the enemy is on your collar before you think you should start resisting him. Learn now who and what you are in Christ. When the enemy comes against you (and he will), you can put him to flight without having to call someone else to pray you out of your troubles.

Just as surely as it takes time to build a house, learning who and what you are in Christ takes time, too. Conditioning yourself to stand automatically, instantly and confidently in the face of a demonic attack takes time-consuming preparation.

C. L. Chapman

Take only five minutes a day at first and dedicate that time to finding out who and what you are in Christ, renewing your mind by those absolute truths. Then when something designed from hell comes against you, you can take your place and take charge of the problem. But don't wait! Start now, TODAY!

1

Considering God and His Word

Two Pillars of Truth

Man has inherent limitations. We know this. Everyone does. But because man has inherent limitations, it often escapes man that God does not have any limitations, much less those with which men are encumbered.

Man's lifespan is limited; God's is not. Man's skills are limited; God's are not. Man's power is limited; God's is not. Man can be only one place physically at any time; God is a spirit who can be (and is) everywhere simultaneously. Man's knowledge is limited to what he garners through his senses and what the Father-God lets him know; but God lacks no knowledge in any area or in any form.

Men tend to think that God is like them and shares some lack, shortcoming or fault with them. He doesn't! He doesn't forget. There are no mysteries to Him. He does not believe lies, not those from men nor those from Satan!

Man's imaginations have led to fallacies like the non-sciences of evolution, global warming (the concept that a warming trend that will wipe out life on Earth) and other political and moral (amoral) social movements. There is much debating related to the politics of these movements and the ramifications of them.

Regardless of how men push their ill-conceived notions, God is not impressed by them. Hardly, the Creator made all things for His pleasure and man's benefit. Godless men have said God used the so-called trial and error methods in creation as presented by evolutionists; others hold conceited ideas that mere man at his worst can destroy what God created and said was good. Both concepts are nothing short of blasphemous!

Having established man's tendencies to be somewhat ignorant of God's limitlessness, let's take time to consider only two aspects relating to God, Jehovah, your Heavenly Father as He relates to His own:

His omnipotence (state of being all-powerful)

His omniscience (having all knowledge)

At this point, if you have not already done so, turn to Appendix 1, "Reasons to Study God's Word from Eight Perspectives." It will help you to appreciate the rest of this chapter.

Now, consider a God who speaks, saying "Let there be light," and light appears. Or One who says "Let Earth appear," and Earth appears. That is omnipotence! This is a quality in His Word called immutability: What He says is, regardless! It is the creative power found only in God's Word.

All of creation came as the direct result of God speaking. He spoke everything into existence. It's not only recorded that way in Genesis 1 and 2, but throughout Scripture.

> Psalms 33: 6—11 By the Word of the LORD were the heavens made, and all the host of them by the breath of His mouth. He gathers the waters of the sea together as a heap; He lays the depths in His storehouses. Let all the earth fear the LORD; let all the inhabitants of the world stand in awe of Him. For He spoke, and it was done; He commanded, and it stood fast. The LORD brings the counsel of the nations to naught; He makes the devices of the people of no effect. The counsel of the LORD stands forever, the thoughts of His heart to all generations.

Not only does His Word have creative power, but it stands eternally firm, even when challenged from rebellious factions in His creation. See in Hebrews 11: 3 where God used His unseen Word to bring about the things we see.

> Through faith we understand that the worlds were framed by the Word of God, so that the things that are seen were not made by things that do appear.

And Peter put it this way:

> II Peter 3: 5: For this they are willingly ignorant of, that by the Word of God the heavens were of old . . . .

Besides having creative power, He knows in advance how things will turn out! As a matter of fact, He sees to it! He is omniscient because He is omnipotent.

> Isaiah 46: 9-11: Remember the former things of old, for I am God, and there is none else; I am God and there is none like Me, declaring the end from the beginning, and from ancient times the things that are not yet done, saying, 'My counsel shall stand, and I will do all My pleasure:' calling a ravenous bird from a far country; yea, I have spoken it, I will also bring it to pass; I have purposed it, I will also do it.

What the Father-God wants, He gets! And He is especially proud of His Word. He won't neglect it.

> Jeremiah 1: 12: Then said the LORD to me, "You have well seen, for I watch over My Word to perform it."

He sends His Word like a workman on assignment, and the results become evident! You can readily see that His prophetic words are backed by His ability to see to the completion of the words' assignment. Thus, His omniscience is linked directly to His omnipotence. That should be reassuring to say the least, especially when you realize that He has said so many wonderful things about you!

> Isaiah 55: 11 So does My Word that goes forth out of My mouth: It does not return to Me void, but It accomplishes what I purpose, and It prospers in the thing to which I send It.

The Workman thus assigned works as well *in* people as it does *for* people—those people who believe.

> I Thessalonians 2: 13: For this cause also we thank God without ceasing because, when you received the Word of God that you heard from us, you received it, not as the word of men but as it is in truth, the Word of God that works effectually in you who believe.

And this Word of God is a convincing, righteous, and overpowering message that is working in you!

> Isaiah 45: 23: I have sworn by Myself, the word is gone out of My mouth in righteousness, and shall not return, that to Me every knee shall bow, every tongue shall swear.

The Word of God is so effective that the Father-God cannot lie, even if He wanted to! Thus, can you not see why there is such a battle over what God has said to and about you, a believer?

Plus, God not only said it, but he confirmed it with an oath.

Hebrews 6: 16—18: For men verily swear by the greater, and an oath for confirmation is to them an end of all strife. Wherein God, willing more abundantly to show to the heirs of promise the immutability of His counsel, confirmed it by an oath, that by two immutable things, in which it was impossible for God to lie, we might have a strong consolation, who have fled for refuge to lay hold upon the hope set before us . . . .

The Word of God is alive, and It is alive FOR you, and It is alive IN you. Because of the creative nature and creative power of God's Word, when He says something about you, a believer, it must be so. It is so overpowering that it is mind-boggling. It is so true that it defies logic; it defies appearances; it defies symptoms; it defies feelings and emotions; it defies the lies from hell and all the demon powers that produce and try to enforce them!

Even if you are a believer, if you do not realize this, your life is not much different than that of a non-believer. Furthermore, until you do realize this truth, your life will never be much different than that of a non-believer.

Your life will never rise above the level of your realization of the Father-God's testimony about you! Realize that the Word of God is alive, active and fruitful in your life; that His Word about you is factual, and then you'll start manifesting the promises of God in reality.

2

The Language (Legalese) of Scripture

The Audiences of Scripture

As a reminder, it doesn't take but a brief glance at the Word to realize that the Old Testament is addressed to one group of people and the New Testament is addressed to another. The Old Covenant was cut with Abraham and his seed. The messages and the promises that came after Abraham were addressed to the Children of Israel, servants of God. The messages and the promises that came after Jesus' ministry was finished were addressed to believers, children of God!

One group cannot jump up and take the message or promise of the other group. The Old Testament people were never born-again and New Testament people should not attempt to play with keeping the Law of the Old Testament. Any attempt by one group to embrace the promises or responsibilities of the other group is folly!

The Purpose of Scripture

The reason for the messages and promises of the Father-God is obvious: The Father-God wants to communicate (commune) with His people, on whatever level. It is the difference in the purposes between the Old Testament and the New into which we want to delve.

Because God is all-knowing, He had to know from the very outset of creation that the Old Law would not work. He knew the people could not keep the Law or any relationship with their God based on it. So the purpose of the messages that were brought regarding the Law and His people was to show the people that they could not keep the Law in their own strength or by their own ability. This point established the necessity of grace, which He brought to the people of the New Covenant.

The New Covenant was established to bring grace, not only to the Children of Israel, but to all mankind (John 1: 12–14; John 3: 16). *All* may enter in and *all* may be received by so entering. The blessing to the New Covenant people was to receive Eternal Life—*Zoe*, the very Life of God the Father Himself!

Look briefly at something that many have overlooked in the fact that they have Eternal Life—*Zoe*. *Zoe* is the same life that God the Father dispenses to anyone and everyone who accepts Jesus as Savior and Lord. It is often overlooked that all the characteristics of Zoe in the Father must maintain themselves in the Zoe of the children. It is like DNA—like Father, like sons!

If the natural father of a child has human characteristics, so will the child. When you are born-again by the Holy Spirit in your spirit, the Father's nature (love, joy, peace, and other fruit of the spirit, as well other characteristics) all begin to develop and manifest themselves in you, the new son or daughter.

The only question remaining is <u>when</u>? On the down side, it may be after you have died and gone to be with the Father before these wonderful characteristics develop. But it could also be now! *It all depends on whether you realize who you are in the Lord and what you are in the Lord or not now and respond accordingly!*

The Verbs of Scripture

Since you left school (if you have), you may have forgotten what the parts of speech are all about. Most students didn't care and basic grammar was soon forgotten. Well, in way of review, I want to show you some basic grammar that is very important in the study of Scripture and how it relates to you.

Verbs as Action Words

The definition of a *verb* is *a word that shows action, being or state of being.* The verb most often plays the role of predicate in a sentence, although there are other uses of verbs. For now we want to look at the verb as a predicate—*the action part of the sentence.*

The verbs of Scripture make some important statements that believers have overlooked for a long time, and now you need to learn how these verbs relate to you and how you relate to them. Here is a basic example of a verb showing action:

Jack bounced the ball.

What did Jack do? He *bounced* the ball. The action is *bounced*. Bouncing shows the action that Jack did to the ball.

Now see some of the typical verbs in the Word. Turn to Chapter 20 of Exodus. Starting with Verse 3, look at the verbs in the Ten Commandments (only those that the Israelite were supposed to do or NOT do).

V. 3 Have,	V.12 Honor,
V. 4 Make,	V.13 Murder,
V. 5 Bow, worship,	V.14 Steal,
V. 7 Take (misuse),	V.15 Commit,
V. 8 Remember,	V.16 Bear,
V. 10 Do,	V.17 Covet.

All of these verbs show action, or lack of it when negated with the *NOT*. The whole relationship with the LORD was based on the action (or non-action) of the Israelites—collectively and individually, as they carried out the directions that the LORD gave them.

Thus, the Ten Commandments and the Levitical rituals were the cornerstones of the Old Testament, or Old Covenant. The Old Covenant was based on the laws of the verbs—the dos and don'ts, and the offerings to make up for the failures of keeping the Law's of dos and don'ts. The Apostle Paul called the Old Law the "Law of Sin and Death" (Romans 8: 2). The writer of Hebrews called the works that Jehovah demanded in the Old Testament "Dead Works" (Hebrews 6: 1 and 9: 14).

One of the most revered passages of Scripture is found in Deuteronomy 28. 1–14.

And it shall come to pass, IF you shall hearken diligently to the voice of the LORD your God, to observe and to do all His commandments that I command you this day, that the LORD your God will set you on high above all nations of the earth; And all these blessings will come upon you, and overtake you, IF you shall hearken to the voice of the LORD your God. (Vv. 1 and 2)

The next 12 verses contain more than two dozen wonderful promises for those to whom the promise was given. However, the <u>Ifs</u> make the promise a reward:

No obedience, no promise!

No verb performance, no benefits!

Non-action Verbs

Here is an example of a verb that doesn't show action. It shows *being*.

Jack's ball is round.

There is no action in this sentence, but there is a statement about the nature of Jack's ball. The ball *is* round, the basic nature of nearly every quality ball except a football. We could have said the ball was a certain size, color, hardness, or a variety of other adjectives, but we chose *round*.

The verb is, of course, *is*. *Is* connects *round* to the ball. This type of verb is a linking verb. (See <u>Italics</u>, "Guidepost 5," Chapter 1, *Book 1*, which further explains the linking verbs in the Scriptures.)

Other linking verbs follow:

That boy there *is* Jack.

Jack and the boy are the same and *is* links them together as the same. Both Jack and boy are nouns and the verb links them together. *Is* re-identifies the first noun as the second.

Another example:

The girls *are* pretty.

In this sentence you see a noun on one side and an adjective on the other. The linking verb relates a noun—in this case *girls*—with a characteristic—in this case, being *pretty*. *Are* links the adjective *pretty* to the noun *girls*.

Hebrew and Greek languages do not ordinarily use linking verbs. In the above examples they would have said *"The ball round," "That boy Jack"*, and *"The girls pretty,"* leaving out the *be* verbs. (All of the following are forms of the *be* verb: *am, is, are, was, were, be, being,* and *been*.)

If you have a good Bible, you will notice that many of the *be* verbs are in italics in both Old and New Testaments, which means that the words were added by the translators or editors for clarity to the English readers. In English, every sentence must have a predicate, whether stated or understood. If we saw a Greek or Hebrew sentence that read *"That boy Jack."* we would know something is missing. Thus, to an English reader, the meaning of *"That boy is Jack."* would be lost. So a translator or editor added the linking verb (*is*) to give the sentence clear meaning to the English reader.

Shifting from Old to New

Now turn to Jeremiah 31: 31 through 33 and see the prediction regarding how the LORD would change things.

> Behold, the days come, says the LORD, that I will make [cut] a new covenant with the house of Israel, and with the house of Judah, not according to the covenant that I made [cut] with their fathers in the day *that* I took them by the hand to bring them out of the land of Egypt, which, My covenant, they broke, although I was a husband to them, says the LORD; But this *shall be* the covenant that I will make [cut] with the house of Israel; After those days, says the LORD, I will put My Law in their inward parts, and write it in their hearts, and will be their God, and they shall be My people.

The terms *will be* and *shall be* are linking verbs that state facts as the LORD will see them. The events predicted will come to pass just exactly as He said. (As a matter of fact, they already did and we believers are the evidence of it!) The New Covenant says that the LORD will be His people's God, and that His people would be His people indeed!

Now notice more of how the LORD made the transition from the Old Covenant to the New.

> Hebrews 10: 16-18: This is the covenant that I will make [cut] with them after those days, says the Lord; I will put My laws into their hearts, and in their minds I will write them, and their sins and iniquities I will remember no more.

This New Covenant is called a new and living way (V. 20). In Hebrews 8: 6 it is called a better covenant based on better promises. The reason of the better covenant is because the Lord did everything Himself! *He did it.* Whatever needed doing, *He did it!*

JESUS PERFORMED ALL THE COVENANTAL ACTION VERBS IN THE NEW TESTAMENT, AND AS A RESULT,

WE BELIEVERS BECAME NEW CREATIONS IN CHRIST, CONFIRMED BY NON-ACTION VERBS.

We could not do it, just as the Old Testament saints could not do it. He did it for us! Look at the action verbs in the New Covenant. The Father-God did them (or is now still doing them) through Jesus!

He came,	He loved,	He lived,
He gave,	He became,	He redeemed,
He healed,	He bled,	He died,
He arose,	He left,	He sits,
He intercedes,	He counsels,	He will return,
He re-creates,	He provides,	He directs,
He governs,	He reigns,	He . . . ,

And He will do anything we ask in His Name!

Where shall the list end? Everything the LORD wants us to be, Jesus *was* and therefore *we become*. This is what we call the Substitutionary Work of Christ: He doing for us what we could not do for ourselves!

The Father-God qualified every believer for the benefits contained in Deuteronomy 28: 1–14. Because He did the verbs for us, we can now receive the benefits listed in those verses. And Hebrews shows us that Jesus Christ has perfected us forever (Hebrews 10: 14)!

Therefore, we can receive these and other blessings.

Blessed in the city,

Blessed in the field,

Blessed fruit of the body,

Blessed fruit of the ground, the cattle, the increase of both cattle and sheep,

Blessed basket and store,

Blessed coming in,

Blessed going out,

Our enemies smitten before us, coming at us one way, retreating seven,

Blessed storehouses and all we put our hands to do . . . .

You read the rest of them. This is about half the list. Yet, even as you read this impressive list of blessings, knowing that you have been qualified to receive them by God's grace, realize that these promises are inferior to the New Covenant standards of the believer!

Hebrews tells us that these promises were replaced by better promises (Hebrews 8: 6). Thus, these Old Covenant promises should be below the bare minimum standards of the believer's life!

The Nouns of Scripture

In the New Covenant the whole emphasis changes from action verbs to linking verbs, and to the nouns and adjectives that we are linked to. This is where we find out what happened when God recreated us! The exact order is found in II Corinthians 5: 14–6: 10:

> II Corinthians 5: 14: For the love of Christ constrains us, because we thus judge that, if one died for all, then were all dead; and that He died for all, that they who live should not henceforth live to themselves, but to Him who died for them, and rose again.

He did die, so we should not live to ourselves but for Him.

> II Corinthians 5: 16 Wherefore, henceforth know we no man after the flesh; yea, though we have known Christ after the flesh, yet now henceforth we know Him no more. Therefore, if any man be in Christ, he is a new creation; old things have passed away; behold, all things have become new.

When you were born again, you became a new species—old things are dead and gone!

> II Corinthians 5: 18 And all things are of God, Who has reconciled us to Himself by Jesus Christ, and has given to us the ministry of reconciliation. To wit, that God was in Christ reconciling the world to Himself, not imputing their trespasses to them, and has committed to us the word of reconciliation.

These are God's Word—not mine, and as a believer, you are not only *bound* by them, but you are *blessed and changed [renewed] by them*.

> II Corinthians 5: 20 Now, then, we are ambassadors for Christ, as though God beseeched you by us; we beg you in Christ's stead, be you reconciled to God. For He [God] has made Him [Christ], Who knew no sin, to be sin for us, that we might be made the righteousness of God in Him[Christ].

If you have ever accepted Christ as your Savior, yet seem to be out of tune with your Heavenly Father, His Word is telling you who you really are and what you really are. Regardless of feelings, former teachings, or accusations from guilt, YOU are the righteousness of God in Christ, or God and Jesus both failed in their mission to save you!

It goes without saying that these identity conditions relate to you, your spiritual identity, and not your manner of living. Your manner of living will eventually conform to who and what you are as soon as you realize what and who you are in Christ. Then you will begin to manifest a complete domination of the enemy and his lures! It is then that you walk in the spirit (your new recreated spirit) and not fulfill the lusts of the flesh!

> II Corinthians 6: 1 We, then, as workers together with Him, beseech you also that you receive not the Grace of God in vain (for He says, I have heard you in a time accepted, and in the day of salvation have I helped you; behold, now is the accepted time; behold now is the day of salvation), giving no offense in any thing, that the ministry be not blamed, but in all things commending ourselves as the ministers of God, ...

Notice that the next ten items Paul lists there are all preceded by *in*. They are not verbs, but NOUNS. The words *watchings* and *fastings* are gerunds, verbs used as nouns.

> II Corinthians 6: 4 and 5: But in all things we commend ourselves as ministers of God: in much patience, in tribulations, in needs, in distresses, in stripes, in imprisonments, in tumults, in labors, in sleeplessness, in fastings;

These are the circumstances in which ministers of God find themselves in their service to the Lord:

In patience,	In afflictions,	In necessities,
In distresses,	In imprisonments,	In stripes,
In tumults,	In watchings,	In labors, and
In fastings.		

The next 13 items, which are also all nouns, are the means whereby these ministers of the Lord cope with the adverse circumstances of the first list in which they serve. II Corinthians 6: 6–8:

> By purity, by knowledge, by longsuffering, by kindness, by the Holy Spirit, by sincere love, by the word of truth, by the power of God, by the armor of righteousness on the right hand and on the left, by honor and dishonor, by evil report and good report;

These are the qualities that produce the ministers' victories. They are preceded with *by*.

By pureness,	By knowledge,
By long-suffering,	By kindness,
By the Holy Spirit,	By unfeigned love,
By the Word of Truth,	By the Power of God,
By honor,	By dishonor,
By evil report,	By good report,

By the Armor of Righteousness on the right hand and on the left.

The next list of seven items, are preceded with *as*. Each item is followed by its antithesis. II Corinthians 6: 8–10:

As deceivers, and yet true; as unknown, and yet well-known; as dying, and behold we live; as chastened, and yet not killed; as sorrowful, yet always rejoicing; as poor, yet making many rich; as having nothing, and yet possessing all things.

These are the world's observations and conclusions of these ministers of the Lord as contrasted to the way things are in reality. The world sees one thing, but in fact the ministers of the Lord are not as they seem to the world.

As deceivers,	yet true;
As unknown,	yet well known;
As dying,	behold we live;
As chastened,	and not killed;
As sorrowful,	yet always rejoicing;
As poor,	yet making many rich; and
As having nothing,	yet possessing all things.

Of these last seven items, there is one noun (*deceivers*), one verb (another gerund, *dying)*, and three adjectives (*unknown, sorrowful, poor*), one participle (a verb form used as an adjective—*chastened*) and one participle phrase (*having nothing*). Concerning the gerund, *dying*, it is not something someone in the right mind sets out to do! But even if that were the goal, the outcome would be to live. All of these negative terms are accompanied by their antithesis, a contradicting positive outcome.

What is all this hoopla? The New Covenant is not concerned with what you *do*, but with what you *are*. Look at the list Paul wrote. A believer *is* these things, *has* these things, and *produces* these things by the new creation nature—not by conscious thought. A goat is a goat. Being a goat takes no concentration or effort for that goat. It's that way because it is that way because God created it that way!

But when the Father changes the goat into a sheep, the goat is a sheep and is a sheep forever. Although converted, there is no conscious effort needed for the sheep to be a sheep. The sheep quits browsing like a goat and starts to graze. It produces wool and lambs. Its offspring are sheep, not goats.

> An Aside: When one considers what Scriptures to meditate on and confess, these passages here contain many qualities and victorious characteristics that believers may want to identify with. Take one or two qualities at a time and absorb them through meditation and then confess them before others as you share.

Now, continuing, look at II Peter 1: 3–8:

According as His divine <u>power has given to us all things that pertain to life and godliness</u>, through the knowledge of Him who has called us to glory and virtue; by <u>whom are given to us exceedingly great and precious promises</u>, that by these <u>you might be partakers of the divine nature</u>, <u>having escaped the corruption that is in the world</u> by lust. And beside this, giving all diligence, <u>add to your faith, virtue</u>; and to virtue, <u>knowledge</u>; and to knowledge, <u>temperance</u> [self control]; and to self-control, <u>patience</u>; and to patience, <u>godliness</u>; and to godliness, <u>brotherly kindness</u>; and to brotherly kindness, <u>love</u>.

For if these things be in you, and abound, they make *you that you shall* neither *be* barren nor unfruitful in the knowledge of your Lord Jesus Christ.

> [Remember the "better promises" mentioned in Hebrews 8: 6? In Deuteronomy there is no mention of anything regarding being partakers in the divine nature! Also remember the information already explained about *might* being a subjunctive use of *may*.]

Of these eight things Peter lists here, seven are added to faith, and all eight of them are nouns! There isn't a verb among them and so that there is nothing to do! We can't do them because we can't do a noun!

These things are all fruit—fruit developed from the knowledge and the life (zoe) of the Lord Jesus Christ!

THEY ARE ALL THINGS THAT YOU ARE TO HAVE, PRODUCE AND MANIFEST!!

And Peter said you would have these things by simply adding them to each other because you have already escaped the corruption of the world.

Did you escape? <u>The Word says you did</u>. Did you? <u>You did, or the Word lied</u>! **So start adding!**

Look at this list and trust what the Father has said about you. All else are lies. You have to be what God said you are or He is a failure!

> I Corinthians 6: 19 and 20: What? Know you not that your body is the temple of the Holy Spirit who is in you, whom you have of God, and YOU ARE NOT YOUR OWN? For you are bought with a price; therefore glorify God in your body and in your spirit, which are God's.

You are bought with the price of the precious blood of Jesus (I Peter 1: 19). You are not your own, neither is your will stronger than God's! So you might just as well cooperate with the Lord as you were told in II Corinthians 6: 1: "We, then, as workers together with Him . . . ."

Examine carefully Galatians 5: 16, 22, and 23 where the Word declares that we do not walk in the lusts of the flesh: This I say then, Walk in the spirit, and you shall not fulfill the lusts of the flesh,

> But the fruit of the spirit is love, joy, peace, long-suffering, gentleness, goodness, faith, meekness, temperance [self-control]; against such there is no law.

Paul has here another list of nouns. Notice, spirit is not capitalized because this spirit is obviously not the Holy Spirit. The comparison in context is the fruit of the flesh and the fruit of the recreated spirit. There would be no sense in comparing the operation of the un-regenerated flesh with the fruit of the Holy Spirit.

> Galatians 5: 22, 23 But the fruit of the spirit is Love, Joy, Peace, Longsuffering, Kindness, Goodness, Faithfulness, Meekness, Self-control; Against such there is no law.
>
> 24 And those who are of Christ Jesus have crucified the flesh with the passions and the lusts thereof. If we live in the spirit, let us also walk in the spirit.

Nowhere does the Scripture tell us that the flesh is renewed or regenerated. Regeneration is only in the spirit. The flesh is to be crucified, reckoned dead (Romans 5). To compare the flesh with the Holy Spirit would be like comparing a pair of rusty roller skates with a new jet airliner!

Therefore those things Paul listed as Fruit of the Spirit are fruit that we produce through our re-created spirits as Branches of the Vine. Because these are things produced by our recreated spirits, they are not dead works. Everything we do to either appease God or "Live for Him" are dead works, even though our spirits may be alive and we are functioning out of ignorance or error.

Whatever is not generated by our re-created spirits in Christ will be only dead works!

You ask, "But how can the fruit of the spirit become evident in me?"

What did James say? He said "Be you doers of the Word and not hearers only." (James 1: 22) That is why you are to read the Scriptures aloud to yourself. Faith comes by hearing and hearing by the Word of God (Romans 10: 17). That is doing the word. Doing the Word is first meditation, then maintaining a consistent positive confession of these wonderful things that God has said to and about you. That is bringing the fruit to bear. Meditation and confession is doing the word.

Learn the other several hundred wonderful things God says about you as a believer, cooperate with the Father, and produce who and what you are, while still being free of the dogmas of the verbs.

3

Laying Hold on Eternal Life!

While on the one hand some people identify the Father-God with their own limitations, some people believe that because God is omnipotent and omniscience that He does everything that needs to be done for them. While this is true on one hand, that fact does not preclude believers from their responsibilities in life on earth.

Therefore the folks who dodge behind their responsibilities often become fatalistic: "What will be, will be!" They become lax and do not engage the Word in their lives and they become ineffective and fruitless. Eventually they believe and practice only the first four words of Ephesians 6: 12: "For we wrestle not."

It is indeed a shame when Christians allow Satan and his cronies to rob, kill, and destroy them. In *Book 1* you saw that you need to fight back, and in *Book 2* you will see how to fight back! "Resist the Devil and he will flee from you" (James 4: 7). Indeed!!

Identity

Because the Bible is the Sword of the Spirit—the Word of God—it is of its own nature, a weapon. Having already set the stage with what to do and what not to do with that weapon, the only thing left to do is to condition the swordsperson—you, the believer. That conditioning will finish you out as the all-conquering victor that you were recreated to be!

So, who are you? If you only think you know who you are, try this question: How can you come before the Father-God unless you know Him as your Father? If you really know who you are, you can come to Him knowing you are His son or daughter? There will be no fear, timidity or condemnation—also known as inferiority!

Let's rephrase the question: Who are you in the Lord? Every person is either a Christian or non-Christian—believer or non-believer—there are no half-and-half's.

You are 100% of something. That means you are 0% anything else. You and the Father alone know the answer regarding who you are. The only factor that determines the answer is your relationship with Jesus Christ.

> He who has the Son [Christ] has life; and he who has not the Son of God has not life (I John 5: 12).

If you have a quality Bible, you have cross-references from this verse that will show you where other Scriptures say the same thing over and over again. John records emphatically that Jesus is the only way to the Father.

> John 14:6: Jesus said to him, "I am the Way, the Truth, and the Life; no man comes to the Father but by Me."

And Jesus said it again in John: 10: 7—10:

> Then said Jesus to them again, "Verily, verily, I say to you, <u>I am the door of the sheep</u>. All that ever came before Me are thieves and robbers; but the sheep did not hear them. I am the Door; <u>by Me if any man enter in, he shall be saved, and shall go in and out, and find pasture</u>. The thief comes not but to steal, and to kill, and to destroy; <u>I am come that they might have life, and that they might have it more abundantly</u>."

Luke also documents that Jesus is the only means of salvation in Acts 4: 12.

So having put aside all sciences, rituals, memberships, ordinances and other religious functions, if you have never placed your trust in Jesus Christ as your own Savior, do it NOW. It isn't hard; and it doesn't take long. Make a conscious decision to follow the Lord wherever He may lead you as He lives within you. (See <u>Audience and Purpose</u>, "Introduction," *Book 1.*)

Regardless of when you accepted Christ as your own Savior, know this: When you accepted the invitation of Christ to come into your life, you became a son or daughter of your Heavenly Father.

Remember that! As you make your way through the remainder of this composition, you will see more details of your identity in Jesus.

Meditation

Read John 3:16:

> For God so loved the world that He gave His only begotten Son, that whoever believes in Him should not perish, but have everlasting life."

Now, read it again—aloud. And one more time, read it aloud.

Now read John 3:16 again, substituting *your name, I* or *me* for the words *the world* and *whoever*. Read it aloud that way slowly four or five times.

> "For God so loved *me* that He gave His only begotten Son, so that [because] *I* believe in Him, *I* shall not perish, but have everlasting life."

Let the full implication of what that verse is saying to and about you soak in. Hearing yourself (or anyone else, as long as it is audible) read the Word reinforces the Word into your consciousness.

"Faith comes by hearing, and hearing by the Word of God" (Romans 10: 17).

The whole idea is to renew your mind so that the Word has first place in your thoughts, all without conscious effort. Because you will have fed your spirit in such a way, your spirit becomes dominant in our walk in life.

Do other Scriptures the same way as we come to them—one at a time, read them aloud several times, and appropriate them for yourself by putting *your name, I,* or *me* in the key places.

This procedure is called *meditation,* and it leads to what the New Testament calls *"renewing the mind"* (Romans 12: 1–3). Several times the Lord told His people to meditate and what the results would be.

Look at Joshua 1: 8 in the Old Testament even:

> This book of the law shall not depart out of your mouth; but you shall meditate therein day and night, that you may observe to do according to all that is written therein: for then you shall make your way prosperous, and then you shall have good success.

Also read Proverbs 4: 20–22; and Psalm 19: 7–11 and 14. Refer to Appendix 4 for a more comprehensive (yet not conclusive) list of Scripture references on this topic and others that will edify you.

A wonderful place for starting meditation is II Corinthians 5: 17 and 21:

> Therefore if any man be in Christ, he is a new creation; old things have passed away; behold all things have become new.

Read it several times. Re-read it now with appropriations:

"Therefore if [because] *I* am in Christ, *I am* a new creation; old things have passed away; behold *I and all of my* things have become new."

Because you have accepted Christ as your Savior, you can drop the *if* clause: "*I* am a new creation; old things have passed away; behold I have become new."

Now try Verse 21:

"For He [God] has made Him [Jesus], who knew no sin, to be sin for us, that we might be the righteousness of God in Him."

Read it aloud four or five times, then appropriate:

"For God has made Jesus, who knew no sin, to be sin for *me,* that *I* would* be the righteousness of God in Him."

(*See <u>Might</u>, Chapter 3, *Book 1.*)

As you read, comprehend what you are reading; do not merely mouth the words.

DO NOT SET OUT TO MEMORIZE THESE OR ANY OTHER MEDITATION VERSES!!! Read them aloud to yourself concentrating on the meaning! They hold vital truths for you. Know the words apply to you, especially after you appropriate them. Those Words are alive and they will make your mind (or soul) renewed as you absorb their meaning into your spirit. (See <u>Might</u>, Chapter 3 of *Book 1.*)

What you are doing is making the spiritual message and life of God's Word part of your psychological makeup through your recreated spirit. You are renewing your mind by the work of the Holy Spirit by the Word of your Heavenly Father by the Son, the Living Word alive in you.

These two verses in II Corinthians 5, along with the verses between them, hold absolutely essential information for Christians who want to manifest their victory in life. If you do not know that you are the righteousness of God in Christ, Satan can rob you of every prayer you pray and of the fellowship with the Father that Jesus died to obtain for you. If you learn nothing else in this book, realize this:

AS A BELIEVER, YOU ARE THE
RIGHTEOUSNESS OF GOD IN CHRIST.

The righteousness of God is more than mere freedom from the guilt of sin.

It is son-ship (John 1: 12, 13)!

It is being one with Christ as a member of His Body (I Corinthians 6: 17; 10: 17; 12: 27)!

It is being an heir of God, and joint heir with Christ (Romans 8: 17).

It is the Father-God seeing you just like He sees Jesus. (Romans 8: 29; Ephesians 1: 15–2: 10)

It is the Life of the Father-God in you (II Peter 1: 3, 4; I John 4: 17; John 14: 12—14).

There are more identity Scriptures in Appendix 4.

These facts are not based on what you have done or what you have not done. God did it all just for you. He did it through Christ and now it is a fact (John 1: 12)! Is it any wonder the writer of Hebrews said the New Covenant has better promises than the Old (Hebrews 8: 6)? It has, and every promise is yours, and they are yours to use and enjoy from now on.

Here is another verse for you to meditate on (already transposed for you):

John 14: 12, 13 . . . "I believe in Him [Christ], *therefore*, the works that He did I shall do also; and greater works than these I shall do because He went to Our Father. And whatever I shall ask in Jesus' name, that He will do, so that the Father may be glorified in the Son. If I shall ask anything in His name, He will do it."

Soon you will be meditating on this verse like this:

"I believe in Jesus, and I do the greater works than He did because He went to the Father to arrange it; I can ask anything in His name and He will do it for me so that the Father will be glorified in the Son. I can ask anything in His name and He will do it."

The Mechanics of Meditation

As alluded to in *Book 1*, the make-up of man is threefold—spirit, soul (or mind) and body. The natural man—the one who does not know the Lord as personal Savior—is sold under sin and his spirit is unknown to him except for the innate longing to be born again.

Therefore he is bound to walk, talk and live habitually in only two of his three domains. If we exclude his physical realm, that means the unsaved person is limited to living in the realm of his soul, or his mind. Most people live in this realm whether they know the Lord as Savior or not. Even though many people know the Lord as Savior, they do not progress or develop enough spiritually to be able to distinguish what is spiritual and what is not.

These spiritually undeveloped or under-developed people, whether believers or not, live strictly in the physical realm and all they know in life is what their senses tell them. This realm is referred to as the "flesh" in the Scriptures. They only see with their eyes, hear with their ears, taste with their mouths, smell with their noses, feel tactically with their body parts, and feel with their human emotions. Some people think the emotions are their spirits, but they are sadly mistaken.

When a person accepts Christ as personal Savior, that person's spirit takes on the life of God (zoe). That life, although all powerful in the Lord, is often dormant as far as the believer is concerned. That dormancy is caused by neglect—like a new-born baby that is unattended.

Again, the believer is like a new-born baby in his or her needs and the food that the new-born believer needs is the Word of God. Because the believer received his or her new life by the Word of God, it is the Word of God that nourishes that new-born spirit.

Peter said it this way (I Peter 1: 22–25):

> Since you have purified your souls in obeying the truth through the spirit in sincere love of the brethren, love one another fervently with a pure heart, having been born again, not of corruptible seed but incorruptible, through the Word of God that lives and abides forever, because "All flesh is as grass, and all the glory of man as the flower of the grass. The grass withers, and its flower falls away, but the word of the Lord endures forever."

Now this is the word that by the gospel was preached to you. You have been born-again by the eternal Word of God and it is that Word that nourishes you now in your recreated spirit. Peter goes on to say this in I Peter 2: 1–3:

> Therefore, laying aside all malice, all guile, hypocrisy, envy, and all evil speaking, as newborn babes, desire the pure milk of the word, that you may grow thereby, if indeed you have tasted that the Lord is gracious.

Meditation is the way to nourish your spirit on the Word of God. Here is the typical end result of a well nourished spirit. Look in the Old Testament at Elisha (II Kings 5:8—23). In a war between Israel and Syria, Elisha kept the king of Israel informed regarding what the king of Syria was up to.

After several episodes of being found out, the king of Syria sought the spies who were ratting him out. It was told to him that it was Elisha who was informing on him. The king of Syria found out where Elisha was and sent his army there to capture him—or maybe even kill him.

When one of Elisha's servants woke up one morning and saw the Syrian army posted all around the city where Elisha lived (Dothan), he hit the panic button. "Alas, master, what will we do!" he cried.

You see, the servant is like the flesh—seeing, hearing, tasting, smelling, feeling tactically and becoming emotional, gripped by fear, fret and consternation. "What are we going to have to do? Die?"

Elisha, typical of the recreated spirit in a believer, banished the servant's fear. "Do not fear because there are more for us than there are with them." Then he prayed, "Lord, I pray, open the young man's eyes that he may see."

The Lord indeed opened the young man's eyes and he saw! What did he see? He saw that the hills were alive—not the sound of music—but with horses and chariots of fire all around Dothan!

In the Old Testament when Elisha said, "There are more of us than there are of them," a New Testament believer would say, "Greater is He who is in me than he who is in the world." It's the same strategy!

You may read the rest of the account of Elisha yourself. But the picture is like a believer who has his spirit well fed on the Word. It is not that a problem does not exist; it is that the believer sees past the problem to its resolution. You see not only the enemy's activities and his army that is against you, but you see how outnumbered and overpowered they are!

A more up-to-date example would be the account of Paul, a prisoner of Rome and under the guard of a Roman soldier as they traveled to Rome for Paul's hearing before Caesar. The complete episode is recorded in the 27th Chapter of Acts.

Paul was forewarned in his spirit that it was not wise to proceed toward Rome because of the dangerous traveling season. Paul warned them and was specific that property would be lost and maybe even lives if they left at that particular time. The centurion was more convinced by the sailors than by Paul, so they proceeded.

On the way, they were taken over by a storm that lasted days— driving the ship where they did not necessarily want to go. Here is a summary of the event as recorded in Acts 27: 20–44:

> After several days without eating, hope was gone. Then Paul stood up among them and reminded them that he had warned them. Then he encouraged them that there would be no loss of life, but

only the ship would be lost. He told them he knew this because an angel had stood by him and told him so.

On the 14th night, as they were driven up and down in the Adriatic Sea, about midnight they came near an island. Fearing running aground on the rocks, they dropped four anchors, and prayed for day to come.

Some sailors tried to escape from the ship and they let a skiff down into the sea. Paul told the centurion who was delivering him to Caesar that is these men left the ship, they cannot be saved. Then the soldiers cut away the ropes to the skiff and let it fall off.

As day approached, Paul urged them and again promised that everyone would be all right. He took some food, gave thanks to God in the presence of them all; and he ate. They joined him.

In all there were 276 persons on the ship. So when they had eaten, they lightened the ship and threw the wheat into the sea.

They did not recognize the land; but they saw a bay with a beach, onto which they tried to run the ship. They let go the anchors, loosed the rudder ropes, hoisted the mainsail and made for shore. They struck a place where two currents met, the ship ran aground, the prow stuck fast and remained immovable. The stern was broken up by the waves.

Now the soldiers' plan was to kill the prisoners, so none would escape, but the centurion, wanting to save Paul, kept them from doing it. He commanded those who could swim to jump overboard first and get to land, and the rest would follow on boards or broken pieces of the ship. They all escaped safely to land with no loss of life.

Paul was on top of the situation because he knew who he was and what he was in the Lord. Everyone should be so openly victorious! These things are for every believer today as well as for Paul then! Jesus promised that greater things than He had done, we would do because He was going to see to it (John 14: 12)!

You cannot fail; you cannot be overcome! You are more than a conqueror (Romans 8: 37) and greater is He who lives within you that he who is in the world (I John 4: 4). These are only three of the many Scriptures that prove who and what you are spiritually and it is these by which you are to nourish your spirit. Meditation is the way to do it!

Confession

The twin of meditation, or renewing your mind, is <u>confession</u>. Confession, the way it is used here, is not what many people think of when they hear the word *confession*. Usually a confession relates to wrongdoing(s) and someone owning up to it or them.

Confession (or profession) is the actual use of the Word of God as the Sword of the Spirit. Once your mind has grasped the Word in all its truth and power, your mind does not operate like it used to. Confession is the speaking of the problem's solution, or speaking to the problem to the problem's elimination!

If a problem arose before your mind was renewed, you saw it as it was—a problem. After your mind is renewed, you automatically look past the same situation to the solution as the Lord would see it according to His Word—all in an instant, all automatically!

When your mouth responds to that solution with positive thoughts and positive words, that's confession!

But all this new insight and understanding is of little value if it is not applied to the problem. It does no good to have a car in the garage if you need to go somewhere. You must get the car out of the garage in order to use it. This is the role of confession—using the Word. Your application of positive words from the Word that you have meditated on concerning a situation rectifies the problem.

Jesus did it continually in His ministry on Earth. He always maintained a confession of Who and What He was, and what He would be, as well as what He could do and have. He always maintained His sights on His goal and He spoke of it to His disciples. He does it still. Read Revelation 1: 9–16. While John was in the spirit on the Lord's Day, he saw Jesus and described Him, "Out of His mouth went a sharp two-edged sword" (verse 16). Jesus came forth saying, in this case, not only who He was, but how things were and would be. We are to maintain a like testimony; we are to say who and what we are in the Lord.

Mark 11: 22–24 relates that Jesus had cursed a fruitless fig tree. The next day Peter noticed that the tree had died from the roots upward. (This is the opposite manner of a normal death to a plant. The top usually has the evidence of death first.)

And Jesus answering said to them, "<u>Have faith in God</u>. For verily I say to you, that <u>whoever shall say to this mountain, 'Be you removed</u>, and be you cast into the sea,' and <u>shall not doubt</u> in <u>his heart</u>, but shall believe that those things that he says shall come to pass; **he shall have what he says.** Therefore I say to you, 'What things you desire, when you pray, believe that you receive them, and you shall have them.'"

First, He gave the command, "Have faith in God."

Second, He said to speak to the problem. He did not say to "ask the problem" or to ask God to take care of the problem. He said for you to speak to the problem!

Third came the condition: Have no doubt in your heart, but believe. It is confession that banishes doubt!

Fourth was the outcome: Possess what was said!

Paul put down the scriptural cornerstone for confession when he told Philemon that the communication of his faith would become effectual when he "acknowledged what all the good things of the Lord were in him" (verse 6):

That the communication of your faith may become effectual by the acknowledging of every good thing that is in you in Christ Jesus.

So it is with you. Acknowledge the good things that are in you by Christ Jesus:

"I AM the righteousness of God in Christ." (II Corinthians 5: 21)

I CAN DO all things in Christ, who is my strength." (Philippians 4: 13)

"The Father-God DOES MEET all my needs according to His riches in Glory by Christ Jesus." (Philippians 4: 19)

"I AM more than a conqueror." (Romans 8: 37)

Not only do we know these things, but we say these things. We have the sharp two-edged sword coming out of our mouths. This is what makes the enemy retreat.

We take charge of our lives rather than allowing circumstance to dictate the terms of our existence.

We declare things that are not as though they are and they become just as God did when He was dealing with Abraham (Romans 4: 17). That is what we as believers seated with Christ have been appointed to do! But we must do it! We must declare it, and continue to declare it, never failing to declare it—*even when it seems to be impossible!!*

When Jesus was hanging on the cross, did He ever say He was a failure, or not the Son of God? NO!! NEVER!! He knew Who He was, and He always said so!

SO DO WE!! Even in the face of certain death and apparent defeat, Jesus did not back off His confession. And neither can we back off of our confession. The warfare is won or lost in what we say because what we say indicates what is in our hearts—defeat or victory! <u>Out of the abundance of the heart man speaks</u>! (Matthew 12: 34 and Luke 6: 45).

Even if you do not feel like confessing what God says about you and your situation, confess it anyway and see what you confess come to pass (Mark 11: 22—24). God does not lie, thus *when you say what He says even in the face of a doubtful situation, the situation must change to conform to God's Word.*

Make the Word of God, not only your confession, but make it your prayer. Pray the Word of God in all its creative ability. Find Scriptures that fulfill your needs and apply them to your situation in both confession and prayer.

If you are ill, see I Peter 2: 24:

Who His own self bore our sins in His own body on the tree, that we, being dead to sins, should live to righteousness; by whose stripes you were healed.

The logic is this: If Jesus bore the stripes for your healing, how can you be sick? Now claim the promise. "Heavenly Father, I claim the promise of my body, my mind and my spirit being healed by the stripes of Jesus and I thank You for my healing. I know it's already done because the Word says so. Now, I speak to the illness or disease in my body and command it to leave in Jesus' name and I speak to my body, mind, and spirit to receive the healing provided for you by Jesus. In Jesus' name, Amen."

<u>Notice</u>: Do not ask the disease or illness to leave. TELL IT!

Do not ask the body to respond to your healing. TELL IT!

Because you are already healed by the stripes of Jesus, the sickness is not your sickness and it must go! If you say you have it, then it is yours. Never admit ownership of a problem because that is a negative confession. Say instead, "I bind up the . . . (ailment, headache, toothache, etc.) . . . in Jesus' name, and I thank You Father, for my healing." Know that the enemy is trespassing to afflict you and he and his must go when you tell them to in Jesus' name.

Look at Isaiah 53: 5 where the Scriptures predict the healing stripes of Jesus.

> But He was wounded for our transgressions, He was bruised for our iniquities; the chastisement of our peace was upon Him; and with His stripes we are healed.

Or maybe your needs are material. Philippians 4: 19:

> But my God shall supply all your need according to His riches in glory by Christ Jesus.

You may have a bill due and your bank account is empty. Do not worry. Give the problem to the Father. "Heavenly Father, you know that I need to pay so-and-so. You promised to supply my need. I speak to money to come in so I can pay . . . . In Jesus' name. I thank You, Father, for supplying . . . (so and so) . . . according to your riches in glory by Christ Jesus. In Jesus' name, Amen."

Leave it there and when you think of the bill you owe, thank the Father for supplying your need and soon it will manifest itself. Don't try to figure out how He will do it or where the wherewithal will come from. Just trust Him to supply your need. And don't express any doubt regarding the problem. Consider it settled and it will be.

Another most wonderful and almost universal prayer and confession Scripture is the 23rd Psalm, especially Verse 1:

The LORD is my Shepherd; I shall not want.

I shall not want for *food*.

I shall not want for *shelter*.

I shall not want for *health*.

I shall not want for *a new tire for the car*.

Whatever your need may be, apply it there and place it as a prayer before the Father and as confession before the world at large and before the enemy.

Make a confession of possession after prayer, and He will manifest it to you. Then, as you wait, indeed, if you have to wait, you have a base in writing for thanksgiving and holding fast to your confidence.

> Hebrews 10: 35: Cast not away, therefore, your confidence, which has great recompense of reward. For you have need of patience that, after you have done the will of God, you might receive the promise.

Remember, you did the will of God when you received Jesus Christ as your Savior. Therefore, the reception of the promise is a certainty instead of a *maybe*. (See <u>Might</u>, Chapter 3, *Book 1*)

WARNING:
The Negative Confession

A double-minded person is discussed in the First Chapter of James:

> If any man lack wisdom, let him ask of God, Who gives to all men liberally, and doesn't upbraid, and it shall be given him. But <u>let him ask in faith, nothing wavering</u>. For he who wavers is like a wave of the sea, driven with the wind and tossed. For let not that man think that he shall receive anything of the Lord. <u>A double-minded man is unstable in all his ways.</u> (Vv. 5–8)

Notice the terms *nothing wavering*. That means when you ask something of your Heavenly Father, you immediately acknowledge your reception of the thing requested whether you see it with your eyes or not. Simply know that you have whatever it is you need.

Read carefully Mark 4: 1–20. Notice that the parable of the sower refers to one who plants, not seeds of wheat or some other crop, but, as the parable indicates, the Word. You sow the Word by praying the Word. Make the Word of God your prayer. Make the Word of God your meditation and confession. The Word brings things to pass in your life as you plant it as you walk through life. After you plant the Word, allow time to let the Word germinate and bring forth its fruit.

Other aspects of James' warning of being double-minded include these waverings:

1. Saying one thing and doing another; (This would include the slip up of admitting ownership of the problem.)

2. Changing what you say to another outcome than what you already established in prayer or confession;

3. Continually dig up your prayer seed to replant;

4. Expressing doubt about the Father's willingness or ability to do for you what needs to be done.

5. The worst one of all: Displaying False Humility!

For instance, if you have a need and you ask the Father for the supply of whatever you need, do not go to someone else and ask them for it. <u>If</u>

you need money, don't ask the Father for it and then go to the bank. If you intend to go to the bank, and you have doubts about the loan, you may ask the Father to see to it. But asking the Father for it first, then turning to the arm of flesh is not honoring the Father. If you ask the Father to bless you with a loan from the bank, and then say He probably won't bless you in the loan, that is also negative confession.

If you have the need of a certain amount of money, say $1000 and you start out asking for the $1000 and as you proceed you start increasing the amount because you see that there are other opportunities where more money could be used. Make up your mind and go to that amount and stick with it!

If you plant a garden, you don't break up the same soil again the next day and replant it. If you seeded the same spot every day, you would never harvest a crop. Re-praying the same prayers again after you have given the matter to the Father is breaking up the soil to re-plant the prayer-seeds. Planting additional or different seeds also breaks up the already planted seeds.

Once you give something to the Father, leave it with Him and allow Him to do whatever is needed to answer your prayer. Go ahead and thank Him for the answer (watering the seeds), even if you don't see it.

DO NOT KEEP TALKING OF THE MATTER AS IF YOU NEVER ASKED THE FATHER TO TAKE CARE OF IT!

The problem, if spoken of, should be in past tense.

Another way to be double-minded is to allow yourself to say that the Father either won't or can't answer your prayer. This is the reason why we need to understand the authority and power (immutability) of His Word. When the Father speaks, things happen! That is how all that we see on Earth exists—by His having spoken His Word.

That is why we should pray the Word of God as much as we know how. If we have the Word on our prayer lips, we have a place to look and find confirmation that the Father is indeed able and willing to answer our prayers. Then we will be less tempted to allow negative words to come out of our mouths.

If the Father has your problem, it is then His problem! As long as you either take it back by your expression of doubt as displayed by re-praying the same prayer or by voicing your skepticism of his ability or willingness to do for you, you are handicapping the Father to perform His Word in and for you.

Another type of problem may then arise due to the person's response to the Word of God. A person will realize that the Word of God is immutable and he or she will accept the message and its benefits as real. But instead of rejoicing over the promises (whether written in His Word or Words of Wisdom, Knowledge or Prophecy) and living in gratitude for the message(s) and their meaning, they abuse their walk with the Lord. They may rely so heavily on the promise that they forget the Lord Himself and quit living before Him responsibly—wisely.

For instance, when Paul wrote that the Lord would supply all your needs according to His riches in glory by Christ Jesus (Philippians 4: 19), a person could take that promise for granted and when the wherewithal comes to fulfill the need, they squander it on other things. They assume that the promise overrides their actions and they continue to look forward for something that the Father has already given.

In other words, because a promise from the Lord is made and received, there is no reason for that person to live irresponsibly, unintelligently or unwisely! A promise does not automatically produce or engender a license to be careless or irresponsible.

There is the account of Jesus and Peter and the Temple-tax (Matthew 17: 24–27).

> And when they [Jesus and the disciples] had come to Capernaum, . . . not your teacher pay the half-shekel?"
>
> Peter said, "Yes."
>
> And when he came into the house, Jesus spoke first to him, saying, "What do you think, Simon? The kings of the earth, from whom do they receive toll or tribute; from their sons, or from strangers?"
>
> And Peter said, "From strangers."
>
> Jesus said to him, "Therefore the sons are free. But, lest we cause them to stumble, you go to the sea, and cast a hook, and take up the fish that first comes up; and when you have opened his mouth, you shall find a shekel. Take it and give it to them for Me and you."

Evidently Peter did as he was told. The miracle of supply was granted and the Lord dealt with it to supply the need that was before them. As believers, we are as diligent to follow sound responsibility when the Father-God supplies us with the wherewithal to meet our needs.

231

Regarding the plight of most people, believers or not, <u>false humility</u> <u>is a robbing spirit that engenders defeat, lack, depression, panic and every</u> <u>other foul attitude that the enemy can get to embrace it!</u>

It is absolutely beneath words what many believing Christians do to themselves by this *false humility.* People who have accepted Christ as Savior are new creations in Christ (II Corinthians 5: 17); they are members of His very Body (I Corinthians 6: 17; 10: 17 and 12: 27); they are one spirit with the Lord (John 14: 20) and there are literally dozens of wonderful things that can be said of a believer regarding who he or she is in the Lord. (See Appendix 4).

For that person to insult himself, herself and the Lord's Substitutionary Work in that person's re-creation by saying something that relates them to being yet unsaved, unworthy, insignificant, or some other vile insult to who and what the Father-God created in him or her as a believer is below decent expression in words!

<u>False humility is a diabolical force</u>—a demon or stronghold—that sets out to rob, kill and destroy by means of one's own mouth! Many clichés have False Humility as a source and none should ever be repeated—not even in jest! One of the main sources for this vileness is the acceptance of the myth of the believer's dual-nature. (See <u>Two Natures</u>, Guidepost 7, Chapter 1, *Book 1.*)

Negative Voices Outside

Still another question may arise: Does the music you listen to or sing contradict the Written Word? It doesn't matter the style of the music you like, but the lyrics are often contrary to what the Lord says in His Word about you and your situation. Whether the music is so-called Christian music or not, listen to the words and if they are not what you want in your life, do not sing them, quote them, think them or repeat them.

Do not re-pray the same prayer again after once giving the problem to the Lord.

> Do not express a doubt regarding God's ability or willingness to do His Word in and for you, not even while you sing a so-called Christian song.
>
> Do not assume a freedom from responsibility based on a promise from the Father.
>
> Do not listen to messages—even in music—that contradict the Word of God.

The Lord's promise of things requested is sure:

If you abide in Me and My words abide in you, you shall ask what you will, and it shall be done to you. In this is My Father glorified, that you bear much fruit, so shall you be My disciples. (John 15: 7, 8)

You have the promises in the Scriptures to stand on. Stand on them firmly! Do not allow doubtful words to come out of your mouth regardless of what things look like or how you feel! It's insulting to the Lord for someone to ask Him for something and then say He didn't give it. It shows doubt and reinforces what the enemy is doing to you—robbing you. Always maintain what God's Word says about you and your situation. Always!

Allow nothing to contradict or corrupt His Word to you. Continue to plant the Word inside you by meditation and reinforce that meditation with a consistent positive confession.

4

Going on the Offense

The Holy Spirit and His Role

The Scriptures show you that you are a new creation in Christ (II Corinthians 5: 17) and that you are the righteousness of God in Christ (II Corinthians 5: 21). These two verses are the bases where many more promises form a network of blessings for believers.

Here is a glance at a few of the blessings the Word has for you as a believer:

> You are more then a conqueror (Romans 8: 37);
>
> You can do anything you need to do by your strength in Christ (Philippians 4: 13);
>
> You can have anything you need (Romans 8: 32; Philippians 4: 19);
>
> Your answers to your prayers are guaranteed (John 14: 13);
>
> You have your diseases healed by His stripes (I Peter 2: 24).

These are only a few of these sorts of promises. Appendix 4 has many more.

Even if you are fully aware of who and what you are in Christ, you still need the power or authority to use that identity and those capabilities. In Acts 1: 7 and 8, Jesus told His followers that it was not for them to know the times or the seasons that were under the Father's power.

> But you shall receive power after the Holy Spirit comes upon you; and you shall be witnesses to Me both in Jerusalem, all Judea, Samaria, and the uttermost part of the earth.

Jesus said that you shall be witnesses to Him after you receive the power of the Holy Spirit. He said this after He had paid the full price for your redemption at Calvary. In other words, He was speaking to His immediate followers (Christians) before His ascension.

You may ask, "Does this Scripture apply to 21st Century Christians?"

Responding to that question, first, look at the wording. He said to the "uttermost," which means *to the farthest*—some lands and peoples yet undiscovered when He said it. If He had meant for just those folks there to witness for Him in the uttermost part of the earth, they would have had a much longer lifespan. So His declaration had to span several generations. Otherwise modern day people would never hear the Word. Yet many did. And many still do!

Look what Peter said in the next point! Peter said of the gift of the Holy Spirit,

> For the promise is to you [the immediate crowd], and to your children, and to all those who are far off, even to as many as the Lord, our God, shall call (Acts 2: 38, 39).

There is no one any farther away from that time and place than we of the Twenty first Century. We are not only geographically removed (not being in Jerusalem), but chronologically distanced as well.

Then we have the divine arrangement to reinforce the previous precepts. In I Corinthians 12: 12 and 13, Paul wrote about the spiritual gifts. He said the Holy Spirit distributes the operations of the gifts of the Holy Spirit to all of us.

> For as the Body is one, and has many members, and all the members of that one Body, being many, are one Body, so also is Christ. For by one Spirit were we all baptized into one Body, whether we be Jews or Greeks, whether we be bond or free; we have all been made to drink into one Spirit.

This means that the empowering of the Holy Spirit is for every believer in all time.

Finally, John the Baptist prophesied that Jesus would baptize with the Holy Spirit and fire (Matthew 3: 11). When John Baptist saw Jesus coming to him, he said he needed to be baptized by Jesus, but Jesus forbade it—reserving the privilege for Christians.

These last two references present two members of the Godhead, Jesus and the Holy Spirit, cross-baptizing believers. That is the Holy Spirit baptizing the lost into the Body of Christ, thus saving them, and Jesus baptizing believers in the Holy Spirit, thus anointing and empowering them.

When you called upon the Lord for salvation—when you first asked Jesus to take charge of your life, the Holy Spirit made you a member of the Body of Christ. At that very instant He did it. At that same instant the Holy Spirit came into your being, too—as an indwelling agent.

But the indwelling agent and the baptism in the Holy Spirit are different. The indwelling agent is One who stabilizes, keeps, and comforts through the recreated spirit (John 14: 16, 17). It is the baptism in the Holy Spirit that anoints, thus empowering you through your recreated spirit and His anointed presence for bearing the fruit of righteousness (Acts 1: 8).

These Scriptures show that Jesus wants to baptize you in the Holy Spirit if you have not already been baptized in the Holy Spirit. There are two extremes people tend to go into before they experience the baptism into the Holy Spirit. Some have an anxious frenzy of eagerness in anticipation, and others seem indifferent, saying, "If He wants to baptize me, He knows where to find me."

Indifference

Both of these extremes cause difficulties. Let's examine indifference first. How did you receive Christ as your Savior? Did you say, "He can save me if He wants to—He knows where to find me."?

No, you called on Him and He did what He promised. Likewise, when you ask Him to baptize you in the Holy Spirit, He will do that, too—simply and just as wonderfully as He saved you.

Anticipation

If the other extreme is your problem, you have no need of eagerness, fear, or any other emotion. It is fitting to be eager enough to want to experience what the Lord has for you—but not to the point of causing a tightness or anxiety. Be anxious for nothing, He will take care of you (Philippians 4: 6).

Remember, perfect love casts out fear (I John 4: 18). What are you afraid of? Rejection? Jesus will reject no one who calls on Him for the baptism of the Holy Spirit (Luke 11: 11—13).

Maybe you are afraid of losing self-control or even losing your identity. Jesus promised those who would lose their lives for His sake would find them (Matthew 10: 39). The idea that there is anything to lose is only doubt that would rob you of what blessings the Lord has for you in Him.

There is no need of fear. No one has ever had a bad experience when the Holy Spirit comes in with His power. If you are seeking an emotional experience, do not bother.

There have been many different reactions to the baptism in the Holy Spirit. No two reactions have been identical. Some have been spectacular, and some hardly a trace of manifestation. Testimonies have indicated that electricity, oil, love, warmth, peace, and a variety of things came over the person. No one can predict what any one person may sense or may not sense when Jesus baptizes him or her in the Holy Spirit. So, do not expect anything or look for anything. Any such expectation will only become a stumbling-block.

Unknown Tongues

Some people teach that when a believer is baptized in the Holy Spirit that the believer will always speak in unknown tongues. They base this teaching on the records in the Book of Acts where believers spoke in unknown tongues when the Holy Spirit came on them in baptism. While not being dogmatic on that particular doctrine, I know of no one, nor have I ever heard of anyone, who was ever used in the operation of the Gifts of the Holy Spirit without first having spoken in unknown tongues.

Unknown tongues are messages to God and are edifying to the speaker (I Corinthians. 14: 2, 4). While both prophecy and love edify the congregation (I Corinthians 8: 1 and 14: 4), speaking in unknown tongues is the only thing the Scriptures indicate that edifies the individual believer (I Corinthians 14: 4).

It is amazing that many ministers will attempt to edify their congregation without first edifying themselves—which is done only by speaking in tongues! Then these same ministers will call the early church (or any church that practices the Gifts of the Holy Spirit) "primitive." It would seem these self-determined ministers are spiritual cripples as they attempt to minister in their churches!

The Baptism in the Holy Spirit

Just as simply as you asked Jesus to take control of you and your life for salvation, ask Him to baptize you in the Holy Spirit. Whisper the request in Jesus' name and expect Him to do it—thanking and worshipping Him for it. Do not be anxious about it regardless of what you experience or do not experience! Put your baptism into Jesus' hands and leave it there.

The Prize—Bringing It All Together

In the presence of the new information, let's look again at meditation. Meditate on this verse: Philippians 4: 13:

I can do all things through Christ, who strengthens me.

You don't even have to recast this verse. Re-read it aloud to yourself several times.

Now, meditate on this one: Mark 16: 16–18:

He who believes and is baptized shall be saved; but he who believes not shall be damned. And these signs shall follow [or accompany] those who believe: In My name they shall cast out devils [demons]; they shall speak with new tongues; they shall take up serpents; and if they drink any deadly thing, it shall not hurt them; they shall lay hands on the sick, and they shall recover.

Now, customize it to yourself (assuming you are baptized in the Lord):

I believe and am baptized and am saved; And these signs accompany me: In Jesus' name. I cast out demons; I speak with new tongues; I take up serpents; and if I drink any deadly thing, it shall not hurt me; I lay my hands on the sick, and they recover.

You are renewing your mind by the Word of God! You are firming your grip on the Sword of the Spirit, God's Word, learning to wield it as a weapon against both any adverse circumstances and the enemy!

Another Scripture for you to absorb is John 14: 12–14:

Verily, verily, I say to you, he who believes in Me, the works that I do shall he do also; and greater works than these shall he do because I go to My Father. And whatever you shall ask in My name, that will I do, that the Father may be glorified in the Son. If you shall ask anything in My name, I will do it.

After you read it aloud a couple of times, recast it to yourself:

Verily, verily, *The Lord* says to *me*, "*You* believe in Me, *therefore*, the works that I do shall *you* do also; and greater works than these shall *you* do because I go to My Father. And whatever you shall ask in My name, that will I do, that the Father may be glorified in the Son. If you shall ask anything in My name, I will do it."

Soon you will be meditating on this verse like this:

I believe in Jesus, and I do the greater works than He did because He went to the Father to arrange it; and I can ask anything in His name and He will do it for me, so that the Father will be glorified in the Son. I can ask anything in His name and He will do it.

Our Outfitting

This may appear to be redundant, but there is sound reason for it. Just as someone may say, "The best defense is a strong offense," someone else may say, "The best offense is a good defense." The message is almost the same—the same words are used and the same order of most of them is incorporated; but the application is different. So is the following:

Earlier in *Book 1* was the following paragraph:

For an adequate defense in any war, game, or sport, the participants need to put on the correct uniform and associated gear. Christians should do the same thing. Here is the armor of God. Look at Ephesians 6: 13—17: [And the Scripture was presented.]

Now let's revisit the words:

For an adequate offense in any war, game, or sport, the participants need to put on the correct uniform and associated gear. Christians should do the same thing. Here is the armor of God. Look at Ephesians 6: 13–17:

Only one word was changed: *Defense* became *Offense*. Here is the Scripture:

Wherefore, take the whole Armor of God, so that you may be able to withstand in the evil day, and having done all, to stand. Stand, therefore, having your loins girded about with Truth, and having on the Breastplate of Righteousness, and your feet shod with the Preparation of the Gospel of Peace; above all, taking the Shield of Faith, with which you shall be able to quench all the fiery darts of the wicked. And take the Helmet of Salvation, and the Sword of the Spirit, which is the Word of God; praying always with all prayer and supplication in the spirit, and watching thereto with all perseverance and supplication for all saints; And for me . . . .

Notice that the list of items that the believer should put on or should take are the very same as the defensive items:

Truth

Breastplate of Righteousness

Shoes of the Preparation of the Gospel of Peace

Shield of Faith

Helmet of Salvation

Sword of the spirit, which is the Word of God

Every item on the list is still spiritual. Unless someone is walking in the spirit (meaning his or her re-created spirit), these armaments will never be manifested. Only the results of these armaments will ever be seen with natural eyes. The only way to get them is directly from the Lord Jesus Christ. He wants you to have and use these things.

> Important Notice: Because of the aim of the message you are reading, the implication is that believers add these pieces of armor to their character or persona as they walk in their recreated spirits with the Lord.

> In reality, these attributes of the armor are already in the believer because of their being complete in Christ (Colossians 2: 10). However, many believers do not manifest these armaments. Because the armor is not manifested, the assertion has been made that they do not have them.

> Believers have these qualities—maybe only in seed form—but they are in every true believer. The goal in this composition is for the qualities and armaments to become manifested, viable and productive. In other words, these qualities are not currently being planted; they are being cultivated!

> It is somewhat redundant, but the strategy now is *offensive* rather than *defensive*. The following instructions deal with the use of the Word as a Sword to route the enemy and do it so that he never comes close to accomplishing his mission.

Your Victory

Be reminded of this fact: Between the Old Covenant and the New there has been a drastic change of audience. The Old Covenant was addressed to the Children of Israel—those to whom all those active verbs were admonished to obey. The New Covenant is addressed to believers—Sons of God, Joint Heirs with Christ, Members of the Body of Christ, Children of God, and the list goes on.

Christ having fulfilled the Law, ended it as it was, the Law of Sin and Death, and He instituted the Law of Life in Christ Jesus. It is the New Covenant that we live in and we were never under the Old One, Christ having ended it long before we came on the scene.

So, not only do the verbs, nouns and adjectives make a difference in the language (legalese) of the Covenants, but so does the Audience. Of course it all follows that the Purpose and Desired Result have also changed.

Therefore, get involved with your relationship with your Heavenly Father and protect what you already have and produce those other things that are yours by the Father's good intentions for you.

The battle is yours. The enemy's head is conquered. Because Jesus defeated Satan, you see the position the Father has put you in. You are seated with Christ in the heavenlies (Ephesians 1 and 2); a son of God (John 1); a member of the Body of Christ (I Corinthians 12), more than a conqueror (Romans 8: 31–39) and many more roles in life. Therefore you are immune to the ways and wiles of the enemy as long as you acknowledge your identity and capabilities in Christ.

Only one thing can stand between you and your manifested victory over the enemy: Your failure to resist the enemy and his attacks on you and yours.

Be ready!! The car does no good if it's locked in the garage! Open the door, get in the car, start it, and drive away! The sword does no good if it's in its sheath! Get the sword out of its sheath, clean off the rust and tarnish, polish it, sharpen it and learn to use it. Use the Word on the enemy in the name of Jesus!

When the enemy knocks, lying to you, attempting to rob, kill and destroy you and yours, use the Sword of the Spirit on him and see him flee from before your face! Assert your authority over him in Jesus' name! Rebuke the enemy in his face, if need be!

I sound the trumpet in your ears! Prepare for the battle. Assert your victory!! See the enemy's backside as he retreats from before you!! In Jesus' Name, so be it!

Appendices

Appendix 4

Faith or Feeling: Good or Bad?

The matter at hand regarding studying at the Word of God through defensive eyes, it would be neglectful to fail to mention the other aspect of defense everyone should be familiar with.

There are times—often many times, and sometimes it seems all the time—that the enemy of our souls puts us on the defensive by personal frontal attacks. There is not enough space or time in this short composition to go into any great depth of teaching in this area, so we will look only briefly at a portion of Psalm 91.

The issues to look at are in Vv. 3–7, although be encouraged to really read and study the whole chapter. Psalms 91: 3–7:

3. Surely He [the LORD] shall deliver you from the snare of the fowler and from the perilous pestilence.

4. He shall cover you with His feathers, and under His wings you shall take refuge; His truth shall be your shield and buckler.

5. You shall not be afraid of the terror by night, nor of the arrow that flies by day, nor of the pestilence that walks in darkness, nor of the destruction that lays waste at noonday.

7. A thousand may fall at your side, and ten thousand at your right hand; but it shall not come near you.

Although you may obviously read the whole Psalm, and you would do well to do it, the points to be made start in Verse 3 where the direct address (second person) starts. The promise there is that He, the LORD, will deliver you out of the snare of the "fowler" and from the noisy pestilence.

A snare is a trap, and this one has been set to capture you. The fowler could be spelled "fouler," because it is the enemy of your soul who set the snare for you. And this fowler is very foul, indeed!

The next point addresses the pestilence. The dictionary has two definitions for *pestilence*: One being a "fatal contagious or infectious disease;" and "anything, as a doctrine, regarded as harmful or dangerous." (Webster's New World College Dictionary, Fourth Edition, Wiley, 2005)

Strong's uses several words in connection with the Hebrew word for perilous and all of them are negative, implying widespread coverage to "very wickedness." So this all adds up to something the modern media seem to desire most for the world—an overpowering pandemic of magnificent proportions.

When all this evil descends on you, whether the trap or the epidemic, Verse 3 promises deliverance. During this experience, your position will be under His wings and His feathers (like a mother hen) and His Word will be your shield and buckler on your arm.

The next two verses depict another perspective of defensive Tactics— still from the enemy personally.

The "terror by night" speaks of the mind's picture of impending doom as the enemy gives you thoughts, imaginations, dreams and/or visions of calamities designed just for you and yours.

The "arrow that flies by day" depicts the accusations that the enemy lays against you before God, your friends and most importantly yourself!

The "pestilence that walks in darkness" alludes to skulking and secret plots that the enemy forms against you.

The "destruction that lays waste at noonday" pertains to warfare and open violence in societies.

None of these diabolical warfare tactics are necessarily caused by incorrect biblical understanding. Any of them can cause emotional strains, depression and could lead to despair to the un-worded person.

But, once again the promise is that none of these things will attach themselves to you or otherwise afflict you.

Herein lies the problem for most people, especially those who do not know the Word of God. They feel the effects of these warfare tactics loosed on them from the enemy and lie there in the middle of their oppressive feelings unable or unwilling to resist him and his sinister plots. They feel incapable, inadequate, useless and therefore unreceptive to the promised delivery!

So what should you do when the enemy comes into your face, calls you names, points his finger at you and accuses you of something (whether real or manufactured)? What should you do when he causes some symptoms of a disease on you or yours? What should you do when all hell breaks out in your front yard and the violence makes you want to stay under your bed? What should you do when the enemy does something across the world that makes your foundations shudder? Yielding to emotions will not do anything for you!

Hebrews tells us that faith is the substance of things hoped for and the evidence of things unseen (Hebrews 11: 1). An easier and more applicable definition for faith as used in this composition is this:

> Faith is acknowledging as fact everything the Father has said in His Word, especially the things about you!

Remember: This faith person is who you are—a member of the Body of Christ! A master! More than a conqueror! You cannot fold under the pressure of your feelings!

Look up in a concordance (any concordance—Strong's or any other) and find all the scriptural references to *emotions* or *feelings* (when used as *emotions*). It won't take long because there aren't any! *Feelings* is mentioned twice, but neither one is used meaning *emotions*.

Then look up *faith*. Among the many references to faith, one of them says that we believers (being justified) live by faith (Romans 1: 17). Then read the whole 11th Chapter of Hebrews and enumerate the great feats accomplished by those who practiced and walked in faith.

So now enter the discipline of Bible-study with an eye on offence knowing that the promises are geared for your success and abundance in life! These promises, once embraced, will put you over the top in every area of your life and they will empower you to bring others with you!

EDIFYING SCRIPTURES

The following are Scriptures for you to appropriate by meditation and confession. Make the Word of God your prayer. Learn to pray the promises of the Father that He has given to you in His Word and see them produced in you. Keep them continually in your mind and in your mouth. Become "God-inside Minded."

Thus you will remember what manner of person you are! Allow nothing contrary to God's Word to remain in your mind or come out of your mouth. Then you will be doing the Word. Then you will understand fully what Hebrews 8: 6 meant when it says the New Covenant has better promises than the Old. The Scriptures show you not only who you are in Him and what you are in Him, but you will find that you can do and have some real benefits by being a Christian.

You will find yourself realizing that you are truly a partaker of the divine nature!

> You will also note that some Scriptures are on more than one list. And be sure to realize that these are not all the verses you may need in your life, so continue to study and add Scriptures to your own list as you need.

Abilities (See also *Ministries*)

You can command and receive in Christ. . . . . Mark 11: 23, 24; John 14: 13, 14; John 15: 7, 8; John 16, 16: 24; Hebrews 10: 35, 36; I John 3: 22, 23; I John 5: 14, 15

You do the same works that Jesus did. . . . . John 14: 12-14; Mark 16:16–18

You will not fear in Christ. . . . . Psalms 23: 1; Psalm 27: 1; I John 4:18; II Timothy 1: 7

The Peace of God keeps your mind and heart. . . . . Philemon 4: 7–9

God has given you the spirit of power,
love and a sound mind. . . . . II Timothy 1: 7

The LORD has good thoughts of you. . . . . Psalm 139: 1–18

The LORD withholds nothing good from you. . . . . . . Psalm 84: 11; Romans 8: 32; I John 3: 22, 23; James 1: 17–25

Christ became poor so you would not have to. . . . . . . II Corinthians 8: 9

You may have divine health in Christ. . . . . Romans 8: 11

Your sins are gone by Christ. Isaiah 43: 25, 26; Romans 4: 8

Deliverance (See *Name of Jesus*)

The Father

Acknowledge the LORD in your life.	Philemon 6
In the Shepherd-LORD, I shall not want.	Psalm 23
There is only one God.	Isaiah 46: 9–11
The LORD is omnipotent.	Ephesians 3: 20, 21; Isaiah 46: 9–11
The LORD is your strength.	Philippians 4: 13; Isaiah 12: 2
The LORD is your salvation.	Isaiah 12: 2
The LORD will not condemn you.	Romans 8: 33, 34; I John 3: 20–24
The LORD does not impute sin to you.	Romans 4: 8
The LORD has good thoughts for you.	Psalm 139: 1–18
The LORD is consistent.	James 1: 17–25
The LORD provides counsel.	Proverbs 8: 14–21
The LORD supplies all your needs.	Philippians 4: 19

Fear (See also *Peace, Identity, Name of Jesus* and *Sanity*)

Perfect Love casts out fear.	I John 4: 18
You shall not fear.	Psalm 23: 1; Psalm 27: 1; Psalm 56: 4; John 14: 1
Satan is afraid of you.	James 4: 7
Greater is He Who is in you than Satan.	John 4: 4
Christ always causes you to triumph.	II Corinthians 2: 14
God does not give you the spirit of fear.	II Timothy 1:7

Healing or *Health* (See also *Name of Jesus*)

By His stripes you are healed. . . . . .I Peter 2: 24; Isaiah 53: 5

You should prosper and be in health. . . . . III John 2

Jesus came to heal the broken hearted. . . . . .Luke 4: 18

Words lead to life, health. .Proverbs 4: 20–22

You are healed and delivered by the Word. . . . . .Psalm 107: 20

Healing comes in Jesus' Name. . . . . Acts 3: 16

You may have divine health in Christ. . . . . Romans 8: 11

The elders may anoint you for healing. . . . . .James 5: 14

The LORD supplies all your needs. . . . . Philippians 4: 19

The LORD has good thoughts of you. . . . . Psalm 139: 1–18

The LORD withholds nothing good from you. . . . . . . Psalm 84: 11; Romans 8: 32; I John 3: 22, 23; James 1: 17–25

In the Shepherd-LORD, I shall not want. . . . . Psalm 23

You can demand and receive in Christ. . . . . Mark 11:23, 24; John 14: 13, 14; John 15: 7, 8; John 16; 16: 24; Hebrews 10: 35, 36; I John 3: 22, 23; I John 5: 14, 15

You do the same works that Jesus did. . . . . John 14: 12–14; Mark 16: 16–18

The LORD is your strength. . . . . Philippians 4: 13; Isaiah 12: 2

The LORD is your salvation. . . . . Isaiah 12: 2

The LORD provides counsel. .Proverbs 8: 14–21

Holy Spirit (Ghost)

Power comes after the Holy Spirit comes on you. . . . . . Acts 1: 8

You were sealed with the Holy Spirit. . . . . Ephesians 1: 13

The Father gives the Holy Spirit. . . . . Luke 11:13

The Holy Spirit comes on all receivers. . . . . Joel 2: 28, 29

The LORD withholds nothing good from you. . . . . . . Psalm 84: 11; Romans 8: 32;
I John 3: 22, 23; James 1: 17–25

The Holy Spirit baptizes you into Jesus. . . . . I Corinthians 12: 13

Jesus baptizes Believers in the Holy Spirit Matthew. . . 3: 11; Mark 1: 8; Luke 3: 16; John 1: 33; Acts 1: 5

Identity

You are one spirit with Jesus. . . . . I Corinthians 6: 17

You are a Son of God. . . . . John 1: 12, 13

You are a member of the Body of Christ. . . . . I Corinthians 6: 17; 10:17; 12: 27

You are an heir and joint heir with Christ. . . . . Romans 8: 17

God sees you just like He sees Jesus. . . . . I John 4: 17; John 14: 12–14

You're more than a conqueror in Christ. . . . . Romans 8: 37; I John 4: 4; I John 5: 4; Isaiah 54: 17

Jesus made an open show of defeating Satan. . . . . Colossians 2: 15

Christ always causes you to triumph. . . . . II Corinthians 2: 14

Satan is afraid of you. . . . . James 4: 7

You have abundant life. . . . . John 10: 10

Greater is He [Jesus] who is in you than Satan. . . . . . . John 4: 4

You are redeemed from the Law's curse. . . . . .Galatians 3: 13

You are no longer in darkness. . . . . Colossians 1: 13

You are a partaker of the divine nature. . . . . II Peter 1: 3, 4

You are the Righteousness of God in Christ. . . . . II Corinthians 5: 21

You are a new creation in Christ. . . . . II Corinthians 5: 17

Your new creation produces fruit. . . . . .Galatians 5: 22, 23

You live, move exist in Him. Acts 17: 28

You are like Jesus now. . . . . .I John 4: 17; John 14: 12–14

You have the mind of Christ. Philippians 2: 5–8

You have wisdom, righteousness, sanctification, and redemption. . . . . I Corinthians 1: 30

You can do all things in Christ. . . . . Philippians 4: 13; Mark 9: 23

You live by the Word. . . . . .Matthew 4: 4

You will not fear in Christ. . . . . .Psalms 23: 1; 27: 1; I John 4: 18; II Timothy 1: 7

You have all your needs supplied in Christ. . . . . Philippians 4: 19; III John 2

The LORD is your righteousness. . . . . .Isaiah 54: 17

You are righteous and free from oppression, fear and terror. . . . . Isaiah 54: 14

You have great authority in Christ. . . . . .Matthew 18: 18–20; II Corinthians 1: 20; I Peter 3: 7

You may receive anything of the Lord. . . . . .Romans 8: 32

You may have accompanying signs. . . . . Mark 16: 17, 18

You are healed and delivered by the Word. . . . . .Psalm 107: 20; Exodus 15: 26; Isaiah 53: 4, 5; I Peter 2: 24

You are wiser than your enemies. . . . . Psalm 119: 98

You have peace with your enemies. . . . . .Psalm 16: 7

Joy

Your recreated spirit produces joy. . . . . Galatians 5: 22, 23

Christ always causes you to triumph. . . . . II Corinthians 2: 14

You are like Jesus now. . . . . I John 4:17; John 14: 12–14

You have the mind of Christ. . . . . Philippians 2: 5–8

Loneliness (See also *Love*)

You are never alone. . . . . Matthew 18: 20; Matthew 28: 20

You shall not want for *fellowship*. . . . . Psalm 23

The Lord will never leave you. . . . . Hebrews 13: 5

The Lord will not leave you comfortless   John 14: 8

Love (See also *Identity*)

Your recreated spirit produces love. . . . . Galatians 5: 22, 23

The Love of God. . . . . I Corinthians 13; I John, 3, 4

Ministry (See also *Abilities*)

You shall receive power from the Holy Spirit. . . . . .Acts 1: 8

You are an able minister. . . . . II Corinthians 3: 6; 6: 4; 9: 10

You have great authority in Christ. . . . . .Matthew 18: 18–20; II Corinthians 1: 20; I Peter 3: 7

You may have accompanying signs. . . . . Mark 16: 17, 18

C. L. Chapman

Miracles (See *Identity, Abilities,* and *Name of Jesus*) *Name of Jesus*

At the Name of Jesus every knee shall bow. . . . . Philippians 2: 9–11

In Jesus' Name, signs follow believers. . . . . Mark 16: 16–18

Healing comes in Jesus' Name. . . . . Acts 3: 16

Whatever you ask in Jesus' Name, He will do it. . . . . . John 14: 13, 14

Whatever you ask the Father in Jesus' Name, He will
give you. . . . . .John 16: 23, 24

Whatever you do, do in the Name of the LORD. . . . . Colossians 3: 17

Jesus made an open show of defeating Satan. . . . . .Colossians 2: 15

The LORD is your righteousness. . . . . .Isaiah 54: 17

Call on the LORD and He will show you things. . . . . Jeremiah 33: 3

Give the LORD all you problems. . . . . Philippians 4: 6, 7

On whatever two or more agree in Jesus Name, the
Father will provide. . . . . Matthew 18: 18, 19

Whatever you bind on earth, bound in heaven;
whatever you loose on earth, loosed in heaven. . . . . . .Matthew 18: 18, 19

Christ always causes you to triumph. . . . . II Corinthians 2: 14

New Creation (See *Identity* and *Abilities*) *Peace*

Your recreated spirit produces peace. . . . . Galatians 5: 22, 23

You have peace with your enemies. . . . . .Psalm 16: 7

The Peace of God keeps your mind and heart. . . . . Philippians 4: 7–9

You have the peace of Jesus. . . . . John 14: 1

The LORD does not impute sin to you. . . . . Romans 4: 8

The LORD has good thoughts for you. . . . . Psalm 139: 1–18

The LORD provides counsel. . . . . .Proverbs 8: 14–21

The LORD supplies all your needs. . . . . Philippians 4: 19

Perfect Love casts out fear. .I John 4: 18

You shall not fear. . . . . .Psalm 23: 1; Psalm 27: 1;
Psalm 56: 4; John 14: 1

Satan is afraid of you. . . . . .James 4: 7

Greater is He Who is in you than Satan. . . . . John 4: 4

Christ always causes you to triumph. . . . . II Corinthians 2: 14

You are like Jesus now. . . . . I John 4: 17; John 14: 12–14

You have the mind of Christ. Philippians 2: 5–8

Prosperity

You should prosper and be in health. . . . . III John 2

You may have enough for all your needs. . . . . II Corinthians 9: 8

You may have enough to share with others. . . . . II Corinthians 9: 10

Words lead to life, health. . . . . .Proverbs 4: 20–22

Words lead to prosperity, success. . . . . .Joshua 1: 8

Christ became poor so you would not have to. . . . . . .II Corinthians 8: 9

The LORD supplies all your needs. . . . . Philippians 4: 19

You live by the Word. . , , , , ...Matthew 4: 4

In the Shepherd-LORD, I shall not want. . . . . Psalm 23

You can command and receive in Christ. . . . . .Mark 11: 23, 24; John 14:
13, 14; 15: 7, 8; 16; 16: 24;
Hebrews 10: 35, 36; I John
3: 22, 23; 5: 14, 15

You do the same works that Jesus did. . . . . John 14: 12–14; Mark 16: 16–18

The LORD is your strength. . . . . Philippians 4: 13; Isaiah 12: 2

The LORD is your salvation. . . . . Isaiah 12: 2

The LORD has good thoughts for you. . . . . Psalm 139: 1–18

Whatever you ask in Jesus' Name, He will do it. . . . . . John 14: 13, 14

Whatever you ask of the Father in Jesus' Name, He will give you. . . . . John 16: 23, 24

Relationships

Your recreated spirit produces love, peace. . . . . Galatians 5: 22, 23; II Timothy 1: 7

You are wiser than your enemies. . . . . Psalm 119: 98

You have peace with your enemies. . . . . Psalm 16: 7

Renewing the Mind (See also *Word*)

Think on things that are true, honest, just, pure, lovely, of good report, or virtuous. . . . . Philippians 4: 7–9

You live by the Word. . . . . Matthew 4: 4

The Word is divine, eternal creative, personal, enlivening. . . . . Psalm 19: 7–11, 14; 33: 6; II Peter 3: 5, 6; Matthew 24: 35; John 1: 1-14; Hebrews 11: 3; I Peter 1: 25

You live by the Word. . . . . Matthew 4: 4

The Word does what the LORD sends it to do. . . . . . . Isaiah 55: 10-13; Jeremiah 1: 12; Ezekiel 12: 23

The Word (Law) converts the soul, enlightens the simple, rejoices the heart, enlightens the eyes. . . . . Psalm 19: 7–11, 14

The Word cleanses. . . . . .John 15: 3; Ephesians 5: 26

Sanity (See also *Fear*, *Peace*, and *Name of Jesus*)

The Lord has given us soundness of mind. . . . . II Timothy 1: 7

The Word

The Word is living, powerful, omniscient. . . . . Hebrews 4: 12, 13

The Word upholds all things. . . . . .Hebrews 1: 3

The Word supplies all your needs. . . . . Isaiah 55: 10–13

The Word ranks higher than the LORD's Name. . . . . . .Psalm 56: 4, 10, 11; 138: 2

The Word works effectually in you. . . . . I Thessalonians 2: 13

You live by the Word. . . . . .Matthew 4: 4

The Word came by the Holy Spirit—not men. . . . . . . .II Timothy 3: 16, 17; II Peter 1: 21

The Word does what the LORD sends it to do. . . . . . . Isaiah 55:10–13; Jeremiah 1: 12; Ezekiel 12: 23

The Word (Law) converts the soul, enlightens the simple, rejoices the heart, enlightens the eyes. . . . . . . Psalm 19: 7–11, 14

The Word is pure, true, righteous, sure, clean, more precious than gold. . . . . .Psalm 19: 7–11, 14

The Word is profitable for correction, instruction, doctrine, reproof. . . . . II Timothy 3: 16, 17; Romans 15: 4

The Word is Spirit, Life. . . . . .John 6: 63, 68

The Word will judge those who reject the LORD. . . . . John 12: 48

The Word cleanses. . . . . .John 15: 3; Ephesians 5: 26

The Word produces the incorruptible re-birth. . . . . . . .I Peter 1: 23

C. L. Chapman

The Word heals and delivers. . . . . Psalm 107: 20; Matthew 8: 5-13, 16

The Word is part of victory's assurance. . . . . Revelation 12: 11

The Word identifies true disciples. . . . . John 8: 31

The Word frees you. . . . . .John 8: 32

Keeping the Word perfects God's Love. . . . . I John 2: 5, 14

If you love the Lord, you will keep His Words. . . . . . . John 14: 23

If you keep His words, the Father will love you. . . . . . .John 14: 23

You keep His words, Son and Father will
live within you. . . . . .John 14: 23

You should hold fast to the Word. . . . . Hebrews 2: 1–4

The Word is the source of your faith. . . . . Romans 10: 17

The Word of Christ dwells in you richly. . . . . Colossians 3: 16

Words lead to life, health. . . . . .Proverbs 4: 20–22

Words lead to prosperity, success. . . . . .Joshua 1: 8

Appendix 5

MEDITATIONS AND CONFESSIONS

A Few Examples

These are not the only verses you will need in your life and in your situation, but the idea is here for you to sample how it may be done. Find other Scriptures as you need them. The first part of each reference states the personalized thought that you may want or need to meditate on; the second part of the entry is the book, chapter and verse of the thought. The goal is to renew your mind and thus become God-inside minded.

JESUS PURGED MY SINS Hebrews 1: 3: Who [Jesus] being the brightness of his [God's] glory, and the express image of His [God's] Person, and upholding all things by the Word of His power, when He had by Himself purged our sins, sat down on the right hand of the Majesty on high.

I HAVE RECEIVED THE EFFECTIVE WORD OF GOD I Thessalonians 2: 13: For this cause also we thank God without ceasing because, when you received the Word of God that you heard from us, you received, not as the word of men, but as it is in truth, the Word of God that effectually works in you who believe.

I RECEIVE MY DAILY SUSTENANCE FROM THE WORD Matthew 4: 4: But He [Jesus] answered and said, "It is written, Man shall not live by bread alone, but by every Word that proceeds from the Mouth of God."

THE WORD SUPPLIES ALL MY NEEDS. Isaiah 55: 10-13: For as the rain comes down, and the snow from heaven, and returns not there, but waters the earth, and makes it bring forth and bud, that it may give seed to the sower, and bread to the eater: So does My Word that goes forth out of My Mouth: It shall not return to Me void, but It accomplishes what I purpose, and It prospers in the thing whereto I send It.

THE WORD

1. CONVERTS MY SOUL

2. MAKES ME WISE

3. REJOICES MY HEART

4. ENLIGHTENS MY EYES

5. WARNS ME

6. REWARDS ME

7. MAKES MY WORDS AND MEDITATION ACCEPTABLE

Psalm 19: 7-11, 14: The Law of the LORD is perfect, converting the soul; the Testimony of the LORD is sure, making wise the simple. The Statutes of the LORD are right, rejoicing the heart; the Commandment of the LORD is pure, enlightening the eyes. The Fear of the LORD is clean, enduring forever; the Judgments of the LORD are true and righteous altogether. More to be desired are they than gold, yea than much fine gold; sweeter also than honey and the honeycomb. Moreover by them is Your servant warned; and in keeping of them there is great reward. Let the words of my mouth, and the meditation of my heart, be acceptable in your sight, O LORD, my Strength and my Redeemer.

I AM PERFECT IN AND BY THE WORD OF GOD, FURNISHED TO ALL GOOD WORKS BY THE WORD II Timothy 3: 16, 17:

All Scripture is given by inspiration of God and is profitable for doctrine, for reproof, for correction, for instruction in righteousness, That the man of God may be perfect, thoroughly furnished unto all good works.

I HAVE HOPE. Romans 15: 4:

For whatever things were written before were written for our learning, that we through patience and comfort of the Scriptures might have hope.

I DO NOT SIN AGAINST THE FATHER BECAUSE I SEE BY HIS LAMP ON MY PATH. Psalm 119: 11,105:

Your Word I have hidden in my heart, that I might not sin against You. Your Word is a Lamp to my feet, and a Light to my path.

I AM CLEAN. John 15: 3:

Now are you clean through the Word that I have spoken unto you.

Ephesians 5: 26: That He might sanctify and cleanse it [The Church] with the washing of water by the Word.

I AM BORN AGAIN OF THE INCORRUPTIBLE SEED OF THE WORD OF GOD. I Peter 1: 23:

Being born-again, not of corruptible seed, but of incorruptible, by the Word of God that lives and abides forever.

I AM HEALED AND DELIVERED BY THE WORD. Psalm 107: 20:

He sent His Word and healed them and delivered them from their destructions.

I HAVE FAITH TO UNDERSTAND. Hebrews 11: 3:

Through faith we understand that the worlds were framed by the Word of God, so that things that are seen were not made of things that appear.

I AM A DISCIPLE AND AM FREE IN IT. John 8: 31, 32:

Then said Jesus to those Jews who believed on Him, "If you continue in My words, you are My disciples indeed; and you shall know the Truth and the Truth shall make you free."

I KEEP THE WORD AND GOD'S LOVE IS PERFECTED IN ME. I John 2: 5:

But whoever keeps His Word, in him verily is the Love of God perfected: hereby we know that we are in Him

I KNOW HIM, AND AM STRONG; THE WORD ABIDES IN ME, AND I HAVE OVERCOME THE WICKED ONE. I John 2: 14:

I have written to you, fathers, because you have known Him from the beginning. I have written to you, young men, because you are strong, and the Word of God abides in you, and you have overcome the wicked one.

I KEEP HIS WORDS; THUS, JESUS AND THE FATHER DWELL WITH ME. John 14: 23:

Jesus answered, and said to them, "If a man loves Me, he will keep My Words; and My Father will love him, and We will come to him, and make Our abode with him."